Volume II

THE DHARMA KINGS

A Collection of Screenplays By

Paul Charles Bailly

For inquiries contact the author: pbailly@live.com

First hardcover edition *December 2023*

Cover art: PCB

ISBN 979-8-9888899-0-8 (dust jacket hardcover)
ISBN 979-8-9888899-1-5 (case laminate hardcover)

TABLE OF CONTENTS

Life isn't about finding yourself, it's about creating yourself.

George Bernard Shaw

First draft was written in Girona, Spain, in the summer of 2020. Left it alone for over a year and then took it up again in Spain and Portugal.

LA GARE

Written by
Paul Charles Bailly

2020

PARIS, 1920s

EXT. PARIS - MORNING

The Parisian skyline - Eiffel Tower, Notre Dame Cathedral, the River Seine.

EXT. TRAIN IN MOTION - MORNING

An early 20th-century passenger locomotive rumbles through northern France. The French countryside, vineyards, and farms pass in the background.

INT. TRAIN - MORNING

MARTN MOREAU (37) sits on the plush velvet banquette of his private rail car. He's got a beautiful young WOMAN on each side of him and an open bottle of Champagne on a small cafe table.

The Women are FRANCOISE (23) and MARIE (24). Marie has her blouse pulled down over her shoulder, and her right breast is exposed. With an extended index finger, M. Moreau draws imaginary circles around the Woman's nipple.

M. MOREAU

The two of you will be staying at the beautiful Hotel Lutetia. My father built it when I was just a boy.

FRANCOISE

But Martin, we wanted to stay with you.

M. MOREAU

That's impossible.

MARIE

They say that you'll never marry. And that your heirs will come from the slums of Banlieue.

FRANCOISE

Because that's where your mistresses live.

M. MOREAU

There's already too much public examination of my life. I don't even have parties at my home anymore.

MARIE

And the radio, you should have heard what they said about you last week.

M. MOREAU

Newspapers, radio, socialists, anarchists, my father, and even the politicians that I pay. At this moment, you two are the only friends that I have.

The two ladies smile at hearing this. Francoise and Marie kiss Martin on his cheeks.

FRANCOISE

We'll always be here for you, Martin.

Frustrated, M. Moreau pours himself another glass of Champagne. The bottle empties into his glass.

INT. MESSEIN APARTMENT, PARIS - MORNING

GUILLAUME MESSEIN (40) and his son, PHILIPPE (7), are getting dressed for the morning.

Guillaume stands in front of the bathroom mirror in his undershirt. With great focus and scissors in hand, he snips at the ends of his mustache. Philippe steps inside the bathroom.

PHILIPPE

Papa. I think I should start using Cream Oil on my hair.

GUILLAUME

No.

PHILIPPE

Why not?

GUILLAUME

Your mother won't like it.

PHILIPPE

But other boys in my class wear Wildroot, and the girls like it.

Guillaume slides the bottle of Wildroot cream oil toward Philip.

GUILLAUME

But not every day, uh?

Philippe smiles.

EXT. GARAGE, PARIS - MORNING

A typical Parisian auto repair garage is nestled between a couple of brick buildings in Paris.

The oversized garage door slides to the side as a MAN pushes it open.

INT. GARAGE, PARIS - MORNING

OCTAVE DE VILLIERS (42), and RENE DEGASTE (31) stand inside the garage and speak. Octave wears a long coat, and Rene wears a suit. They both wear Bowler hats.

The two stand next to a table where several firearms are lying. Another man, ANDRE (24), checks and loads the weapons - some repeating pistols, a shotgun, and a lever-action rifle. JULES (22), who opened up the garage door, leans against the wall smoking a cigarette.

OCTAVE

Make sure those pistols are well-oiled. The gunpowder in those shells is very messy.

ANDRE

Will do.

OCTAVE

Also, I want you to use the shotgun again.

A large yellow limousine pulls into the garage. The driver, RAYMOND (31), wears a driving cap and goggles. He jumps out and speaks to the men over the top of the car.

RAYMOND

Let's go!

Raymond looks over to the open garage door. The others follow his eyes and look to the door themselves.

RENE

Have you been spotted?

RAYMOND

You never know.

Octave looks over to Andre.

OCTAVE

Are you ready?

ANDRE

Take these. I'll get the shotgun.

The Men step over to the table and load the pistols in their coat pockets, as Andre dashes off.

INT. PRIVATE RAIL CAR, TRAIN - MORNING

Martin Moreau is finishing his breakfast with another bottle of Champagne. Francoise and Marie are already smoking cigarettes and drinking cafe. M. Moreau waves at the smoke from the cigarettes as he eats.

MARIE

Martin, when will you finish eating?

M. MOREAU

I'm sorry. This omelette is so exquisite that I had to have another.

M. Moreau looks up to the car's Chef.

M. MOREAU

This omelette. Monsieur Crespier, is it yours?

M. CRESPIER

It's from Mont Saint-Michel. A restaurant there - run by a Madame Poulard.

M. MOREAU

It's so simplistic and so...perfect.

Martin Moreau drains his glass of Champagne. He stands and looks down at the ladies with mild frustration.

M. MOREAU

I need some air.

He walks off to the rear of his private rail car.

INT. TRAIN VESTIBULE - MORNING

M. Moreau opens the door and steps inside the vestibule. As the door closes behind him, he is dumbstruck and stares through the glass panel in the door and into the first-class passenger car beyond.

ANGLE ON: GENEVIEVE MESSEIN

A half-full first-class passenger car. Passengers are talking amongst themselves; some read the morning papers. In the very back of the car sits Genevieve Messein. She sits quietly, looking out the window at the passing scenery. She has a faint smile on her lips.

She turns and looks over at Martin Moreau. He smiles at her, and she smiles back, then turns her attention back to the scenery outside the train.

M. Moreau's smile fades as Genevieve fails to turn his way again. The Porter opens the door from the private rail car and pops his head inside.

PORTER

Eight minutes to Gare Du Nord, sir.

M. MOREAU

Alright.

M. Moreau turns and heads back into his private car.

INT. APARTMENT - MORNING

Guillaume and Philippe put on the finishing touches of their toilette and s'habiller. They both look very dapper - Guillaume wears a vested suit and top coat. Philippe wears a handsome boy's suit jacket with shorts. His hair is slicked back with Cream Oil.

Guillaume looks at his pocket watch.

GUILLAUME

We're late.

Guillaume grabs his grey felt Homburg hat and slides it onto his head.

GUILLAUME

Grab your beret.

PHILIPPE

Okay.

Philippe snatches his beret off the hat rack, and they both step out of the door.

EXT. APARTMENT BUILDING - MORNING

Guillaume and Philippe step out of the front door of the building and strut down the sidewalk.

PHILIPPE

Where will we go for lunch today?

GUILLAUME

Cafe de la Paix.

PHILIPPE

The poet, T.S. Elliot, eats there often. Do you think we'll see him?

Guillaume looks over to Philippe.

GUILLAUME

Is it common these days for seven-year-old boys to admire poets?

PHILIPPE

No. But I have Genevieve Messein as my mother.

GUILLAUME

That would do it.

Guillaume grabs hold of his son's hand and pulls him into the street.

GUILLAUME

This way!

As they step beyond the parked wagons and cars in the street, the yellow limousine we saw earlier in the garage goes rushing by them.

GUILLAUME

Be careful.

INT. LIMOUSINE - MORNING

Octave, Rene, Andre, and Jules sit in the back of the spacious limousine. They speak as they double-check their weapons. Raymond is driving the car.

Guillaume and Philippe are seen walking through the rear windshield in the background - they cross the street behind them.

OCTAVE

The gold should be in a strongbox. We don't act until we see that strongbox on the platform. Also, I want to make sure Martin Moreau is dead before we leave.

Rene smiles as he holds up two automatic pistols - one in each hand.

RENE

I'll kill Moreau myself.

OCTAVE

Don't be so bloodthirsty.

Octave gives the Men a severe look.

OCTAVE

No. I'm killing Martin Moreau. Give me the shotgun.

Andre and Octave exchange weapons; the double-barreled shotgun for a repeating pistol.

ANDRE

What if there are guards?

Octave looks over to Andre and then to Rene and Jules.

OCTAVE

If they get in the way...shoot them.

Andre and Jules smile at each other. Octave now has the shotgun.

RENE

Okay! Here we go!

EXT. GARE DU NORD, PARIS - DAY

The expansive symmetrical triple-arched facade of the historic Parisian train station. People hustle in and out of the tall entrance doors.

The yellow limousine pulls up in front of the station, and the rear doors fly open. Well armed, Octave, Rene, Andre, and Jules quickly storm out of the car and through the station's main portal. Raymond stays behind the steering wheel.

INT. PLATFORM 13, GARD DU NORD - MORNING

The train from Brussels pulls into platform 13. Martin Moreau is standing in the vestibule, prepared to disembark.

ANGLE ON:

Two GUARDS jumped off the train. They slide a strongbox off the train and onto a hand lorry. They immediately wheel it down the platform. One manages the lorry, and the other holds a bolt-action rifle.

In the background, the Octave De Villiers Gang rushes through the station lobby towards the train.

ANGLE ON:

Martin Moreau steps off of the train and walks up the platform. He's followed by Genevieve Messein and the two Guards with the lorry.

Octave, Rene, Andre, and Jules appear on the platform. Octave stops, pulls up the shotgun, and fires.

The shotgun pellets hit Martin Moreau in the face and shoulder. He falls back immediately. Behind him, Genevieve stumbles for a moment and then collapses.

Rene and Jules exchange a near point-blank volley of gunshots with Guard #1. Jules' head whiplashes backward as he takes a bullet to the forehead.

Rene holds an automatic pistol in each hand and bangs away at Guard #1 as he falls back against the train. Without pause, Rene turns to Guard #2 and continues his onslaught until both pistols are empty and the Guards lie dead on the platform. Jules, too, lies dead on his back - blood dripping over his face.

OCTAVE

Get the strongbox!

EXT. GARD DU NORD - MORNING

Guillaume and Philippe walk by the yellow limousine. Philippe looks curiously into the car and makes eye contact with Raymond. Raymond gives him a stern glare.

INT. GARE DU NORD - MORNING

Octave, Rene, and Andre run through the station's lobby as Guillaume and Philippe stumble into them.

Octave and Guillaume lock eyes as the Gang rushes by them and out the entry door. Rene holds open the large door as Andre pushes the lorry out of the station.

The heads of Guillaume and Philippe swivel to the platform, where there is an obvious commotion. They run over to the platform.

INT. PLATFORM 13, GARD DU NORD - MORNING

Train and Station Attendants help Martin Moreau and Genevieve as they lie on the platform. Also, there are the bodies of the Guards and Jules.

Guillaume and Philippe run over to Genevieve and crouch down over her.

GUILLAUME

Darling!

PHILIPPE

Mother!

Guillaume holds Genevieve's head up, and she looks into their eyes. She is struck by a shotgun pellet on her cheek, just below her left eye - a single drop of blood drips from her wound.

She speaks to them - faint and unsteady.

GENEVIEVE
My men. I love you two.

She looks at Guillaume.

GENEVIEVE
Let him read, Guillaume...and not play out in the street so much.

GUILLAUME
Of course, my darling.

Genevieve pulls both of their faces down to hers and kisses them together.

Genevieve's head goes limp.

PHILIPPE
Mama!

With tears streaming down his cheeks, Philippe hugs his mother. Guillaume wraps his arms around them both.

INT. OFFICE OF THE CHIEF, DEPARTMENT OF POLICE - DAY

CHIEF AUBERT GOUGET (40), and DETECTIVE ETIENNE BONHOMME (27), sit around the Chief's desk. The office has a glass partition wall that looks out onto the desks of the other detectives. Gouget lifts a piece of paper and reads from it.

CHIEF GOUGET
There was gold in the box. Thirty-two thousand francs worth.

DETECTIVE BONHOMME
This was more than a robbery. They're sending a message by murdering Martin Moreau in the station.

CHIEF GOUGET
Obviously.

DETECTIVE BONHOMME
It has to be De Villiers.

DETECTIVE HUCHE (30), enters the office.

DETECTIVE HUCHE

The car that they used was stolen
from Madame Boulanger this morning.

CHIEF GOUGET

What about the witnesses?

DETECTIVE HUCHE

No one is speaking. They're saying
that they didn't notice them.

DETECTIVE BONHOMME

This is maddening. Has everyone in
this city become an anarchist?

Chief Gouget looks out through the glass partition to Guillaume and Philippe sitting outside at Detective Bonhomme's desk. Guillaume stands and looks at them in frustration. He and Detective Bonhomme lock eyes.

CHIEF GOUGET

What about them?

DETECTIVE HUCHE

They can't I.D. anyone.

CHIEF GOUGET

They killed his wife.

DETECTIVE BONHOMME

She was a schoolteacher.

CHIEF GOUGET

Get what you need, and let them go.

Detective Bonhomme stands and walks out of the office.

EXT. DEPARTMENT OF POLICE - DAY

Detective Bonhomme walks out of the building with Guillaume and Philippe. He leads them a few steps down the sidewalk.

DETECTIVE BONHOMME

I'm very sorry about your wife.
She'll be missed by many.

Guillaume gives the Detective a questioning look.

DETECTIVE BONHOMME

My niece was in her class at school.

Guillaume smiles.

GUILLAUME

Oh.

DETECTIVE BONHOMME

She's in the city morgue, near the river. You need to go there and sign some papers.

GUILLAUME

Yes, tomorrow.

PHILIPPE

Detective, why would they shoot my mother?

DETECTIVE BONHOMME

They didn't mean to shoot her. She was struck by a stray round. Their target was Martin Moreau.

PHILIPPE

What about the man that the guards shot?

DETECTIVE BONHOMME

He died on the platform.

GUILLAUME

Thank you for your help, Detective.

Guillaume puts his hand on Philippe's shoulder and leads him away. As they walk off, Philippe turns to Detective Bonhomme.

PHILIPPE

Goodbye, Detective.

DETECTIVE BONHOMME

Goodbye.

EXT. MESSEIN APARTMENT BUILDING - EARLY MORNING

Candlelight shines from the window of the upstairs apartment. A newspaper kiosk is just taking delivery of the morning papers. The NEWSPAPER MAN unwraps the bundles of newspapers and starts setting up his stand.

A couple of passersby snatch a newspaper off the counter and toss a coin in the dish there.

NEWSPAPER MAN

Je vous remercie, Monsieur. Merci.

INT. MESSEIN APARTMENT - MORNING

A single candle burns at a small table. Smoke waifs around the room as a sad-faced Guillaume sits in a chair drinking and smoking. He stares at a revolver sitting on the table in front of him.

Also on the table, there is a small framed black and white photo of Genevieve, Philippe, and himself. There's a mostly empty bottle of absinthe and a mostly full ashtray.

Guillaume has a little beard growth and a tired look. The whimpering sound of crying is heard off-camera.

Philippe is sleeping on the couch on the other side of the living room. He's still wearing yesterday's clothes and covered with his father's coat as a blanket. A tear runs down his cheek as he's crying in his sleep. Guillaume looks over at him.

Philippe's eyes flutter open. He wipes the tears from his eyes as he sits up and looks at his father.

PHILIPPE

Have you been up all night?

GUILLAUME

I'm okay.

Philippe slides out from under the coat and off of the couch. He eyes the bottle of absinthe, the ashtray, and the revolver on the table. He steps over to the window, opens it, and looks down at the Newspaper Man.

PHILIPPE

Le Libertaire et deux croissants
s'il te plait!

The Newspaper Man looks up to him.

NEWSPAPER MAN

D'accord!

Philippe steps over to his father's table and stares at the almost empty bottle of absinthe.

PHILIPPE

What is that you're drinking?

Guillaume reaches over and twists the bottle around so Philippe can read it.

PHILIPPE

Absinthe? That's poison.

GUILLAUME

I wish it were.

PHILIPPE

They say it causes hallucinations.

GUILLAUME

I've heard that, too

PHILIPPE

And?

Guillaume eyes Philippe.

GUILLAUME

Nothing yet.

There is a knock on the door. Philippe snatches up the bottle of absinthe and the ashtray, then walks off.

PHILIPPE

I'll make some cafe.

Guillaume watches Philippe as he walks into the kitchen.

INT. CAFE - MORNING

Octave De Villiers sits at a small table, smoking a cigar and drinking brandy while he handwrites a letter with a fountain pen.

His wife, MICHELLE (23), quietly sits with him - a teapot and teacup sit on the table in front of her. Michelle stares at Octave, she wears a pair of sunglasses - even though they are indoors.

Octave takes a sip from his cafe and then looks over to Michelle.

MICHELLE
What are you writing?

OCTAVE
Oh, I'm just penning a letter to the Chief of Police.

Octave smiles at her as she turns away from him.

OCTAVE
Would you stop acting so disheartened all the time?

Michelle adjusts the sunglasses on her face and takes a sip of tea.

MICHELLE
How do you expect me to endure this life with you?

Angry, Octave leans over to her and tears off her sunglasses, and then slings them back at her.

OCTAVE
You want more!?

Michelle reclines away from him. There's a purple bruise under her left eye. They both turn to find a little girl standing near their table, watching them. She's GABRIELLE (8), Rene's daughter. Rene walks up behind her.

RENE
What's the word?

OCTAVE
Nobody's talking.
(half-whisper)
I'm nervous about the gold.

GABBIE
We're going to bury Tiger.

OCTAVE
Tiger?

GABBIE
My doggy.

RENE

He died last night, and I promised Gabbie that we would have a proper funeral at the Cimetiere des Chiens.

OCTAVE

A dog cemetery?

MICHELLE

That's a wonderful idea, Gabrielle.

Gabbie looks over to a smiling Michelle.

GABBIE

Will you come?

MICHELLE

Thank you, but I don't think -

Octave leans in.

OCTAVE

Yes. We'd love to come to your puppy's funeral. When is it?

GABBIE

After lunch.

Octave flags over the Waiter.

OCTAVE

We'll meet you there. And Rene, get the nicest coffin that they have - I'll pay for it.

INT. MESSEIN APARTMENT - MORNING

Guillaume sits at the breakfast table drinking a cafe, while Philippe is eating a croissant with hot chocolate. Philippe is wearing eyeglasses. While reading the newspaper aloud.

PHILIPPE

(reading newspaper)

...the criminals are thought to be from the local anarchist movement that had been terrorizing Paris over the early part of this year. The police call them Illegalists,

PHILIPPE (CON'T)

and it is believed that their leader is the notorious Octave De Villiers.

Philippe leans over and writes some notes in a small notebook, and then looks over to the revolver on the table.

PHILIPPE

Where did you get that revolver?

GUILLAUME

The Great War. It's a Lebel 1892. Standard infantry issue.

PHILIPPE

I've never seen it.

GUILLAUME

I've never told you this, but on two separate occasions, I killed a man.

PHILIPPE

I know.

Philippe locks eyes with his father.

PHILIPPE

Mother told me.

GUILLAUME

When? Why?

PHILIPPE

Last year. To help explain some things.

GUILLAUME

I see.

Philippe goes back to reading aloud from the newspaper.

PHILIPPE

(reading newspaper)

De Villiers led the late-morning robbery yesterday that killed Martin Moreau and an innocent bystander named -

GUILLAUME

Stop!

The two stare at each other for a beat.

BEAT

GUILLAUME

We have to leave.

EXT. CITY MORGUE, PARIS - DAY

The City Morgue is located at the edge of Ile de La Cite, behind the Notre Dame Cathedral. The building is a lower, single-level stone structure.

A black horse-drawn Hearse is in front of the entrance. Some MEN are there, opening up the back of the wagon.

INT. CITY MORGUE, PARIS - DAY

A couple of BYSTANDERS are standing inside the lobby of the morgue. They stare through the wide glass partition at some corpses on display. The bodies lie on white marble slabs, with a slow drip of ice water that keeps them fresh.

Also, there is MADAME GARNIER (65). She stares, entranced at the insensitive display of human flesh - covered only by a small white towel over their private parts.

The MEDICAL EXAMINER, dressed in a white medical smock, steps out of a door and over to Madame Garnier.

MEDICAL EXAMINER

Good morning, Madame.

MADAME GARNIER

My god, man! I can only hope that my daughter's body was not on display for the entertainment of these people!

MEDICAL EXAMINER

That was many years ago, Madame. In the new morgue, only employees and family members of the deceased are allowed inside.

The Examiner's ASSISTANT walks over to them, carrying a marble tray with a white cloth draped over something. He places it on a side table.

MEDICAL EXAMINER

Here is what you ordered, Madame.

He pulls off the cloth to expose a white plaster 'death mask' of her daughter, Genevieve Messein.

Madame Garnier gasps at the sight.

MADAME GARNIER

Dear!

Madame Garnier turns to find Guillaume and Philippe walking into the morgue lobby. She puts her hand over Philippe's eyes.

MADAME GARNIER

No, Philippe. I don't think it wise that he views Genevieve's mask.

GUILLAUME

What mask?

Madame Garnier gestures towards the plaster cast on the marble tray.

Guillaume's face goes blank as he peers down at the mold.

GUILLAUME

How could you?

MADAME GARNIER

It's for the sculptor that I've hired to create her sarcophagus.

Guillaume looks over to Madame Garnier.

GUILLAUME

I won't allow it.

MADAME GARNIER

What do you mean?

Guillaume lifts the plaster cast off of the table and crushes it with his bare hands.

MEDICAL EXAMINER

Sir! I'll have you arrested for that!

Guillaume punches the Medical Examiner in the jaw with a straight right hand, and he collapses to the floor.

The Assistant attends to the fallen Medical Examiner as Madame Garnier pushes Guillaume and Philippe back out of the same door they just entered.

EXT. CITY MORGUE, PARIS - DAY

Guillaume, Philippe, and Madame Garnier stumble out onto the cobbled walk outside.

Madame Garnier looks over to the Men wheeling a black hand-carved wooden coffin on a lorry.

MADAME GARNIER

Be careful with her. It's a long ride back home, and we're not in a hurry.

GUILLAUME

What are you doing?

MADAME GARNIER

I'm so sorry, Guillaume. I'm just so distraught with all of this.

She embraces Guillaume. She breaks off from him and bends down to hug Philippe.

MADAME GARNIER

How sad you have lost such a wonderful woman as your mother.

Philippe weeps into his grandmother's arms.

PHILIPPE

Oh, Grandmother. There is already such a gap in our lives without her.

GUILLAUME

This is Genevieve?

MADAME GARNIER

I'm taking her home to be buried with her family. Of course, there's a place for the two of you, next to her.

Guillaume and Philippe put their hands on top of the coffin as the Men are loading it into the back of the Hearse.

GUILLAUME

My love.

MADAME GARNIER

She should never have come to Paris. I told her that. She could have educated children anywhere in the world. This city is dreadful.

Madame Garnier signals for the Men to lift the casket and get it loaded. They do so as Guillaume and Philippe lift their hands from it.

GUILLAUME

She came to Paris because I was here. She was my wife. We both wanted to build a family.

MADAME GARNIER

Yes. And you did.

She looks down at Philippe.

MADAME GARNIER

A wonderful family. The funeral will be this Friday. You and Philippe should come a day early and spend a couple of nights.

The coffin is loaded up, and the Men climb aboard for the journey home.

PHILIPPE

Goodbye, grandmother.

MADAME GARNIER

Goodbye, my dear.

GUILLAUME

Thank you for everything, Madame Garnier.

Guillaume puts his hand on Philippe's shoulder, and they both turn and walk off.

EXT. CIMETIERE DEX CHIENS, PARIS - DAY

Rene, his wife Sylvie (28), and their daughter Gabrielle stand in the dog cemetery next to a freshly dug grave. There are many headstones and statues of dogs on the cemetery grounds.

Octave driving, he and Michelle arrive on an old one-horse wooden cart. A burlap cloth covers a box that sits on the flatbed.

OCTAVE

Sorry if we're late.

RENE

Where did you get the cart?

Octave jumps off of the cart.

OCTAVE

Borrowed it from a fruit vendor at the market.

He walks up to the small fancy white coffin.

OCTAVE

The dog is in here?

RENE

Yes.

OCTAVE

Open it up, and let's get the gold inside.

Rene starts prying the lid off of the coffin.

GABBIE

It's bad luck to open a coffin once it's closed.

OCTAVE

Bad luck for whom? The dog?

GABBIE

No. For you.

SYLVIE

Gabbie, don't wish bad luck on Uncle Octave.

MICHELLE

She's okay.

Octave leans over to Gabbie.

OCTAVE

It's fine, Gabrielle. When one behest bad luck upon me, it then brings me good luck.

GABBIE

Fine, then.

RENE

Let's load it.

Rene and Octave walk around to the rear of the cart and peel away the burlap, exposing the strongbox stolen from the train.

INT. GUN SHOP - DAY

The dark wood and leather interior give the feel of a hunting lodge. There is a boar's head hung on the wall. Several rifles and shotguns are displayed on a gun rack behind the sales counter.

The PROPRIETOR of the shop sits on a stool at the counter. There is a disassembled shotgun lying out on the counter that the Man is cleaning.

Guillaume and Philippe walk through the front door.

GUILLAUME

Hello.

PROPRIETOR

Good day, sir.

They step up to the counter.

GUILLAUME

We're interested in purchasing some cartridges for this.

Guillaume places his military revolver on the counter.

PROPRIETOR

Uh. Lebel M-1892, eight millimeter. I haven't seen one of those is a while.

GUILLAUME
I kept it after the war.

PROPRIETOR
As many did.

The Proprietor smiles at Philippe as he lifts the pistol up and inspects it - smells it.

PROPRIETOR
Hasn't been fired in a while. Why do you want to fire it now?

GUILLAUME
Protection.

PROPRIETOR
You could find some military issue cartridges around town, but I wouldn't recommend them.

EXT. CIMETIERE DEX CHIENS, PARIS - DAY

Octave and Rene finish shoveling dirt and filling the grave. Gabrielle steps over to the grave and looks down at the disappearing coffin.

GABBIE
Goodbye, Tiger.

OCTAVE
I've got to return this cart. Need a lift?

RENE
Yes, we have to leave, too.

Octave and the others climb onto the one-horse cart. Octave looks down at Michelle.

MICHELLE
I think that I'll just stroll back.

Octave gives her a frustrated look.

OCTAVE
Suit yourself.

All onboard, Octave slaps the reins, and the horse responds - pulling the cart down the path.

SYLVIE
Au revoir, Michelle.

GABBIE
Goodbye.

Michelle stands at the grave for a few moments. The cemetery CARETAKER comes trotting up to her.

CARETAKER
Excuse me; I'm looking for Monsieur Degaste?

MICHELLE
He just left.

They each look off to the horse-drawn cart in the distance.

CARETAKER
I have the deed for him.

MICHELLE
Deed?

CARETAKER
The ownership document for the animal's grave.

The Caretaker hands the document to Michelle, and she looks it over.

MICHELLE
It's all so formal looking.

CARETAKER
It's similar to a deed for real estate. It's the only proof of ownership for this plot.

Michelle looks at the deed and then to the Caretaker.

MICHELLE
I'll make sure he gets it.

INT. GUN SHOP - DAY

The Proprietor pulls a box of cartridges off of the shelf behind him.

PROPRIETOR
These will work well. They're rimmed, black powder, 111 grains.

PHILIPPE
What kind of gun do you use?

The Proprietor reaches under the counter again and pulls out a tiny, palm-size double-barrel Derringer, and puts it on the counter.

PROPRIETOR
This little thing. I keep it loaded and in a handy place near the cash register. It's a six-millimeter.

Philippe gives the tiny pistol an interested look.

PROPRIETOR
It would fit well in your little hands, son.

Philippe and the Proprietor share a smile.

GUILLAUME
These cartridges are fine.

PROPRIETOR
How many boxes?

GUILLAUME
One, please.

INT. CAFE - MORNING

Chief Gouget is standing at the bar counter of a cafe. Detective Bonhomme walks up to join him.

CHIEF GOUGET
I didn't want to mention this at the office, but this business with De Villiers has become personal.

DETECTIVE BONHOMME

How’s that?

Chief Gouget signals the Bartender.

CHIEF GOUGET

I went to school with Martin Moreau, and I think he knew that.

DETECTIVE BONHOMME

High school?

CHIEF GOUGET

University.

The Bartender steps up.

CHIEF GOUGET

Un galopin, s’il te plait.

DETECTIVE BONHOMME

Double expresso.

CHIEF GOUGET

Anyway, he killed two birds yesterday - three if you count the gold.

DETECTIVE BONHOMME

What do you want to do about it?

CHIEF GOUGET

I want you to find De Villiers so that I can kill him.

Detective Huche walks up and joins them at the bar. As the Bartender drops off their order - a tiny glass of beer and a double espresso.

DETECTIVE HUCHE

(to Bartender)

Scotch, up.

CHIEF GOUGET

Wait a minute. You’re on your way back to the office.

DETECTIVE HUCHE

So?

CHIEF GOUGET

You can't drink scotch now.

DETECTIVE HUCHE

You're drinking beer, so I thought -

CHIEF GOUGET

I want you sharp.
(to Bartender)
Espresso.

DETECTIVE BONHOMME
(to Chief Gouget)
So, I'll take care of that. Just give me a little space.

CHIEF GOUGET

D'accord.

Detective Bonhomme drains his double espresso and smacks his cup on the counter.

DETECTIVE BONHOMME

See you.

Detective Bonhomme walks off as Chief takes a sip of his beer.

INT. MESSEIN APARTMENT - MORNING

Guillaume sits at the small breakfast table, drinking absinthe while smoking a pipe. Philippe walks up and puts a cafe on the table in front of him.

PHILIPPE

Please drink some cafe, Papa.

GUILLAUME

Read.

Philippe lifts the newspaper and reads.

PHILIPPE
(reading)
De Villiers and his Gang are wanted for extortion, robbery, and murder. The Gang has found sympathy among the French working class, who flock

PHILIPPE (CON'T)
to the site of their most famous heist and shootout at the Bank Societe Generale in Nogent-sur-Marne.

ANGLE ON: Philippe pauses as he watches Guillaume pour himself a glass of absinthe.

PHILIPPE
I read that absinthe makes people insane and that drinkers end up killing their whole family.

Guillaume eyes Philippe as he takes another gulp of absinthe.

GUILLAUME
You know that's not true.

PHILIPPE
Yes. But it sounds scary.

GUILLAUME
Continue.

PHILIPPE
(reading)
It is believed that the murder of Martin Moreau and robbery of over thirty thousand in gold bars was retribution for the comrades that were killed at Nogent-sur-Marne. The trial of Michel Jacob, one of the Gang members captured at the robbery, continues today at the Palais de Justice.

Philippe continues staring at the newspaper momentarily and then at his father.

GUILLAUME
There is a trial this morning. Court usually commences at ten o'clock.

PHILIPPE
Father. I know that you've been to meetings at the Socialist Federation. These men are anarchists, which means they're most likely socialists.

GUILLAUME

Yes. In many ways, I support the Socialists Federation, as I also have supported the anarchists. But what I don't support, is Illegalism. Robbery, violence, and murder. And, of course, I could never forgive the men that killed your mother. Could you?

BEAT

PHILIPPE

Never.

EXT. PALAIS DE JUSTICE DE PARIS - DAY

A sweeping, and steep staircase leads up to a Second Empire stone building with a central pavilion - four stone columns and a curved mansard roof.

Some Anarchists Protesters are in front of the Court House picketing.

INT. COURTROOM, PALAIS DE JUSTICE - DAY

Court is in session. A Prosecuting Attorney is interviewing a Witness on the stand. The gallery is partially filled with people - Michelle De Villiers among them.

The doors to the gallery open, and Guillaume and Philippe enter the courtroom. Michelle de Villiers looks back to the father and son as they shuffle over to an aisle bench and slide into a seat.

Guillaume is focused on courtroom litigation as Philippe makes eye contact with Michelle.

The Prosecuting Attorney addresses the Witness in the background.

PROSECUTING ATTORNEY (O.S.)

So, in the deposition you gave three weeks ago, you claimed that you saw the Defendant at the robbery. Now you're saying that you're not sure?

WITNESS (O.S.)

Yes. I'm not certain that it's him.

PROSECUTING ATTORNEY (O.S.)
Have you been threatened by strangers or persons affiliated with this case?

WITNESS (O.S.)
Not that I know -

PROSECUTING ATTORNEY (O.S.)
...And what does that mean, sir?

Philippe continues looking around the room and finds Detective Bonhomme sitting in the back row.

WITNESS
It means...no.

PROSECUTING ATTORNEY
Well, I think that you have!

INT. COURTROOM, PALAIS DE JUSTICE - DAY

The Judge slaps the gavel down on his desk to end the day's court proceedings.

JUDGE
This hearing is called for lunch and will not resume again until tomorrow at ten o'clock in the morning.

SLAP SLAP SLAP

All of the courtroom participants and bystanders rise and start filing out of the space. A couple of the Defendant's supporters shout out as their identity gets lost in the mass of bodies moving about the courtroom.

SOMEONE #1
He's innocent!

SOMEONE #2
Let him go!

The Judge glares out amongst the crowd as he disappears through his private door.

INT. COURTROOM CORRIDOR, PALAIS DE JUSTICE - DAY

People are milling about the corridor outside the courtroom. Guillaume and Philippe stop and talk there.

PHILIPPE

I think that I saw that man over there in front of the train station on the morning mother was killed.

Guillaume follows his son's eyes over to Raymond.

PHILIPPE

He was driving the automobile.

Raymond is standing alone. He locks eyes with the Witness that was being questioned in the courtroom. Raymond nods at the Man.

Raymond walks over towards Michelle and two other Women who are talking amongst themselves. The two others are Sylvie and Jules' wife, EDITH (27).

Philippe eyes Raymond, and then the three Women.

ANGEL ON:

Michelle, Sylvie, and Edith, as Raymond approaches the three Women. Philippe walks away from his father and subtly blends into the group without them noticing.

Guillaume watches from the background as Philippe stays low and unnoticed, as the group speaks to each other.

RAYMOND

You, ladies, shouldn't stand around outside the courtroom.

MICHELLE

Shall we rush home to our place in the kitchen?

Raymond gives Michelle a hard stare.

SYLVIE

When is Jules' funeral?

EDITH

Tomorrow afternoon at two. A small gathering at Cemetery Montrouge.

EDITH

Do you think Octave will come?

MICHELLE

No. The police are certain to be watching.

Raymond notices Philippe nestled into the group listening to them.

RAYMOND

Hey, boy. Who does this kid belong to?

The Women shake their heads. Michelle smiles. Philippe looks at Michelle, and they share a smile.

PHILIPPE

Why do you wear your cap backward when you drive?

Raymond is shocked at this statement. He pushes Philippe to the floor.

RAYMOND

Go!

MICHELLE

Don't push him, Raymond!

Philippe stands back up and stares at Raymond. Then, he looks over to Michelle and smiles.

PHILIPPE

Thank you, Mademoiselle.

Philippe turns and walks off.

MICHELLE

Raymond. Your shoes are untied.

All in the group look down at Raymond's shoes - and indeed, the laces of both shoes are untied.

RAYMOND

What the hell?

ANGLE ON:

Guillaume and Philippe walk through the Courthouse corridor.

PHILIPPE
Tomorrow they're burying their friend that was killed at the station.

GUILLAUME
Where?

PHILIPPE
Montrouge, at two.

INT. DRAFTING ROOM - DAY

Guillaume sits on a stool as he leans over a large drafting board. With the help of drafting tools, he's drawing a complicated machine part by hand with a pencil. He adjusts the light fixture which hangs over the board. There are several other MEN at similar desks, all drawing machine parts.

The SUPERVISOR enters the room and walks over to Guillaume's table, and looks down at his drawing.

SUPERVISOR
Excellent, Guillaume.

GUILLAUME
I'm going to draw two isometrics on the side here, so it will all be on one page.

SUPERVISOR
Good idea.

The Supervisor points to an area of the drawing.

SUPERVISOR
Double-check these dimensions with the floor manager.

GUILLAUME
I've already confirmed them.

SUPERVISOR
Listen. We're all very sad here about Genevieve. And we appreciate your coming in today.

GUILLAUME

Thank you. I do have to leave for the day at one-thirty.

SUPERVISOR

Something important?

GUILLAUME

Funeral.

SUPERVISOR

Oh. Of course. Well, please let us know if you need anything.

GUILLAUME

Thank you.

EXT. SCHOOLYARD, PARIS - DAY

Guillaume walks along the fence of a schoolyard. Many children are playing in the yard. He looks over and makes eye contact with Philippe, and nods his head. Philippe and his TEACHER walk over to the fence.

TEACHER

I wanted to say that there's no need to rush Philippe back to school. He's already ahead of the class in his studies.

GUILLAUME

He likes school, and I've got to work, anyway.

TEACHER

I was thinking of making an appointment with a child psychologist to help Philippe through these difficult times.

Guillaume looks over to Philippe.

GUILLAUME

Would you like to see a psychologist, Philippe?

PHILIPPE

No, thank you.

The Teacher gives Guillaume an awkward look.

TEACHER
Those men, they're horrible. They have to be dealt with.

GUILLAUME
We're working on that.

The Teacher gives Guillaume another awkward look as Guillaume gives Philippe a hand signal. He immediately starts climbing over the fence.

TEACHER
So, Philippe is...leaving for the day?

GUILLAUME
The funeral.

Philippe jumps down from the fence, on Guillaume's side.

TEACHER
Oh, of course.

EXT. CEMETERY MONTROUGE, PARIS - DAY

Guillaume and Philippe walk through the cemetery toward a group of people who are gathering at a gravesite. Philippe holds a dozen pink chrysanthemums (flower of death).

When they arrive, they find Michelle, Edith, Sylvie, Raymond, and several other adults and children. At the head of the grave, a Priest stands wearing a black cassock cloak and holding a Bible.

The grave is surrounded by bronze urns - each filled with flowers.

Michelle gives Guillaume a once-over and then makes eye contact with Philippe. He smiles at her, and she hesitantly returns his smile.

PRIEST
Everyone, please gather around the grave and keep silent.

EXT. JULES'S GRAVESITE, CEMETERY MONTROUGE, PARIS - DAY

All stand around the grave as the Priest is at the end of his burial service.

PRIEST

...now, let us pray. God, we thank you for the life that you give us. It is full of work and of responsibility, of sorrow and joy. Today we thank you for Jules Valet for what he has given and received. Does anyone have anything they would like to add?

Nobody moves for a beat.

BEAT

Philippe takes a couple of steps forward and stands just at the edge of the grave.

PHILIPPE

(speaking in Latin)

Diabolus enim mihi miserere animae tuae ut expendas dabis tamen in inferno aeternum.

Amen.

Translation: May the devil have mercy on your soul as you will surely spend eternity in hell.

Amen.

ALL

Amen.

The Priest doesn't say amen - he just stares at Philippe.

The ceremony is over, things become relaxed.

Everyone gives Philippe a questioning look as only the Priest understood what he said.

EDITH

Was that Latin?

MICHELLE

It must have been.

EDITH

How could a little boy like that speak Latin?

Still stunned, the Priest watches Philippe as he walks over to FLEUR (8), a little girl standing next to Edith. Philippe speaks to her.

PHILIPPE

I'm sorry that you'll have to live the rest of your life without a father.

FLEUR

Thank you. But I will see him in heaven one day.

PHILIPPE

What makes you believe that he'll be in heaven?

FLEUR

Why wouldn't he?

The two stare at each other for a beat.

BEAT

PHILIPPE

I suppose that one could discover a certain hell in heaven, but I don't believe that one could find any kind of heaven in hell.

The two smile at each other.

FLEUR

Would you like to come to our house after the funeral?

PHILIPPE

I don't think so but thank you for your invitation.

Philippe smiles at Fleur, and she smiles back.

EXT. CEMETERY MONTROUGE, PARIS - TWILIGHT

It's getting dark outside. Dressed in a hat and overcoat, Octave

De Villiers steps through the iron gates into the cemetery. He looks around apprehensively as he walks the path toward Jules Valet's gravesite.

As he gets closer to the grave, something gets his attention. He looks puzzled.

ANGLE ON:

Jules Valet's gravesite. The coffin and grave are covered by earth now. All of the urns filled with flowers that surround the grave are burning - engulfed in flames.

BACK TO:

Octave continues his curious approach until he's only ten meters from the grave. He stops and stares at the sight. The pink chrysanthemums that Philippe had brought to the funeral lay flat on the freshly filled earth.

ANGLE ON:

Philippe, in the shadow of a nearby mausoleum. In the safety of the darkness, he quietly watches Octave from 100 meters off.

EXT. PARIS STREETS - NIGHT

Philippe follows Octave down the sidewalks and through the streets of Paris as he walks home. Octave has his coat collar pulled up high to help obscure his face. Some PEDESTRIANS and cars pass him in the street.

Philippe stands off and watches Octave disappear around the side of the house. He looks over to a Brasserie Pied-Noir, that sits across the street and has a good view of the house.

INT. BRASSERIE PIED-NOIR - DAY

INTERCUT: Between Guillaume and Philippe's table and Michelle and Detective Bonhomme at the bar counter.

Guillaume and Philippe are having lunch at the brasserie across from De Villiers' house. They both sit on the same side of the table to keep watch on the front of his house.

A glass of sauvignon blanc sits in front of Guillaume.

A Woman and a Man sit in the dimness at the rear of the bar.

A WAITER approaches their table, holding a couple of plates.

WAITER

Okay. Cod provencal and bouillabaisse.

He places the bouillabaisse in front of Guillaume.

ANGLE ON:

At the rear of the cafe, in the shadows, at the far end of the bar counter, Michelle sits with Detective Bonhomme. Michelle is eyeing Guillaume and Philippe up front in the dining area.

Michelle is drinking absinthe. They speak in a whisper voice.

DETECTIVE BONHOMME

Listen, I could arrest you right now and have you thrown in jail.

MICHELLE

Why don't you then?

DETECTIVE BONHOMME

Because I love you.

MICHELLE

You're a fool.

DETECTIVE BONHOMME

Why are we always meeting here?

MICHELLE

Why do you always come?

DETECTIVE BONHOMME

Does he live nearby?

MICHELLE

I don't even know where he's living. He sets me up in a house and then just pops in and out as he wishes.

Michelle nods towards Guillaume and Philippe's table.

MICHELLE

I think that boy is following me.

Detective Bonhomme looks over to Philippe.

DETECTIVE BONHOMME
His name is Philippe Messein. His mother was killed at the Gard Du Nord robbery.

MICHELLE
(gasps)
No!

DETECTIVE BONHOMME
And that's his father he's with.

Entranced, Michelle stands from the barstool and slowly walks towards their table.

BACK TO:

Guillaume and Philippe's table. They're eating.

GUILLAUME
Bring me a little green salad, please.

WAITER
Very well.

The Waiter walks off.

PHILIPPE
Look.

They both look towards the front of De Villiers' house. A WOMAN walks up the side of the house.

GUILLAUME
I wonder who that is?

MICHELLE (O.S.)
The housemaid.

They both look over to find Michelle, drink in hand, sitting on the barstool nearby.

She and Guillaume eye each other for a beat.

BEAT

MICHELLE

I'm so sorry.

PHILIPPE

Papa. This is Madame De Villiers.

Michelle and Guillaume look at each other for a beat.

BEAT

GUILLAUME

(to Michelle)

I believe you.

MICHELLE

Why are you watching my house?

Guillaume stands and steps over to an empty chair at their table. He pulls it out for her.

GUILLAUME

Please, won't you join us?

Michelle steps over to the chair and sits down. She shows slight, unstable drunkenness as she does so. She places her drink down awkwardly.

Guillaume lifts her drink and sniffs it. Michelle smiles slightly.

MICHELLE

That's my little green fairy.

Guillaume smiles at her.

GUILLAUME

Please, excuse me for a moment.

Guillaume eyes the BARTENDER and Detective Bonhomme at the far end of the bar. Drink in hand, he walks over to them.

ANGLE ON:

Guillaume walks up to the two Men. He addresses the Bartender and places Michelle's drink on the counter.

GUILLAUME

What is this?

BARTENDER

Absinthe.

GUILLAUME

I know what she thinks it is, but what is it, really?

Guillaume lifts the glass and pours what's left of the drink over the counter. His eyes locked with the Bartenders.

The Bartender and the Detective give each other a look.

BEAT

GUILLAUME

Bring her a Pernod Fils, avec sucre.

The Bartender gets to work as Guillaume turns to Detective Bonhomme.

GUILLAUME

You should be ashamed of yourself, Detective.

Detective Bonhomme stares at Guillaume.

BEAT

DETECTIVE BONHOMME

It's not what you think.

GUILLAUME

You're taking advantage of a woman in need.

Detective Bonhomme stays silent as Guillaume turns and walks back to the table.

BACK TO:

Guillaume walks over to his table and sits. He lifts an oversized spoon.

GUILLAUME

You'll excuse me, Madame. I didn't come here for cold bouillabaisse.

He looks over to Philippe.

GUILLAUME

Eat your lunch, Philippe.

MICHELLE

Why are you spying on my house?
What can I do for you?

Holding a small tray, the Bartender walks up to their table. He places a 10oz Napoleon Tumbler on the table and then adds a small strainer with a sugar cube.

Michelle watches with interest as the Bartender pours the absinthe over the sugar cube - the soft green liquid elegantly filters through the cube and into the glass.

MICHELLE

Wow.

GUILLAUME

If he's doing this to you, you should leave him immediately.

MICHELLE

He'd find me again. He beats me...he takes me at his will. You see, he owns me.

GUILLAUME

How could that be -

MICHELLE

When I leave him, he terrorizes my family.

PHILIPPE

Why is he so popular with anarchists?

MICHELLE

Because they don't know him. Octave and his Gang...they're all ruthless. They enjoy what they do.

An upstairs window opens in De Villiers' house.

PHILIPPE

Somebody just opened the window.

Michelle turns around to look.

MICHELLE
I have to go. That's my signal.

She takes another gulp from her drink and stands. Guillaume also stands.

GUILLAUME
We didn't see him enter.

MICHELLE
He uses the kitchen door.

PHILIPPE
Madame, are you in love with Octave De Villiers?

MICHELLE
I stopped loving him two years ago.

GUILLAUME
Are you sure?

MICHELLE
(half-whisper)
He's leaving tomorrow morning for Chantilly. A bank robbery. That's how much I love him.

The three stare at each other for a beat.

BEAT

MICHELLE
I have to go.

Michelle rushes over to the door - she turns back to them as she pulls it open.

MICHELLE
Please, be careful.

She smiles as she hurries out the door.

Guillaume looks back towards the Detective - he's gone. He sits down and looks over at Philippe as he lifts his spoon.

GUILLAUME

Eat your lunch. We have to get home and pack if we're going to make the six-fifteen train.

PHILIPPE

We're going to Chantilly?

GUILLAUME

Of course.

EXT. POLICE STATION PARKING LOT AREA, PARIS - DAY

INTERCUT: Raymond, Policeman #1, Attendant, and a yellow limousine.

Raymond stands in the shadows of the late afternoon sun. He eyes the Police parking lot and its ATTENDANT from across the street. Madame Boulanger's yellow limousine is parked against the wall at the far end. Raymond crosses the road and creeps along the lot's fence. SERGEANT DEGROOT walks out to the lot and speaks to the lot Attendant.

DEGROOT

The Boulanger chauffeur is coming to pick up their car tonight.

ATTENDANT

Shall I clean it up for them?

DEGROOT

Give it a once over, and tell him it was Sergeant Degroot's order.

ATTENDANT

Okay, Sergeant.

Degroot smiles, and then turns and walks back into the Police Station. The Attendant walks over and pushes the lot's long security gate open. He walks over to the limousine, starts it, and pulls it up near his Guard's Station.

Raymond watches curiously from behind the fence. He keeps a lookout for street walkers and tries not to look too suspicious.

RAYMOND

Uh?

The Attendant fills a bucket with water and soap, carts it over to the yellow limousine, and starts wiping it down.

RAYMOND
(softly to himself)
Well, thank you very much, Officer.

INT. MESSEIN APARTMENT - DAY

Guillaume and Philippe hurry through the front door of the apartment.

GUILLAUME
Your mother's funeral is tomorrow afternoon. So pack your church suit.

Philippe stares at his father.

GUILLAUME
No Wildroot cream, tomorrow.

Guillaume walks over to the little cafe table and the half-full bottle of absinthe that sits on it. He grabs the bottle by the neck and walks it over to the kitchen sink. He pours the absinthe down the drain.

Guillaume then packs a shirt into a small valise. He lifts the revolver and gives it a look for a beat.

BEAT

Guillaume looks over to his son. Philippe is standing at the large front window staring down at some BOYS playing football on the street.

Guillaume joins him at the window.

GUILLAUME
I promised your mother I'd limit your time playing in the street. But you'll be back scoring goals soon.

Philippe turns and smiles at his father.

PHILIPPE
There will be plenty of time for football, Papa.

Guillaume shoves the revolver into the valise as Philippe slings a small duffle over his shoulder.

PHILIPPE

I'm ready.

EXT. POLICE STATION PARKING LOT, PARIS - DAY

While the Attendant washes the automobile, Raymond sneaks around to the back of the lot. He quietly climbs over the fence and drops down onto the pavement. He pulls out a pistol as he walks up behind the Attendant.

RAYMOND

Excusez-Moi.

As the Attendant turns around, Raymond slams the pistol over his head.

INT. TRAIN, SECOND CLASS CAR - TWILIGHT

Guillaume sits while Philippe stands at the window. He gazes out to the Chateau de Chantilly in the distance.

PHILIPPE

It's beautiful.

Guillaume looks out to the Chateau.

PHILIPPE

Who owns it, Papa?

GUILLAUME

The Duke d'Aumale.

The sound of the train's wheels sliding in the background.

GUILLAUME

We're arriving.

EXT. DE VILLIERS HOUSE - EARLY MORNING

The sun rises over the house, and a few lights illuminate the windows. A FARMER rides a horse-cart through the street into town.

INT. DE VILLIERS HOUSE - SAME

Octave is hustling around, getting ready for the morning. Michelle helps him.

OCTAVE

This is the address of our new house.

He hands her a paper.

MICHELLE

But I like this place.

OCTAVE

You know the routine. Hopefully, I'll be there to join you tonight. If not, soon.

Michelle looks off and stares into space for a moment.

OCTAVE

Also, I'm sorry about last night. But you should know better than to irritate me when I'm drinking.

Michelle nods her head in agreement.

MICHELLE

It's my fault.

Octave looks out as an auto pulls up behind the house.

OCTAVE

I have to go.

He grabs a bag and starts out the backdoor. Michelle follows him as he disappears outside to the yellow limousine waiting in the back alley.

Michelle watches from a window as the limousine drives off.

Raymond climbs out of the driver's side and looks over the top of the auto. Rene and Edith step out and help Octave into the back of the limousine.

INT. HOTEL ROOM, CHANTILLY - MORNING

Guillaume stands at the front window looking down at the street. Philippe's head rises from his bed pillow.

PHILIPPE
What time is it?

GUILLAUME
Seven. There's a Societe Generale Bank on the corner.

Guillaume turns to Philippe.

GUILLAUME
De Villiers has been targeting them.

PHILIPPE
Shall we contact the police?

GUILLAUME
No. I'm going to kill Octave De Villiers myself.

BEAT

PHILIPPE
What about me?

GUILLAUME
You stay at the hotel. You can watch from upstairs, here.

PHILIPPE
I want to go with you.

GUILLAUME
It's too dangerous.

PHILIPPE
Will you shoot him before the robbery, or after?

GUILLAUME
I'm going to let the circumstance present itself. As soon as I have a clean shot, I'll take it.

Philippe stares at his father for a moment.

PHILIPPE

Papa.

GUILLAUME

Yes, Philippe?

PHILIPPE

You're not allowed to die.

EXT. COUNTRYSIDE, CHANTILLY - MORNING

The yellow limousine parked among some trees. Octave, Raymond, Rene, Edith, Sylvie, Andre, and a new man, ETIENNE Soudy, stand around the automobile talking about strategy.

OCTAVE

(speaks quickly)

Raymond will stay with the auto and stand outside as a lookout. I'll be the first in the door, and Rene will deal with the front Guard - there shouldn't be more than one. The ladies will have shotguns.

Andre hands a shotgun to Sylvie and one to Edith.

EDITH

I've never shot a gun before.

OCTAVE

It's okay; just point it at the middle of what you want to shoot.

Octave gestures with his hand over the center of his torso.

EDITH

I'm nervous. What if I miss it?

ANDRE

(frustrated)

Okay, try this.

Andre pulls an empty wine bottle out of the car, walks off about five meters to a tree trunk, places the bottle upright on the trunk, and steps aside.

OCTAVE
(to Edith)
It has some kick to it, so spread your legs a little for balance.

Edith spreads her feet apart. She pulls the shotgun up to her shoulder, points at the bottle, and fires.

The recoil from the shotgun firing blows Edith backward two meters. As that happens, the glass wine bottle explodes from a direct hit.

Rene bends over and helps a shaken Edith to her feet. Everyone laughs for a moment.

OCTAVE
Well done, Edith.

ALL
Great!

EXT. SOCIETE GENERALE BANK, CHANTILLY - MORNING

A quiet morning in the village of Chantilly. A bank GUARD steps outside and unlocks the front doors of the bank.

ANGLE ON:

Guillaume sits at a cafe across the street, having a drink. He looks up the road to find the yellow limousine approaching. The automobile pulls up next to the bank and stops. Guillaume stands at his table as he watches.

Guns in hand, the De Villiers Gang quickly files out of the back of the limousine and into the bank.

INT. SOCIETE GENERALE BANK - MORNING

The bank has a polished wood interior, iron-barred teller windows on one side, and small offices on the other. There are a few bank CLIENTS and half a dozen bank EMPLOYEES.

The De Villiers Gang charges through the front door and into the bank's lobby.

Octave pulls out a semi-automatic pistol and fires it into the air.

OCTAVE

Everybody! Hands up! Don't make a move!

The Gang fans out over the lobby. Rene climbs up on the teller counter for a better vantage point. He holds an automatic pistol in each hand and spreads his arm like a giant bird as he fires several shots into the air.

Bank EXECUTIVE #1 sneaks out the rear of the lobby through the back door.

OCTAVE

You! Freeze!

De Villiers grabs hold of bank EXECUTIVE #2 by the suit collar and drags him over toward the vault.

OCTAVE

You're opening the vault!

Octave looks over at her as he pushes Executive #2 through the lobby towards the vault.

OCTAVE

(to Edith)

I need you over here!

Edith follows Octave to the vault and stands back a few meters as Octave pushes Executive #2 into the vault door.

OCTAVE

Where's the Guard?

The Executive gives Octave a silent stare.

OCTAVE

Tell me!

Nothing from Executive #2, but he glances over to a wooden door near the vault.

Octave looks over at the wooden door, and then to Edith.

OCTAVE

Watch that door.

Edith raises her shotgun towards the door - then eyes Octave.

OCTAVE

The door!!

The sudden jolt from Octave startles a nervous Edith, and she accidentally pulls the trigger of the shotgun.

The blasts blows apart the wooden door. Edith recoils backward about two meters and ends up on the floor.

Behind the busted-up wooden door is the Guard, now wounded from the shotgun blast - blood on his left arm and leg.

Octave signals to Sylvie.

OCTAVE

Help her!

Sylvie helps Edith to her feet.

Octave gives Executive #2 a stern look. Then pistol whips him across the forehead.

EXECUTIVE #2

Uhh!

OCTAVE

It's not your money!

Executive #2 quickly starts turning the vault's combination dial.

INT. POLICE STATION, CHANTILLY - MORNING

The station is quiet in the mid-morning. The DESK SERGEANT keeps an eye on the front lobby from his perch at the high counter. A few other POLICEMEN wander around the office.

Suddenly, escaped BANK Executive #1 rushes through the front door.

BANK EXECUTIVE #1

Hurry! They're robbing the bank!

DESK SERGEANT

Who!

BANK EXECUTIVE #1

De Villiers!

The Desk Sergeant looks over to a nearby Policeman.

DESK SERGEANT

All foot Policemen! Close off the road!

The Policeman rushes through a door into the back offices. The Desk Sergeant rushes through the backdoor and outside.

The Desk sergeant hurries into the horse stables. The LIEUTENANT and several Mounties are working there.

DESK SERGEANT

De Villiers is robbing the Bank!

LIEUTENANT

Chantilly?

DESK SERGEANT

Yes!

The Lieutenant turns towards the Mounties scattered throughout the interior of the stables.

LIEUTENANT

Mount up!

All the Mounties scurry about as they saddle their horses.

EXT. SOCIETE GENERALE BANK - MORNING

Guillaume makes his way up the street as he keeps an eye on Raymond, who holds a lever-action rifle next to the limousine.

INT. POLICE STABLES, CHANTILLY - MORNING

Five of the Mounted Police stand at attention next to their saddled horses as the Lieutenant stands in front, giving them their orders.

LIEUTENANT

This is an opportunity to bring great honor to these stables! They've come from Paris to rob our bank! They have no respect for us! I was born for this moment - we were all born for this moment! Were we not?!

MOUNTIES

Yes, sir!

LIEUTENANT

Present arms!

With perfect synchronization, the Mounties present their bolt action rifles to the Lieutenant.

INT. SOCIETE GENERALE BANK - MORNING

The bank's vault door is open. Octave, Rene, and Andre quickly load cash and gold into satchels as the Women hold the bank Clients and Employees at bay.

The wounded Guard is being cared for by Bank Executive #2 and one of the female tellers.

INT. POLICE STABLES, CHANTILLY - MORNING

The Mounties, still at attention - present their arms. The Lieutenant takes a Policeman's rifle, inspects it, and then hands it back.

LIEUTENANT

Mounted Police, mount your horses!

INT. SOCIETE GENERALE BANK - MORNING

Rene and Andre have satchels of money and gold slung over their shoulders. The Gang starts backing their way toward the front entrance.

EXT. POLICE STABLES, CHANTILLY - MORNING

With a burst, six horseback and uniformed French Mounted Policemen charge out of the Great Stables of Domaine de Chantilly. They all ride matching soft-grey Arabian horses.

They race at full gallop over the dirt roads toward the Societe Generale Bank.

EXT. SOCIETE GENERALE BANK, CHANTILLY, COUNTRYSIDE - MORNING

INTERCUT: Raymond, Octave's Gang, Police, and Guillaume - engage in a shootout in the street and countryside.

Octave and his Gang back out of the bank. Octave looks over to Raymond.

OCTAVE

Get in the automobile!

Raymond hears something.

RAYMOND

Wait a moment!

He runs around the limousine and looks up the road.

The six Mounted Police are charging up Main Street - only 300 meters from the bank

RAYMOND

The police!

The rest of the Gang rushes out of the front entry to confront them. They immediately start firing shots at the fast-approaching Mounted Police. The Mounted Police, pistols in hand, return fire at the Gang while at full gallop.

LIEUTENANT

Disperse!

The Mounted Police fan out away from each other and dismount. They take up positions and start firing their rifles.

Guillaume watches all of this with fascination. He's ducked down behind an oxcart across the street from the bank. He watches Octave with interest.

Philippe watches the gun battle from the upstairs hotel room window. He runs over to the door and rushes out.

Octave and his Gang struggle to get loaded into the limousine. The limousine, too, is taking a beating from the carbine rifles of the Mounted Police. Gang member, Etienne Soudy, takes a gunshot to the shoulder and falls to the ground.

Octave exposes himself a bit, and Guillaume takes a couple of shots. He misses him, but he does attract Octave's attention. Octave spots his attacker behind the post and takes a few shots at Guillaume, himself.

One of the Mounted Policemen takes a bullet in the chest and falls. Gang members, Andre and Sylvie, also take a couple of bullets but nothing lethal.

Octave is more focused on his mano-a-mano with Guillaume, and the two continue to exchange gunfire with each other.

Another Mountie takes a bullet in the arm and struggles to use his rifle. He's trapped against a storefront wall. A shotgun blast blows out the storefront window just above his head, and bullets fly.

The storefront door opens up a little, and Philippe is there. He waves the Mountie over to him. The Mountie obliges and clambers across the boardwalk - Philippe reaches out and helps him escape through the door.

With the Gang loaded up into the limousine, Octave stands on the step outside the limo's rear door as Raymond maneuvers the automobile away from the bank and down the street.

As the limousine pulls away, Guillaume shouts out to Octave.

GUILLAUME

Octave!

Octave turns and looks at his aggressor, and the two engage in a final round of gunfire. They each strike a direct hit - Octave takes a bullet in the left shoulder, and Guillaume in the left arm.

Octave jumps into the limousine as bullets continue to fly. The yellow limousine zooms away from the battle. The Lieutenant stands and shouts orders to his Men.

LIEUTENANT

Mount up!

The Lieutenant and the three other Mounties ride off through the forest.

INT. YELLOW LIMOUSINE, CHANTILLY - MORNING

Raymond races the automobile along the dirt road out of town. It's animated inside the limousine. There's blood everywhere. Octave, Andre, and Sylvie are wounded and bleeding.

SYLVIE

My arm! Help me!

Edith and Rene tend to Sylvie's cries. Rene tears part of his shirt away and wraps it around Sylvie's arm. As he does so, Rene looks over to Octave, who's attending to his own wounds.

RENE

Are you okay?

OCTAVE

I can deal with it.

Octave tears away part of his shirt and wraps it around his upper left arm.

RENE

We should have brought more shirts!

Octave and Rene eye each other and chuckle.

EDITH

What's so funny!?

The two Men straighten up.

OCTAVE

It's only my left shoulder.

Andre is grimacing.

ANDRE

I think mine hit the bone.

Octave and Edith take a look at Andre's wound.

OCTAVE

Can you raise your arm?

ANDRE

Not really.

Octave and Rene wear torn-up bloody shirts with undershirts exposed. Octave looks around.

OCTAVE

Who's got a spare shirt?

Raymond starts working his shirt off.

RAYMOND

Take mine.

EXT. ROAD, CHATEAU DE CHANTILLY - MORNING

Five Policemen have the road blocked with a couple of oxcarts. They're waiting for the Bandits with their guns drawn and ready.

The Chateau de Chantilly sits resplendently in the background.

POLICEMAN #1

There they are!

All look up the road towards the distant but fast-approaching yellow limousine.

INT. YELLOW LIMOUSINE, CHANTILLY - MORNING

The yellow limousine group is a bit calmer as Raymond slams on the breaks. The auto skids to a stop.

RAYMOND

Merde!

All look up.

RAYMOND

They've got the road blocked!

OCTAVE

Let's get out here!

EXT. YELLOW LIMOUSINE ON THE ROAD, CHANTILLY - MORNING

Octave is the first out, and the Gang follows - filing out of the automobile.

OCTAVE

Stay behind the vehicle!

Octave opens the rear trunk as the others climb out and make their way to the rear of the auto.

The Policemen down the road start to fire shots at the Gang.

OCTAVE

Get everything out! Load up your guns!

As bullets strike the limousine, they drag the guns and the satchels behind the auto.

EDITH

More!

Edith points towards the Mounted Policemen riding two hundred meters off through a clearing in the forest.

OCTAVE

That's the road we want!

Rene carries the other satchel, and all are loaded up as they rush into the forest for better cover.

EXT. ROAD, CHATEAU DE CHANTILLY - MORNING

The Mounted Policemen ride up to the foot Policemen at the roadblock. Policeman #2 points off towards the limousine stranded on the road.

POLICEMEN #1

They've abandoned their auto, and they're heading through the forest.

The Lieutenant looks out towards the De Villiers Gang. He sees Edith helping Sylvie - they both disappear into the woods.

LIEUTENANT

They're headed towards the other road! You five cut across down this direction, and we'll follow them!

POLICEMAN #1

Yes, sir!

The Mounties ride off towards the yellow limousine, and the foot Policemen work they're way directly into the forest.

EXT. TRAIN STATION, CHANTILLY - MORNING

Guillaume and Philippe manage their small bags as they walk across the station platform toward a waiting train. Guillaume wears his coat over his shoulders and has his left arm in a sling.

The train CONDUCTOR is standing near one of the cars.

CONDUCTOR

Fontainebleau! Leaving in two minutes!

EXT. CHANTILLY FOREST - MORNING

The De Villiers Gang stays close together as they work their way through the Chantilly Forest. Bandaged up, they're all blood, sweat, and tired. Octave stops and looks back behind them.

OCTAVE

They're coming.

ANGLE ON:

In the distance, the Mounties make their way through the forest.

BACK TO:

OCTAVE

Give me the rifle. I'm going to slow them down a little.

Rene exchanges the lever-action rifle for Octave's pistol. Octave slides open the chamber of the gun to confirm it's loaded.

RENE

It's loaded up.

OCTAVE

Keep everyone going. Try to get a vehicle.

Rene turns, and they all start moving again.

OCTAVE

Hurry!

Octave looks back to the Mounties. They're about one hundred and fifty meters back.

Octave fits the rifle into a small wedge between a tree trunk and a branch and takes careful aim at one of the Mounties.

He fires the rifle, and the Mountie rolls over backward from his horse. The other Mounties quickly obstruct themselves behind the trees.

Octave fires another shot just to keep them down longer. He then turns and moves through the forest to join the others.

EXT. OTHER ROAD, CHANTILLY FOREST - MORNING

Rene, Raymond, Andre, Edith, and Sylvie work their way out of the forest and onto another dirt road. Rene spots an automobile driving along the road toward them.

RENE

Down! Everyone, down!

They all crouch. Rene puts his gun away and walks out onto the road. He waves his hands over his head to stop the approaching automobile.

The automobile is a four-door sedan and is occupied by a MAN and a WOMAN. When they reach Rene, the Man pulls the automobile to a stop.

Rene pulls out his pistol and points it at the Man. The rest of the Gang appears - all holding guns pointed at the Couple.

Sylvie boldly steps up to the Man, three meters off. She points the shotgun at him.

SYLVIE

Get out!

The Man's concern reverts to a smile as he looks at Sylvie.

MAN

What is this?

SYLVIE

We're taking your automobile!

The Man looks around at the Gang and then suddenly pulls out a pistol of his own.

Sylvie pulls the trigger, and the shotgun blasts just as the Man pulls the trigger on his pistol.

The shotgun's recoil again blows Sylvie backward a couple of meters and onto her back. The Couple in the auto are both blown back from the shotgun blast - both of the auto's front doors are blown off. The two are reclined - bloody, mangled, and dead in the front seats.

Edith hurries over to help Sylvie, but she's not moving.

EDITH

My god!

RAYMOND

What is it?

EDITH

She's dead. Shot in the heart.

Octave comes walking out of the forest.

OCTAVE

Great!

Octave looks down at Sylvie.

OCTAVE

Oh.

RENE

The Mounties!

All look back to the forest.

ANGLE ON:

The Mounties riding out of the forest eighty meters off - they're firing rifles at the Gang.

OCTAVE

Let's go!

All jump into the auto. Before joining them, Octave pulls up the rifle and takes careful aim at the Mounties. He fires off one last shot.

ANGLE ON:

The Lieutenant takes a bullet in the chest, and he crumples forward over his mount.

Octave smiles to himself, taking pride that he hit his mark.

All inside the auto - Raymond steers them off and down the road away from Chantilly.

RAYMOND

Merde!

All in the automobile, look up.

ANGLE ON:

The foot Policemen from the earlier roadblock are standing on the new road with their weapons pointed at the fast-approaching automobile.

OCTAVE

Get down!

They all duck down as they race head-on through a hail of bullets. The sound of gunfire, breaking glass, and steel popping.

Raymond swerves a bit and plows over two Policemen shooting at the automobile. The other Policemen continue the gunfire as the automobile disappears down the dusty road.

Safe at a distance, Octave cautiously raises his head and takes a couple of breaths. He makes eye contact with Rene, and they both look over to find Edith and Andre shot dead in the backseat.

INT. TRAIN - DAY

Guillaume and Philipe are now in formal dress. The door to the train's bathroom is open, and they stand together grooming themselves. Guillaume's arm is in a homemade sling.

Philippe has the comb and works on his hair.

A young GIRL walks by and eyes Philipe. He smiles at her; she smiles back and runs off.

EXT. EGLISE SAINT-LOUIS DE FONTAINEBLEAU - DAY

The centuries-old baroque-style church sits on a primary corner in the village of Fontainebleau.

Guillaume and Philippe hurry up to the church and disappear beneath the portico.

INT. EGLISE SAINT-LOUIS DE FONTAINEBLEAU - DAY

The church's nave is full - barely an empty seat - every soul there is dressed in black. Genevieve's father, GÉNÉRAL GARNIER (72), stands at a podium at the altar. Genevieve's ornately carved wooden coffin sits below him. He's delivering a eulogy.

GÉNÉRAL GARNIER

She'll surely be missed by everyone here. But Genevieve only had one father. I am that man, and I will feel this loss like no other.

There is a subtle thud of a closing door as Guillaume and Philippe enter the church's rear-center aisle. Général Garnier stops speaking and stares at them. The two stand out - Guillaume wearing a medium gray vested suit and Philippe wearing a matching brown outfit with short pants.

Everyone in the church twists around and looks at Guillaume and Philippe. Philippe smiles at them.

EXT. GARNIER ESTATE, ENTRY GATE/CEMETERY - DAY

On foot, the large funeral party follows the two-horse black hearse carrying the coffin.

Guillaume and Philippe walk with Général and Madame Garnier.

GÉNÉRAL GARNIER
Well, the two of you barely made it here.

PHILIPPE
We had to come directly from Chantilly.

GÉNÉRAL GARNIER
Chantilly? What on earth were you doing in Chantilly?!

Général Garnier gives Guillaume a hard stare. Guillaume looks over to Philippe.

PHILIPPE
We...we saw some horses.

GÉNÉRAL GARNIER
I guess if you want to see horses, that's as good a place as any.

MADAME GARNIER
Guillaume, your arm is in a sling, what happened to you?

GUILLAUME
I was...thrown from a horse.

GÉNÉRAL GARNIER
But, you're a Cavalryman.

The General gives Guillaume a questioning glare.

EXT. GENEVIEVE'S GRAVESITE, GARNIER CEMETERY - DAY

Genevieve's coffin sits suspended over an open grave. Guillaume and Philippe stand next to the coffin - Général and Madame Garnier are beside them. The balance of the funeral party fills out around the area surrounding the gravesite.

PRIEST #2

Death reminds us that we live in a fallen, imperfect world of humanity's failings, flaws, and limitations. Anytime we stand at the graveside, we are reminded of a shadow that has been cast over society. There is a period of time when we are, as the Bible describes, absent from the body and present with the Lord. For Genevieve, this is that time. Amen.

ALL THERE

Amen.

MADAME GARNIER

Everyone is invited to the east parlor for the reception. Please, come.

Guillaume and Philippe stay standing there, while the others wander off.

Now they're alone with Genevieve. With tears in his eyes, Guillaume steps up to her coffin and places his arm over the coffin, embracing it.

GUILLAUME

Oh, my dear, I miss you so. I had always assumed that I would go first and that I'd never have to endure these moments. When we said that we'd never part, somehow, I imagined that it was possible.

A tear rolls down his cheek.

GUILLAUME

I'll never stop loving you, dear. I'll see you in heaven.

Guillaume leans over and kisses the coffin, as Philippe approaches - tears rolling down both cheeks.

PHILIPPE

Mother. I promise you that I will grow to be the man that you had always dreamed that I'd become. You may be gone, but I will always feel your dear, caring presence. We'll be together again, one day.

Philippe leans forward and kisses the coffin.

INT. EAST SALON, GARNIER MANOR HOUSE - DAY

People are wandering about. Others are gathered in clusters while drinking tea or brandy. In the corner, amongst some bookcases, Général Garnier is holding court with a group of Gentlemen. They're all drinking brandy.

GÉNÉRAL GARNIER

...I have been thinking of putting up a sum for the capture of that scoundrel. He and his murderous gang will surely end up in hell, and I'd like to take him there.

Philippe watches his father from the background. Guillaume walks up and joins the Gentlemen. Général Garnier signals to one of the men.

GÉNÉRAL GARNIER

Give this man a brandy. It'll help to wash the pacifism out of his soul.

Guillaume waves it off.

GUILLAUME

No, thank you.

MAN #1

Capitaine Messein, I'm very interested to know why a military man with so much promise would retire just before his biggest promotion?

Guillaume looks at Man #1.

GUILLAUME
The War, it was too violent.

MAN #2
Violent?!

MAN #1
But the War was over.

GUILLAUME
Sir, there is always another war.

GÉNÉRAL GARNIER
What about this Octave De Villiers Gang?! Are you going to let them take your wife? Your son's mother?

GUILLAUME
No.

GÉNÉRAL GARNIER
So, what will you do?!

GUILLAUME
That, sir, is my concern. Excuse me.

Guillaume turns and walks off.

GÉNÉRAL GARNIER
Well, I hope it is.

EXT. DE VILLIERS HOUSE, PARIS - MORNING

Rene and Raymond walk together on the sidewalk up the street. Rene is wearing clear-lens eyeglasses and Raymond sunglasses. They turn and walk up to a house and knock on the door.

INT. DE VILLIERS HOUSE, PARIS - MORNING

There is a knocking at the front door. Michelle walks up and opens the door to find Rene and Raymond. They barge right inside and close the door behind them.

MICHELLE
Rene, I'm so sorry to hear about Sylvie.

RENE
She was just another soldier.

MICHELLE
And Edith, too.

RENE
Yes. And Andre was killed; he was much more valuable.

MICHELLE
Yes, but you loved Sylvie.

Rene and Michelle hold a stare.

BEAT

RAYMOND
Where is he?

MICHELLE
In the back, outside.

The two men walk off as Michelle remains. She stands there for a moment considering her own value to the Gang.

EXT. REAR PORCH AT HOUSE, PARIS - MORNING

Octave reclines on a Le Corbusier chaise-longue on the elevated back porch of the house. The view looks out to the city.

Octave's left arm is in a sling, and he struggles a bit with pen and paper. He finishes writing and pushes the sheet of paper away, and then caps the pen.

Rene and Raymond walk out onto the porch.

RAYMOND
Working on your memoirs?

OCTAVE
Finishing a letter to the Chief of Police.

RENE
You shouldn't antagonize him.

OCTAVE

I can't help myself.

Octave smiles at them both.

RAYMOND

This place looks expensive.

OCTAVE

That's because you prefer to live in the slums.

RENE

Now that Sylvie is gone, Raymond is moving in with me.

Octave eyes Raymond.

OCTAVE

Well, he's a better cook.

The Men chuckle among themselves.

INT. UPSTAIRS SUITE, GARNIER MANOR HOUSE - MORNING

Guillaume sits at the upstairs window drinking a cafe and smoking his pipe. He has a white bandage wrapped around his left hand and forearm.

The door opens up, and Philippe steps inside. He's got a folded newspaper under his arm.

GUILLAUME

Did you see the pistol that De Villiers carried?

PHILIPPE

No.

GUILLAUME

It was far superior.

PHILIPPE

Papa, have you ever thought that maybe we should leave De Villiers for the police?

GUILLAUME

I've thought of it many times.

PHILIPPE

And -

GUILLAUME

Philippe, I fought out of a mud ditch for seven months and watched many people around me die - all in the name of patriotism. If I can do that, I can surely fight for the one person who brought me back to life.

They stare at each other for a beat.

PHILIPPE

I'll be there with you, father.

GUILLAUME

I don't want you to do anything that will haunt you for the rest of your life. And that's what killing another human being does to a person.

BEAT

GUILLAUME

Perhaps you should stay with your grandparents until it's over.

PHILIPPE

Never. I swear, I will run away and follow you as soon as you leave me.

Guillaume smiles.

GUILLAUME

Understood.

Philippe pulls out the newspaper and holds it up for his father to see.

PHILIPPE

They mention us.

GUILLAUME

What?

PHILIPPE

The Mounted Policeman that I helped told them about me. And here's you...

(reads)

...along with Chantilly's Mounted Police, De Villiers had to fend off an armed civilian who was firing off shots from the storefronts near the bank. After the shooting was over, the authorities searched for this civilian, who seems to have completely disappeared.

GUILLAUME

I hit him in the shoulder. I'm surprised they didn't notice that.

Philippe pulls out his notebook and jots down some notes.

PHILIPPE

Well, De Villiers noticed it.

The two smile at each other.

PHILIPPE

Grandmother wants us to come down for breakfast.

EXT. REAR PORCH AT HOUSE, PARIS - MORNING

Octave is now sitting up on the chaise-longue, Rene and Raymond sit in a couple of chairs near him.

RENE

What's our next job?

OCTAVE

I'm working on that. You two should be prepared to leave Paris on short notice.

Rene smiles.

RENE

For where?

OCTAVE

I'll let you know.

RAYMOND

Did you read the newspaper about that boy in Chantilly?

OCTAVE

Yes. And that man on the street.

RENE

What man?

OCTAVE

In front of the bank, there was a man shooting at me. We nicked each other.

Octave touches his wounded shoulder.

RENE

I didn't see him.

RAYMOND

Neither did I.

OCTAVE

I think that man was at Gard Du Nord last week.

RENE

Gard Du Nord?

OCTAVE

And I read that the woman who was killed had a young son.

RENE

You're talking crazy, Octave.

OCTAVE

Yes. Perhaps.

Raymond and Rene eye each other.

RAYMOND

We need some money.

OCTAVE

I have it right here for you.

Octave lifts two envelopes from a low table and hands them to Rene.

OCTAVE

I'm keeping the gold safe.

RAYMOND

We can't use it anyway.

OCTAVE

Also, I've got a broker in Belgium who might be able to unload it for us.

RAYMOND

Sounds good.

There is a squeak noise from near the door to the house.

They all look over towards the door to the house.

ANGLE ON:

Just inside, Michelle is behind the door to the porch. She'd been listening to the Men talk. She walks off.

BACK TO:

Rene quietly walks over to the door and looks around. No one there. He looks back at Octave and shakes his head.

INT. CAFE BAR - DAY

Chief Gouget and Detective Bonhomme sit at a table in the back of the cafe. A beer and a cafe sit on the tabletop.

CHIEF GOUGET

Five policemen dead and three wounded, in Chantilly. And who is this boy? And the man that was shooting at De Villiers?

DETECTIVE BONHOMME
I think I know.

CHIEF GOUGET
What? Who?

DETECTIVE BONHOMME
Remember the husband of Genevieve Messein? They had a son.

CHIEF GOUGET
The girl killed at the station? Why would they be there?

Detective Huche walks up to their table - they look up to him.

CHIEF GOUGET
Huche, today you're coming with me to Chantilly.

HUCHE
For what?

CHIEF GOUGET
To take a look at the scene of the crime. And bring back De Villiers' wounded comrade, Etienne Soudy.

The Chief and Bonhomme smile at each other.

DETECTIVE HUCHE
This came for you this morning.

Huche hands Chief Gouget a white envelope.

He opens it up and pulls out a single sheet of stationery paper, and looks it over.

CHIEF GOUGET
It's from De Villiers.

All ears perk up as Chief reads it allowed.

CHIEF GOUGET
(reading)
Chief Gouget - You and I have so much in common, it is a shame that we must fight against each other. But alas, a skillful adversary only

CHIEF GOUGET (CON'T)

makes one a more accomplished foe. One day soon, I'll disappear, and you will never hear from me again. I wonder, will you miss me? Or will my absence make you grateful for the calm and simple life you will have - post Octave De Villiers.

Chief Gouget drops the letter on the table, and looks over to Detective Bonhomme.

CHIEF GOUGET

Where do they live? Messein and his son.

DETECTIVE BONHOMME

Saint-Michel.

CHIEF GOUGET

Put a surveillance detail on them. Immediately.

EXT. ORPHANAGE, PARIS - DAY

A two-story building - Louis XIII architecture. Red brick, stone, and a blue slate Mansard roof.

Michelle walks up the cobbled walk to the front door and alerts her presence using the iron door knocker.

The door opens.

INT. ORPHANAGE - DAY

As Michelle steps inside, she's immediately confronted by an older woman, the HEADMASTER of the orphanage.

HEADMASTER

Good morning.

MICHELLE

Good morning.

HEADMASTER

What can we do for you?

MICHELLE

I'm here to visit a child who arrived yesterday, Fleur Valet. I'm a friend of her parents.

HEADMASTER

Madame, her parents were criminals.

BEAT

MICHELLE

I just want to make sure that she's alright.

HEADMASTER

I'm afraid that's impossible. Visitors are by appointment only, and -

FLEUR (O.S.)

Michelle!

The two look over to find Fleur rushing up to Michelle.

HEADMASTER

Fleur! Please control yourself!

Fleur wraps her arms around Michelle.

FLEUR

Are you here for me?

Michelle gives the Headmaster an awkward look.

MICHELLE

I'm afraid not, dear.

HEADMASTER

Well, the two of you are already together, so I'll give you two minutes in the drawing room. Not a minute more.

INT. DRAWING ROOM, ORPHANAGE - DAY

The Headmaster leads Michelle and Fleur into the next room, and they both step inside.

HEADMASTER

Two minutes.

The Headmaster walks off.

FLEUR

You're not here to take me home?

MICHELLE

I'm afraid not. We have to try to find your mother's family in Corsica.

FLEUR

But I don't know them. Can't you adopt me, Michelle?

Michelle holds her firmly and looks into her eyes.

MICHELLE

(whispers)

Look into my eyes, dear. Be here, and don't make trouble. Just know that I'm on the outside doing everything in my power to get you out.

FLEUR

They just sent a couple of girls to the workhouse this morning.

MICHELLE

Shhh. They don't send children to workhouses anymore.

FLEUR

Yes, they do!

MICHELLE

Just be patient. I'll do everything I can.

FLEUR

Will you promise to get me out?

BEAT

MICHELLE

Of course, I will.

The Headmaster steps inside the room.

HEADMASTER
I'm sorry, but your time is up.

The Headmaster takes Fleur by the arm and leads her away.

MICHELLE
I'll come back again soon.

FLEUR
Please! Help me, Michelle! Please!

The Headmaster and Fleur disappear through the large double doorway.

EXT. GUN SHOP, PARIS - DAY

Guillaume and Philippe walk the sidewalk and turn into the gun shop.

INT. GUN SHOP - DAY

The Proprietor sits on his stool with a disassembled Thompson's Submachine gun lying on the counter. It's recognizable by its circular magazine clip. Guillaume and Philippe walk up to the Proprietor.

PROPRIETOR
Good afternoon.

GUILLAUME
Hello.

Guillaume pulls his military service revolver out of his coat and slaps it down on the counter. The Proprietor looks down at the pistol, then at Philippe, and finally at Guillaume.

PROPRIETOR
What is this?

GUILLAUME
It's too slow.

The Proprietor lifts the pistol and looks it over.

PROPRIETOR
That was always the problem.

GUILLAUME
And trying to reload it while under fire was also quite burdensome.

PROPRIETOR
Under fire? How were you using this weapon, sir?

GUILLAUME
Well...uh...?

Guillaume and Philippe eye each other. Philippe turns and smiles at the Proprietor.

PHILIPPE
We had a bit of a shootout in Chantilly.

Guillaume gives Philippe a questioning look. The Proprietor smiles broadly and chuckles.

PROPRIETOR
In Chantilly?

The three have a short laugh.

GUILLAUME
Anyway, we'd like something with a little more efficiency.

The Proprietor pats on the Tommy Gun laid out before them.

PROPRIETOR
Would this do?

PHILIPPE
What is it?

CUT TO:

Guillaume, Philippe, and the Proprietor are in the yard behind the gun shop. Guillaume is holding the Submachine gun loosely.

PROPRIETOR
Okay. Now -

The Proprietor walks over to the wall at the far end of the space. He places a cardboard target on a stand and then returns to the Father and Son.

The Proprietor helps Guillaume position himself with the gun.

PROPRIETOR

Hold it tight with both hands and bring it in against your hip here.

The Proprietor reaches over and slides a lever down - chambering a shell - the gun is ready to fire.

PROPRIETOR

Okay. Hold on tight, point the gun, and pull the trigger.

Guillaume does so.

BLAM! BLAM! BLAM! BLAM! BLAM! BLAM!

Bullets from the machine gun tear through the target and surrounding area. Shell casings fly out from the chamber. After five seconds, Guillaume stops and takes a deep breath. He looks over to the Proprietor.

PHILIPPE

I think it’s a little too destructive.

GUILLAUME

I agree.

The Proprietor smiles at them.

PROPRIETOR

I do have something else.

EXT. THE PLATFORM, PARIS STREET - DAY

Many pro-anarchists are celebrating in the street in front of a small building with a sign over the entry reading: THE PLATFORM.

They’re holding signs reading; We Do Not Fear Anarchy - We Invoke It, The Platform, Unity, and Collective Responsibility. Some signs only have the symbols of the Anarchists and Platformism movements.

There is also a MAN wearing a typesetter’s UNION SUIT with The Platform printed on the back. He’s handing out five-franc notes (one dollar) to everyone who passes. There’s a small crowd gathered around him.

The Franc takers are wearing big smiles as they run off with their new-found wealth.

UNION SUIT

Five francs! One Five Francs for everyone! Courtesy of The Platform! The people's newspaper! Get your Five France note right here!

ANGLE ON: Police Chief Gouget, Detectives Bonhomme and Huche. A few uniformed Policemen are there.

CHIEF GOUGET

What the hell is this?

DETECTIVE BONHOMME

They've opened a new Journal called The Platform. Pro Anarchists.

CHIEF GOUGET

Socialism is one thing, but anarchism is quite another.

UNION SUIT (B.G)

Five Franc notes! Get your Five Francs!

DETECTIVE HUCHE

They're going to publish a daily newspaper.

CHIEF GOUGET

Where do they get their money from?

The two Detectives give Gouget a look, and a light goes on in Gouget's brain.

CHIEF GOUGET

That son of a bitch!

DETECTIVE BONHOMME

The word is: Illegalists.

Union Suit walks across the road to where the Policemen are watching. He holds out a Five Franc note for Chief Gouget.

UNION SUIT

Five Francs, Chief?

CHIEF GOUGET

Sure, financed by your friendly neighborhood bank robber.

DETECTIVE HUCHE

Killer.

DETECTIVE BONHOMME

We just might decide to arrest you!

UNION SUIT

For what?

Passers-by bark out at the Chief and company.

WOMAN #1

Hey! Leave him alone; he's not bothering anyone!

The Policemen look over to the Woman.

UNION SUIT

Here you go, madame!

He hands her a Five France note. She eagerly snatches it out of his hand.

MAN

(walking past)

Don't the police have anything to do other than bother people?

Bonhomme looks over to Chief Gouget.

DETECTIVE BONHOMME

And you wonder why De Villiers is so popular.

CHIEF GOUGET

It doesn't sound like you do.

INT. GUN SHOP - DAY

At the counter, the Proprietor is showing Guillaume and Philippe a Bergmann-Bayard 9mm semi-automatic pistol. They're both very impressed. It has a 15cm barrel and a built-in magazine for the shells.

PROPRIETOR

It's more expensive, but it's a big step up - made in Belgium.

Guillaume lifts the pistol for inspection. He shows it to Philippe.

PROPRIETOR

It's a nine-millimeter semi-automatic and will hold ten shells in the magazine.

GUILLAUME

Is it fast?

PROPRIETOR

It's as quick as you can pull the trigger. And, you can purchase this unique stock that easily bolts onto the pistol.

The Proprietor pulls out a wooden rifle stock and connects it to the pistol's handgrip.

Guillaume holds it up to his shoulder and aims - he pulls the trigger, and with an empty chamber - the firing pin clicks.

Philippe eyes the Proprietor's double-barrel Derringer sitting on the counter.

GUILLAUME

We'll take it.

Guillaume slides the gun into its case as the Proprietor makes some notations on a piece of paper.

PROPRIETOR

Very good. I've added the case and two boxes of shells.

He hands Guillaume a receipt.

Guillaume and Philippe walk out of the door. The Proprietor smiles as he looks down at a newspaper folded up at the end of the counter.

A bold caption reads.

MYSTERY BOY HELPS POLICEMAN IN CHANTILLY SHOOTOUT

The Proprietor contemplates to himself for a moment. And then he smiles and shakes his head.

EXT. OPEN AIR FARMERS MARKET, PARIS - MORNING

Michelle strolls the aisles and shops the produce 'en plein air' Farmers Market. She stops and speaks to a FRUIT VENDOR.

MICHELLE
These strawberries look so small, and their color is faint.

FRUIT VENDOR
It's the first pick early in the season.

MICHELLE
I will take some mirabelles and the Melon du Quercy, s'il te plait.

Michelle raises her head and looks around the market.

ANGLE ON:

A Woman, the Chevalier's COOK (40), is shopping a couple of stalls over. The Cook looks over and makes momentary eye contact with Michelle and then turns away.

Michelle looks back at the Fruit Vendor.

MICHELLE
This melon, here.

She takes out a couple of coins and hands them to the Vendor.

MICHELLE
Put them in a bag. I'll pick them up later.

Michelle meanders her way over toward the Cook, but the Cook seems to avoid her by picking up her step as they pass each other. Michelle gives the Cook a frown.

Michelle turns around and follows the Cook until she bumps her from behind.

COOK
I beg your pardon, Madame.

MICHELLE
(under her breath)
There's been a change of plans.

COOK
Yes, from my end, too.

MICHELLE
I want to come by the house and see you tomorrow.

COOK
That's impossible.

MICHELLE
Nothing is impossible.

COOK
I'm discontinuing our relationship.

MICHELLE
You made a deal with him. You can't walk away from that.

COOK
Watch me.

BEAT

MICHELLE
Okay. You're a Roma, and wanted by the police in Hungary.

The Cook's head swivels as she looks Michelle in the eye.

MICHELLE
I know more than you think, and a lot more than you want me to. Tell me, how would Chevalier Moreau feel if he found a Gypsy working in his kitchen?

COOK
Look, we can't talk in public like this.

MICHELLE
We already have.

COOK

That was my mistake.

MICHELLE

Perhaps this would help ease your anxiety.

Michelle slips the Cook a small gold bar. The Cook gives it a peak.

COOK

Chantilly?

MICHELLE

I'll be at the kitchen door tomorrow morning at nine.

The Cook makes a sharp turn and walks away from Michelle.

EXT. SOCIETE GENERALE BANK, CHANTILLY - DAY

Chief Gouget and Detective Huche walk the street where the bank robbery took place. There are several others there, including Etienne Soudy - the wounded Gang member.

Chief Gouget points and talks as he walks the area. He enumerates the robbery step by step.

CHIEF GOUGET

So, Madame Boulanger's limousine, the escape vehicle, was waiting here. Who was driving yesterday?

Chief Gouget looks over to Soudy. But Soudy just stares at the ground. The Chief walks up to Soudy and slaps his head, knocking Soudy's cap off and onto the ground.

CHIEF GOUGET

Your problem is you don't think that you have to help me.

Chief Gouget walks over to a spot where Soudy was hit by gunfire.

CHIEF GOUGET

You were shot right here! They left you to die like a dog! Oh, I know! You are an anarchist! But those who left you are not anarchists. They are murderers. They don't give a 'merde' about your anarchism!

Soudy looks up to the Police Chief.

SOUDY
You've always been considered sympathetic to the cause.

CHIEF GOUGET
What I care about is innocent people and policemen dying. And a little bit less than that; I care about robbery and political assassination.

SOUDY
You'll get nothing from me.

INT. MESSEIN APARTMENT, PARIS - NIGHT

Guillaume and Philippe sit at a table having dinner. A roasted pheasant sits in the center of the table.

PHILIPPE
Mother always loved rosemary pheasant.

GUILLAUME
This meal is in her honor.

The two smile at each other.

PHILIPPE
Do you think that we'll have another chance? What if De Villiers disappears from Paris? From France?

GUILLAUME
Your mother's trust account has a balance of sixty thousand francs. We could travel around Europe for many years with that money. We'll find Octave De Villiers. Sooner or later.

Philippe smiles at his father - his father smiles back.

PHILIPPE
May I have a leg, please?

Guillaume reaches over the table and starts carving out a piece of the bird for Philippe.

Knock Knock Knock

They both look over as there is a knock on the front door.

PHILIPPE
I'll get it.

Philippe stands as Guillaume works on the pheasant.

Philippe walks over to the door and opens it. He looks back at his father and then again at the person at the door.

PHILIPPE
Please, come inside.

The visitor steps into the apartment. It's Michelle De Villiers. She's wearing sunglasses.

MICHELLE
Hello.

Philippe nods toward Guillaume, and she turns to look.

MICHELLE
I'm sorry to interrupt your dinner, but I come here as a desperate woman.

She takes off her sunglasses and exposes some fresh bruises.

GUILLAUME
Would you like to join us?

Michelle shakes him off.

MICHELLE
No, thank you.

PHILIPPE
It's pheasant, in honor of my mother.

MICHELLE
Thank you, but I have no appetite at this time.

PHILIPPE
How did you know where we live?

MICHELLE

The Detective.

GUILLAUME

Please, have a seat.

Michelle takes a seat at the table.

MICHELLE

I have so much emotion and fear in my life. I haven't enjoyed a meal in months. Mostly I've been drinking my meals.

Guillaume stands and walks over to a cabinet.

GUILLAUME

I don't have any absinthe, but I do have some cognac.

MICHELLE

That will be fine, thank you.

Guillaume pours one centimeter of brandy into a common drinking glass.

Michelle looks at Philippe.

MICHELLE

It was you, wasn't it?

Philippe stares back at Michelle for a beat. He smiles.

Guillaume walks over and hands Michelle her drink. She grabs Guillaume by the left arm, and he flinches in pain.

MICHELLE

So, it's true. You did get shot in the left arm.

Guillaume soothes his left arm as he steps over to his seat at the table - he chuckles to himself.

GUILLAUME

You were right to grab my arm. We would never have told you.

MICHELLE

You have to kill my husband for me.

GUILLAUME

For you?

MICHELLE

For me...for all the other women
and children of these men. For you
and your son...for Paris, and
France.

EXT. TRAIN, CHANTILLY - NIGHT

The train is pulling out of the station at Chantilly.

INT. HORSE CAR, TRAIN - NIGHT

Etienne Soudy is handcuffed to a rusty iron eyelet hook screwed into the upper sidewall of an equine transport car. Soudy's is weak and glazed in sweat, as he's already taken a beating.

Chief Gouget and Detective Huche take turns punching Etienne Soudy in the ribs and head as they try to work information out of him.

Huche punches Soudy in the ribs as Gouget talks to him.

CHIEF GOUGET

Don't worry, Soudy. We're going to
stay away from your pretty face.

SOUDY

So it's not so obvious.

CHIEF GOUGET

Where is De Villiers?!

SOUDY

I could tell you where he was, but
his wife moved him the morning of
the bank hit.

Huche punches Soudy again in the ribs, and he groans in pain.

CHIEF GOUGET

What's the next job?!

SOUDY

We robbed Societe Generale six times and killed little Moreau. You figure it out.

Gouget punches Soudy in the ribs, and he winces in pain.

CHIEF GOUGET

Tomorrow the bank is announcing a reward for his capture. I could make sure ten thousand goes to your wife and children.

SOUDY

I wouldn't sleep with your wife for ten thousand Francs.

BEAT

CHIEF GOUGET

Don't ever think about my wife again.

Gouget slams Soudy hard in the mouth with his fist.

Soudy teeters back against the wooden wall of the car and then looks back at Gouget. He then spits a broken tooth into Gouget's face and smiles - an incisor is missing from his upper row of teeth.

Shocked, Detective Huche laughs, and Gouget turns and knocks Huche out with a right cross.

A shocked Soudy watches and then looks back at Gouget as the Chief of Police nails him with another right and knocks him unconscious.

INT. MESSEIN APARTMENT, PARIS - NIGHT

Michelle and Philippe sit in the living room while Guillaume stands, smoking a pipe.

MICHELLE

They're going after the gold at Moreau's mansion.

PHILIPPE

They did that already.

MICHELLE
No. The father. Chevalier Aubert Moreau.

GUILLAUME
When?

MICHELLE
Any day, now. I've been working on his cook.

GUILLAUME
Is he one of them?

MICHELLE
She, is not. But she is a fugitive, who's wanted for forgery and fraud in Budapest.

Guillaume and Michelle eye each other.

MICHELLE
Anyway, your time is limited.

Michelle strolls over to the large street-front window.

GUILLAUME
Why is that?

Michelle points through the window to a couple of MEN standing in the shadows of the shops across the road.

MICHELLE
The police are watching you.

PHILIPPE
The police!

Guillaume and Philippe rush over to the window to take a look.

GUILLAUME
How do you know this?

Michelle stands and gathers her things.

MICHELLE
That doesn't matter. Octave is sleeping at home tonight.

She hands Guillaume a folded piece of paper. And then gathers her things and readies to leave.

MICHELLE

He usually leaves early in the morning for meetings.

Guillaume looks at the piece of paper as Philippe opens the front door for her.

GUILLAUME

Why not tell Detective Bonhomme?

Michelle steps over to Philippe at the door. She looks back to Guillaume.

MICHELLE

I'm far from innocent, Monsieur. And the Detective is only a boy, while you were a military hero.

GUILLAUME

And?

Guillaume and Michelle stare at each other for a beat.

BEAT

MICHELLE

You are right, Monsieur. We have foolishly fallen in love.

GUILLAUME

Good night, Madame.

PHILIPPE

Be careful.

Michelle smiles at Philippe as she disappears through the door.

INT. PASSENGER CAR, TRAIN - NIGHT

Chief Gouget and Detective Huche sit next to each other. They both wear serious faces and stare straight ahead. Huche has a bruise on his chin.

BEAT

HUCHE

You didn't have to hit me.

Huche rubs his jaw with his hand.

CHIEF GOUGET

I'm sorry. I'm just so fed up with De Villiers and his Gang. And the letters he writes to me. These fools and their idealism, and their senseless killing.

HUCHE

We'll be at the station in five minutes.

CHIEF GOUGET

Let's get Soudy ready to go.

HUCHE

Hopefully, he's conscious.

Gouget stands from his seat.

CHIEF GOUGET

Bring some water from the bar.

Gouget walks up the aisle towards the back of the car as Huche walks over to the bar.

INT. HORSE CAR, TRAIN - NIGHT

Soudy hangs lifeless from the cuffs and the iron hook. White foam surrounds his mouth and slowly drips onto the floor. The door slides open, and Chief Gouget steps inside. He notices Soudy and quickly steps over to inspect him.

He spots something on the floor, so he kneels down to take a look. It appears to be a small glass vile that held some type of liquid.

Huche steps inside, holding a cup of water.

HUCHE

What happened?

CHIEF GOUGET

Prussic Acid. He must have had it hidden somewhere.

Chief Gouget reaches over and takes the glass of water from Huche's hand.

CHIEF GOUGET
Go and tell the Engineer that he's going to have to drop this car.

HUCHE
Right, Chief.

Huche turns and exits, as Chief Gouget eyes Etienne Soudy's lifeless body.

EXT. EIFFEL TOWER, PARIS - EARLY MORNING

Octave, Raymond, and Rene walk the upper first level of the iconic 19th-century structure. The sun is just breaking the horizon over the Parisian cityscape beyond.

OCTAVE
We're making our move this morning.

RENE
This morning?

OCTAVE
Yes. They're expecting us to lay low, so they'll never expect it.

Octave takes out a couple of cigars and hands them to the two men. They take them.

RAYMOND
Shouldn't we celebrate after the job?

OCTAVE
Well, you never know.

He lights a match and leans over with the flame and lights Rene's cigar.

OCTAVE
Some of us might not make it. This cigar is to celebrate our fortitude and audacity to try it.

Octave and Raymond light their cigars.

RAYMOND

Yes, but is it set up properly? What does Michelle say?

OCTAVE

She says and does what I tell her.

Rene and Raymond stare silently at Octave for a beat.

BEAT

Octave smiles and then begins a stroll along the catwalk, and the two Men follow him.

OCTAVE

She's meeting with Moreau's cook later this morning, and we'll crash in right behind her.

RENE

And our escape?

OCTAVE

I've got a first-class berth to Brussels at noon. And you two are going to Bruges.

Octave hands them each a train ticket.

OCTAVE

I'm meeting with a gold dealer tomorrow afternoon.

RENE

And the gold with the dog?

OCTAVE

If this works, I'll return for that gold and do it again. We'll all meet in Bruges next month.

RAYMOND

Why Bruges?

OCTAVE

Because the three of us speak Flemish, and they don't know that. We'll blend in more easily.

RENE

Michelle doesn't speak Flemish.

Octave stops in front of the Eiffel Tower Radio station that exists in a small office/studio on the corner of the first landing. For a moment, they look at the NEWS REPORTER who sits behind a glass partition in the studio behind them.

The muffled sound of the live broadcast is heard.

Octave gives the Men a stern look.

OCTAVE

She won't need to. Rene kills Moreau, Raymond kills the cook, and I'll take care of Michelle.

RENE

But -

OCTAVE

It's okay. She's a liability, and it has to be done. You two put the guns together and pick me up with a coach in an hour.

They all turn and look at the News Reporter through a glass partition as he speaks into a microphone.

NEWS REPORTER

(muffled)

...skies should be mostly overcast, and temperatures in the afternoon between fourteen and seventeen degrees.

INT. MESSEIN APARTMENT - MORNING

A radio is sits on an end table, and through it, the slightly muted Eiffel Tower Radio report plays in the background.

Philippe is taking notes while reading the newspaper and munching on a piece of toast. Guillaume sits at his small table while smoking his pipe and sipping his cafe. He watches his son - reading and scribbling in his notebook.

NEWS REPORTER (O.S.)

...with possible rain tonight and tomorrow morning....

GUILLAUME

Why are you always taking notes when you read the newspaper?

PHILIPPE

I don't want to forget any of it.

GUILLAUME

That's peculiar because I'd like to forget it all.

Philippe reaches over and turns up the volume of the radio.

NEWS REPORTER

...In local news, Chief Aubert Gouget of the Parisian Police has scheduled public disclosure outside the Hotel de Ville for this morning at nine o'clock.

Their interest piqued, Philippe and Guillaume look over at each other with curious expressions.

NEWS REPORTER

The focus of the announcements is the recent assassinations and robberies believed perpetrated by the De Villiers Gang, which includes the fantastic bank robbery and gun battle in Chantilly a couple of days ago. The general public is invited.

Philippe reaches over and turns off the radio and looks at his father.

PHILIPPE

Shall we go to L'Hotel De Ville this morning?

Guillaume stares at Philippe for a beat.

BEAT

GUILLAUME

No. Get dressed. We're dealing with Octave De Villiers this morning.

Philippe stares at his father as Guillaume stands and walks out of the room.

EXT. PLACE DE L'HOTEL DE VILLE, PARIS - MORNING

Chief Gouget, Detective Bonhomme, and Detective Huche walk out of the large front doors of the Paris City Hall.

A large group of News Reporters surrounds them. Chief Gouget stands up on one of the balustrades to speak.

CHIEF GOUGET

Thank you, everyone, for coming today. I thought that it would be an excellent time to get the story straight about the De Villiers Gang, make a few announcements, and perhaps take questions from the press.

REPORTER #1

There's a rumor that you murdered Etienne Soudy.

Chief Gouget looks over to Reporter #1 and gives him a short stare.

CHIEF GOUGET

That is not true. But as I said, I'll be taking questions shortly.

EXT. DE VILLIERS HOUSE, PARIS - MORNING

A two-horse coach pulls up in front of De Villiers' house. The COACHMAN wears a 'Le Montmartre' cap and smokes a 'Briar Bent Apple' pipe. Rene steps out of the rear cab and gives the street a cursory inspection as he walks across the cobbled walk.

ANGLE ON:

Guillaume and Philippe stand in the Recessed doorway of a shop down the road from De Villiers' house. They're watching the coach at the front of the house. Guillaume is smoking his pipe.

BACK TO:

Octave De Villiers steps out of the house and over to the coach. Rene follows him inside and closes the door. The COACHMAN maneuvers the coach back out onto the road.

Guillaume and Philippe lean back into the shadow of the shop stoop as the coach drives past them.

INT. DE VILLIERS HOUSE, PARIS - MORNING

Michelle puts the finishing touches on her appearance as she stands in front of the bedroom mirror. She looks off-camera and calls out.

MICHELLE

You've had a busy morning. What are you up to?

She finishes her work at the mirror and walks out of the bedroom to the terrace.

MICHELLE

Octave?

There is no one there - no answer.

EXT. DE VILLIERS HOUSE, PARIS - MORNING

Michelle steps out of the side door. She walks out to the sidewalk and then turns and starts down the street.

EXT. PLACE DE L'HOTEL DE VILLE, PARIS - MORNING

Chief Gouget stands on the balustrade while he speaks to a large group of News Reporters that surround him. Detective Bonhomme stands by Gouget.

There is also a group of ANARCHISTS DEMONSTRATORS there - several carrying signs as they chant in the background.

DEMONSTRATORS

Police are the enemy!
Octave is a friend of me!
Police are the enemy!
Octave is a friend of me!

CHIEF GOUGET

I've also been informed by Chevalier Moreau that the Bank Societe Generale is offering a one hundred thousand Franc reward for information that leads to the arrest of Octave De Villiers.

REPORTER #2

Where is Etienne Soudy?

DEMONSTRATOR #1

Bring him here! We want to see him!

Chief Gouget leans over to Bonhomme and whispers to him.

CHIEF GOUGET

(to Bonhomme)

Get some men and move these agitators out of the plaza.

DETECTIVE BONHOMME

Will do.

Detective Bonhomme steps over to a uniformed Police Sergeant standing guard near them.

DETECTIVE BONHOMME

(whispers)

Sergeant, I want some officers here as crowd control on the double.

The Sergeant steps off and hand signals some orders out to a couple of uniformed Policemen.

EXT. TWO-HORSE COACH, PARIS - MORNING

An upscale Parisian neighborhood. The COACHMAN directs the horses over to the side of the cobblestone road.

EXT. STREETS OF PARIS - MORNING

Guillaume and Philippe are lurking in the shadows of the storefronts on a cobblestone street. They're spying on the coach from 150 meters.

Guillaume and Philippe speak to each other in half-whisper.

GUILLAUME

That's the Chevalier Moreau's mansion over there.

Philippe cranes his head to look further up the street.

PHILIPPE

The Chevalier?

INT. TWO-HORSE COACH - MORNING

Octave, Rene, and Raymond are sitting in the passenger cabin of the coach. Octave reaches over and pulls the curtains closed.

Rene and Raymond start checking their weapons as Octave pulls out a rough-drawn sketch of the property and spreads it out over his lap.

OCTAVE

This is the property.

The other two lean over and take a look.

OCTAVE

The kitchen and servant's entry is down this path to the far side of the manor house.

RAYMOND

Looks simple enough.

OCTAVE

There's always an armed Guard at the front gate.

Octave and Rene lean over and look out from the coach window towards the mansion.

ANGLE ON:

A single uniformed GUARD stands at the entry gate. A long rifle over his shoulder.

BACK TO:

Inside the coach, Octave leans back and addresses the men.

OCTAVE

One Guard?

RAYMOND

Better for us.

RENE

But where's the other?

The men eye each other for a beat.

BEAT

OCTAVE

We're going to have to kill the Guard at the gate.

Abruptly the flap door atop the coach interior opens again.

COACHMAN

Excuse me, gentlemen. I've got a pick-up at Jardin du Luxembourg at 9:15.

RENE

It'll be a few more minutes!

COACHMAN

Well, I'm leaving in two minutes, with or without you gentlemen in the cab.

RENE

Just hold on!

Raymond pulls the flap door closed.

OCTAVE

And kill the Coachman, too.

RENE

When?

OCTAVE

Now.

Octave and Rene look over to Raymond.

RENE

Please.

Raymond smiles as he flips out the blade of a switch knife - opens the door, and climbs out of the coach.

INTERCUT: Exterior between Guillaume/Philippe, the De Villiers' coach, and Michelle arriving at the scene.

Guillaume and Philippe watch the De Villiers' coach from the shadows.

PHILIPPE

Someone is getting out.

Raymond is out of the coach and walks towards the front. He looks up and converses with the Coachman.

The Coachman climbs down off of the coach, and he and Raymond are obstructed from Guillaume and Philippe's view behind the carriage.

Suddenly, Michelle appears. She walks up the street towards the Chevalier's mansion.

PHILIPPE

Michelle!

Inside the coach, Octave is looking out the window. He spots Michelle crossing the street.

OCTAVE

(whispering)

She's arriving!

Rene helps Raymond to drag the now-dead Coachman inside of the coach.

They just get the Coachman inside the coach, and the coach door quietly shut as Michelle glances over to them, and then addresses the Guard at the entry gate.

The Guard tips his hat at Michelle as she passes him and walks up the path towards the servant's entrance along the side of the house.

GUILLAUME

They were waiting for her.

PHILIPPE

Why?

Guillaume turns to Philippe.

GUILLAUME

Do you know where the Hotel De Ville is from here?

PHILIPPE

Uh...yes. It's across the river and up the street a few blocks.

GUILLAUME

Right. Hurry over there and tell Chief Gouget to come here

GUILLAUME (CON'T)

immediately. Tell him that De Villiers is raiding the Chevalier's mansion!

PHILIPPE

Okay!

Philippe starts off.

GUILLAUME

And be careful.

Philippe runs off in the opposite direction from the coach.

EXT. PLACE DE L'HOTEL DE VILLE, PARIS - MORNING

Chief Gouget is still atop the balustrade speaking to the news reporters. At the same time, Detective Bonhomme is trying to control some Anarchist Protesters.

CHIEF GOUGET

Etienne Soudy was wounded during the bank robbery a couple of days ago. He was captured and held in a Chantilly jail. I personally went to Chantilly to transfer him to Paris, and along the way, Mr. Soudy poisoned himself and died on the train.

REPORTER #2

That sounds rather convenient, Chief. Over the last seven months, two other anarchists have died in your custody.

CHIEF GOUGET

Soudy would have been much more valuable to us alive than dead.

EXT. PARIS STREETS - MORNING

Philippe runs across a bridge and up the street towards the Hotel De Ville.

EXT. TWO-HORSE COACH, STREET - MORNING

Raymond wears the Coachman's cap and pipe in his mouth. He sits atop the coach and steers the carriage slowly down the street towards the Chevalier's mansion.

The Guard stands firmly at attention at the entry gate with his rifle over his shoulder.

The coach pulls up and stops directly in front of the Guard. The Guard looks over to the coach.

Suddenly, the coach door swings open, and Rene appears, holding a rifle. Immediately Rene fires a single shot that hits the Guard in the chest.

EXT. STREETS OF PARIS - MORNING

Responding to the gunfire, Guillaume steps out of the shadows and into the street. His view of the entry gate area is partially obstructed by the coach parked just in front.

He pulls out the Bergmann-Bayard semi-automatic pistol with its rifle-stock grip. He slides a clip into the magazine and chambers a round.

EXT. TWO-HORSE COACH, STREET - MORNING

Octave and Rene rush out of the carriage. They catch the Guard as he stumbles forward, and together they rush the Guard through the door and into the coach compartment.

Octave helps by grabbing the Guard by his lapels and pulling him in through the carriage door. He quickly jumps into the coach while shutting the door.

The street is silent. Taking care of the armed Guard at the gate was done in a swift and efficient manner.

EXT. PLACE DE L'HOTEL DE VILLE, PARIS - MORNING

Chief Gouget stands on the balustrade as he speaks to Reporters. Detective Bonhomme is standing on the ground next to him.

REPORTER #3

What about the boy in Chantilly? Have the police been able to locate him?

CHIEF GOUGET

No. We have yet to determine who he is or what his involvement was in the robbery.

Philippe comes running up to Chief Gouget and pulls on his coat.

REPORTER #3

Is that the boy!?

Chief Gouget and Detective Bonhomme look down at Philippe.

CHIEF GOUGET

Yes! What is it?

PHILIPPE

De Villiers! He's attacking the Chevalier's mansion!

DETECTIVE BONHOMME

What?!

PHILIPPE

The gang is there now! Hurry!

Chief Gouget looks over at several mounted police, some standing and some mounted. Chief Gouget rushes over to them.

He pushes an officer to the side as he steps into the horse's stirrup and mounts the horse. Detective Bonhomme follows Gouget's lead and mounts another empty-saddled horse.

CHIEF GOUGET

(to other Mounties)

You three follow us!

DETECTIVE BONHOMME

Let's go!

Detective Bonhomme leads Chief Gouget and the three officers on horseback galloping down the road.

INT. TWO-HORSE COACH - MORNING

Octave and Rene pull over and prop up the Guard so he's sitting upright next to the Coachman. Raymond is doing a final check of the weapons.

OCTAVE

We'll leave the horses tied off here.

Raymond hands out the weapons. Octave leans over and pulls all of the curtains down as he speaks.

OCTAVE

We'll use the carriage for our escape - I'm the coachman.

The three exit the carriage door and onto the walk.

EXT. PARIS STREETS - MORNING

Chief Gouget, Detective Bonhomme, and the three Mounties are in a full gallop down the cobbled street. Bonhomme's horse leaps up and over a Vendor with a wheelbarrow filled with produce in the street.

EXT. CHEVALIER'S MANSON, STREET FRONT - MORNING

The De Villiers' Gang makes their way through the gate and quickly struts around the side of the large house.

OCTAVE

We'll crash into the servant's entrance and rush them into the kitchen. Shoot anyone you see.

EXT. STREETS OF PARIS - MORNING

Gun in hand, Guillaume quickly moves across the cobblestone road toward the mansion.

INT. KITCHEN/HOUSE, CHEVALIER'S MANSION - MORNING

Michelle and the Cook are standing in the kitchen, talking.

MICHELLE

You have to leave today. They're going to kill you, whether we help them or not.

COOK

I can't just leave.

MICHELLE

Your choice is to leave, or die. They're ruthless, and there's no third option!

There is a crash in the other room as the Gang breaks down the servant's door and enters the house.

Both turn their heads as the Gang comes charging into the kitchen - all with guns drawn.

The Cook bolts for the door.

MICHELLE

Don't!

Raymond rushes over and fires a double-barrel blast with the shotgun right through the closing door.

The blast shatters the door apart and also blows up the Cook, fleeing on the other side.

Michelle looks at Octave.

MICHELLE

What did you do?!

Octave steps over and violently grabs Michelle by the arm.

OCTAVE

Change of plans, dear! We're taking down the Chevalier today!

Octave looks over to Rene.

OCTAVE

You two go upstairs and get the old man.

Rene leads Raymond through the splintered door.

OCTAVE

You were going to double-cross me. Weren't you?

MICHELLE

No!

The Gang rushes through the great room towards the stairs. Guillaume is seen through the glass of some French doors as he arrives in the backyard.

Guillaume spots the gang and fires several shots through the panes of glass with his Bergmann-Bayard semi-automatic. Rene and Raymond take cover.

The Gang fires their guns back at Guillaume. Raymond fires another cannon shot from the double-barrel that blows apart a pair of French doors.

Octave rushes Michelle through a door to another part of the house.

There is another shooter - shots coming from the mezzanine upstairs. It's the CHEVALIER (75), shooting his pheasant gun at the intruders from over the balustrade on the second level.

Suddenly, one of the Mounties crashes through the large glass window in the salon and into the house. Glass and wood shards flying about everywhere - another Mountie and Chief Gouget follow him through the door inside.

The three are immediately in a near-point-blank shootout with Rene and Raymond. Two of the Mounties are shot dead.

Rene and Raymond both take a few bullet wounds but keep battling.

Chief Gouget is shot in the shoulder, falls from his mount, and continues the fight from behind a large cabinet.

EXT. CHEVALIER'S MANSION - MORNING

Octave drags Michelle through the garden and out front as he trades shots with Guillaume.

Octave takes several shots, as does Guillaume. Philippe arrives, and Guillaume quickly grabs him and pulls him to safety, closer to the ground.

Michelle manages to push Octave off of her and hide behind a wall - Octave cannot recover her because Guillaume is all over him, firing shots, with the Bergmann-Bayard semi-automatic.

Guillaume is nicked up a bit. Blood drips from his mouth.

PHILIPPE

No more! You've done it already!

GUILLAUME

No!

Guillaume and Philippe stare into each other's eyes.

GUILLAUME
He's not dead.

PHILIPPE
But you're wounded.

Tears roll down Philippe's cheek as Guillaume clutches his son.

GUILLAUME
Philippe, you'll soon enough learn in life; that sometimes a man has to do, what a man has to do.

Guillaume stands and fires a couple of shots at Octave. He's hit again in the arm, but Octave makes a break for the getaway carriage they left parked on the street.

INT. GREAT ROOM, CHEVALIER'S MANSION - MORNING

Detective Bonhomme and the last Mountie charge into the great room through the broken window. They're in full force and firing their weapons in support of Chief Gouget. Raymond is killed immediately as Rene stands there, an automatic pistol in each hand, he fires away like a kamikaze madman as he takes bullets from Gouget, Bonhomme, and the Mountie.

Riddled with bullets, Rene falls back against the wall and slides down - dead.

EXT. CHEVALIER'S MANSION - MORNING

Octave manages to climb onto the Coachman's bench and get the horses moving.

Guillaume looks over to find one of the Mounties' horses nervously wandering about.

Guillaume grabs the horse's reins and controls him. He grabs Philippe and lifts him onto the horse and then lifts himself onto the animal.

Michelle watches as Guillaume and Philippe ride off, following Octave up the street.

Gare Du Nord stands only a few blocks away in the distance.

Detective Bonhomme comes riding up to Michelle. He jumps off of his mount and holds her.

DETECTIVE BONHOMME
Are you all right?

MICHELLE
I'm fine. But the boy and his father - they've gone after Octave!

Detective Bonhomme starts to mount his horse.

DETECTIVE BONHOMME
Where did they go?

Michelle points towards the Gard Du Nord.

MICHELLE
Towards the station.

Bonhomme readies to take off.

MICHELLE
Take me with you!

DETECTIVE BONHOMME
It's too dangerous.

MICHELLE
The boy will need me!

Bonhomme hesitates for a moment and then leans over.

Michelle grabs his arm, and he swings her up and onto the back of the horse. They ride off towards the train station.

EXT. PARIS STREETS AND GARD DU NORD - MORNING

Octave pushes the two horses to the maximum but struggles to manage the coach. He's bleeding from his head and shoulder - his white linen shirt is covered in blood.

Guillaume and Philippe are approaching on a galloping horse.

Octave crashes the coach into the Gare Du Nord entrance. He climbs off the carriage and stumbles through the large doors inside.

INT. GARD DU NORD - MORNING

INTERCUT: Between Octave, Guillaume, Philippe, Michelle and Detective Bonhomme.

People inside the station flee as a bleeding, and floundering Octave De Villiers drags himself across the lobby. He's holding a semi-automatic pistol in one hand and firing shots randomly at the station's entry door.

Out of ammunition, he pops out a clip and shoves another into the handle of the gun.

Guillaume and Philippe ride their horse through the large entry doors and into the station lobby.

On Platform 13, the train's ENGINEER stands with a couple of CONDUCTORS near the engine. Octave rushes up to them. He grabs the Engineer by the collar and pushes the pistol into his neck.

OCTAVE

You're going to get this train going now!

ENGINEER

I can't! The boilers are just being fired!

Octave clubs the Engineer over the head with his pistol, then turns to find Guillaume, standing at the far end of the platform, and the two immediately exchange gunfire.

Octave is hit on the left side, twists around, and falls to the ground.

Guillaume also is hit. He stumbles to the ground.

Philippe runs over to Guillaume and throws himself over his father's body to protect him from further harm.

PHILIPPE

Papa!

Guillaume looks up to his son and struggles to speak.

GUILLAUME

Be strong, Philippe. You have to be strong now.

Philippe stares down at his father for a beat - tears flow over his cheeks.

BEAT

Detective Bonhomme and Michelle rush into the station lobby.

Philippe stands and walks over to Octave De Villiers.

Octave's head leans against a column on the platform. He can't move, and he's barely alive himself. There is blood dripping down his face and all over his shirt.

Philippe stands over Octave, just a few meters off.

PHILIPPE

My father didn't want me to have to live my life as a killer. So, I'm going to just let you die.

Octave struggles to speak.

OCTAVE

Who are you, boy?

PHILIPPE

I'm the son of Genevieve Messein. And you are the coward that killed her.

Philippe and Octave stare at each other for a beat.

BEAT

Philippe turns away from Octave and takes a few steps back toward his father.

Octave somehow musters up enough strength to lift his pistol and aim it at Philippe's back.

He'll kill Philippe sure as hell!

BEAT

Octave pulls back the hammer of the gun with a click.

Click

It's ready to fire!

MICHELLE

No!

In a flash, Philippe twirls around with the gun shop Proprietor's Derringer in his hand. Octave and Philippe each fire their weapons.

Philippe is knocked backward and falls to the platform.

The bullet strikes Octave in the cheek, just below his left eye - identical to the wound that killed Philippe's mother. Octave's head jerks back against the column's base. He's dead.

Michelle rushes over to Philippe and lifts his head off of the hard surface of the platform.

Blood trickles from Philippe's lip.

BEAT

Philippe's eyes open, and he sits up and looks over to a lifeless Octave.

MICHELLE

You're not hit?

PHILIPPE

No. I think I bit my lip.

Philippe stands, turns, and rushes back to his father. He bends down and kisses his father on the forehead. Guillaume's eyes open, and he smiles at Philippe.

PHILIPPE

(to Guillaume)

...and sometimes that man, is a boy.

GUILLAUME

I love you, Philippe. We will see you soon.

Guillaume's eyes softly close as he dies.

Philippe bends down and hugs his father's body again.

Michelle joins him. She bends down and comforts the boy.

Detective Bonhomme is standing in the background, watching.

THREE YEARS LATER

EXT. CIMETIERE DEX CHIENS, PARIS - AFTERNOON

Detective Bonhomme drives an automobile through the cemetery. Michelle sits in the passenger seat - Philippe, now ten years old, sits in the backseat with Fleur and Gabrielle.

PHILIPPE
There's a man walking over.

MICHELLE
Yes. Let me talk to him.

The cemetery CARETAKER walks up to them as Detective Bonhomme pulls the auto up to Tiger's gravesite - Gabrielle's dog that was buried that sunny afternoon three years earlier.

The automobile stops, and they all climb out.

CARETAKER
(to Michelle)
I received your telegram.

MICHELLE
Thank you for being here.

Detective Bonhomme pulls a shovel from the back of the auto and walks over to the grave with the two Girls. Philippe stays behind with Michelle.

CARETAKER
It's funny because I've never had anyone disinter an animal before.

Michelle hands the Caretaker the deed to the plot that he had given her five years earlier.

MICHELLE
We've decided to move Tiger to our family cemetery.

The Caretaker opens the deed and takes a look.

CARETAKER
You see, this deed is in the name of Rene DeGaste.

MICHELLE

Yes, and that's his daughter right over there.

CARETAKER

Does she have identification and a death certificate for her father?

Detective Bonhomme starts digging in the background. The two Girls stand nearby, watching him.

PHILIPPE

Excuse me.

The Caretaker looks at him and smiles.

PHILIPPE

Is that a copy of my book in your hand?

CARETAKER

It sure is. I was hoping that you'd be here.

The Caretaker hands a book over to Philippe.

CARETAKER

Do you mind?

The boy smiles at him as he takes the book.

PHILIPPE

Not at all.

Philippe signs the book with a pen that was wedged into the binding.

CARETAKER

My compliments. It's quite an enthralling story.

PHILIPPE

Thank you.

Philippe hands the autographed book back to the Caretaker. As he does so, he smoothly slips the deed for Tiger's plot out of the Caretaker's hands.

Philippe hands the deed to Michelle behind the Caretaker's back as he speaks.

PHILIPPE

There was a lot more to the story that I'd be happy to tell you sometime.

CARETAKER

Well, that would be thrilling.

Philippe puts his hand out, and the two shake hands.

PHILIPPE

Thank you for all of your help today. I appreciate it.

The Caretaker gives him a big smile.

CARETAKER

Uh...no problem.

Philippe and Michelle walk off. Leaving the Caretaker, book in hand, standing alone.

The Caretaker smiles as he watches them for a moment and then turns and walks off himself.

INT. CEMETERY SHED - MORNING

The Caretaker walks into the shed and puts the book down on a small desk that sits in front of a window. Outside the window Bonhomme, Philippe, and the Girls are seen pulling Tiger's casket up and hauling it over to the back of the auto.

The title cover of the book comes into focus - it reads, 'LA GARE.'

EXT. CIMETIERE DEX CHIENS, PARIS - AFTERNOON

Drone shot of Tiger's dug-up gravesite, the gravesite party, and the shed - zoom out.

THE END

First draft written in Cascais, Portugal, autumn of 2021.

MIRAMAR

Written by
Paul Charles Bailly

2021

MIRAMAR, PORTUGAL

EXT. PORTUGUESE COASTLINE - DAY

Scattered clouds help to defuse the sunshine of the rugged Portuguese coastline.

A film crew is set up to shoot a scene of two WOMEN standing on some large rocks. The beach and the Atlantic Ocean are in the near background - waves pound the shore.

A group of twenty-odd local spectators watches the shoot with interest. A couple of local uniformed Policemen monitor the scene. One is CHIEF GARCIA (42) - he casually leans against a squad car away from the action. The other, POLICEMAN #1 (26), is closer to the scene, wears a big smile - obviously more interested in the shoot.

The actors are LUCI Taylor (35), British and blonde, and ALICE Miranda (23), Portuguese and brunette.

OTTO Varga (45), the director, sits next to the cinematographer and large movie camera. The rest of the film crew surrounds them.

One of the spectators who watch with great interest is ALBA Monjardino (26), a woman with dark, fringe-punk-looking hair.

Close-up of a film production 'clapperboard' reading MIRAMAR, scene 77, take 3.

The clapperboard slaps down with a snap.

OTTO

Action!

ANGLE ON:

Luci and Alice.

LUCI

(British accent)

I do love you, Alice. I'm just not ready to commit to being gay.

Alice shakes her head slightly.

ALICE

(Portuguese accent)

After all you've been through, you can't let him go?

LUCI
Yes. I mean, maybe.

ALICE
Look, even bisexuals have to make a choice if they want a life partner.

BEAT

ANGLE ON:

Alba, watches Luci and the scene intensely.

BACK TO:

LUCI
Maybe, I am making a choice.

ALICE
So you don't love me.

LUCI
I do, I do. Just not in the way you deserve to be loved.

ALICE
You mean the way that I love you?

BEAT

LUCI
I'm sorry.

ALICE
So am I.

Alice turns and walks off. Luci watches her as the camera zooms out.

OTTO
Cut!

Luci takes a deep breath and then bows slightly to the scattered applause of the spectators and film crew.

Alba is infatuated and deeply focused on Luci. She's not applauding like the others.

Luci looks over to Otto and smiles. She hurries over to him, wraps her arms around his neck, and attempts to kiss him on the lips. Otto rebuffs her by turning his head away - she kisses him on the cheek as he pushes her off.

OTTO
(British accent)
I was hoping to get a little more emotion from you.

LUCI
I gave it honest emotion, Otto.

PRODUCTION MANAGER (O.S.)
Okay, everyone, that's a wrap!

Alice walks up to them - Otto turns to her and smiles.

OTTO
You were great.

ALICE
Thank you.

Luci watches as Otto walks off with the Production Manager.

Alba stands alone in the background, watching Luci.

INT. MIRAMAR BAR/CLUB - NIGHT

The film production crew is having a wrap party at a local club. Everyone is drinking and dancing to the music played by a rock band on stage.

ANGLE ON:

Alba is the singer of the band. She sings hard while she grips the microphone stand with both hands.

INT. HOTEL ROOM, HOTEL MIRAMAR - NIGHT

Luci is getting dressed for the party. She's wearing a stunning red, mid-length, late-summer dress. Her daughter, BETTE (5), lies under the covers in bed as she watches her mother.

BETTE
(British accent)
Mommy, is Daddy going to come and tuck me in tonight?

LUCI

I don't think so, honey. It's a busy night for your father; he's hosting a party for all the people who worked so hard to make this film.

INT. MIRAMAR BAR/CLUB - NIGHT

Loud rock music plays in the background. Otto and Alice are affectionately huddled up in the flickering shadows of the bar.

ALICE

Take it easy, Otto.

INT. HOTEL ROOM, HOTEL MIRAMAR - NIGHT

Luci puts some lipstick on as she finishes up her makeup. She then turns to Bette.

LUCI

Am I ready?

BETTE

You're ready.

Luci walks over and kisses Bette as her Assistant, NAOMI (26) female, knocks on the door lightly as she enters.

NAOMI

Phillip is here.

LUCI

Okay.

Luci leans down and kisses Bette on the forehead, then addresses Naomi.

LUCI

I'll only be an hour or two.

Luci smiles as she exits the bedroom door.

LUCI

Sweet dreams.

BETTE

Bye, mommy.

PHILLIP HAZLETON (55), the film's producer, stands just inside the Hotel Room door.

PHILLIP

Let's get out of here. I haven't had my first drink yet.

Luci smiles.

LUCI

Really? And it's after ten already.

INT. MIRAMAR BAR/CLUB - NIGHT

Loud music as the Film Crew is partying in the club.

Alba is singing with the band onstage.

Otto and Alice are nestled in the pale light of a cafe table while watching the band.

Otto is all over Alice. He holds her in his arms as he kisses her neck. Alice is somewhat disinterested in Otto but tolerates the affection. She smiles as she sips her martini and watches Alba sing on stage.

Luci and Phillip enter the club. While she sings on stage, Alba notices Luci as she and Phillip walk over to the bar.

Luci turns, and the eyes of the two meet as Alba finishes her song.

Between songs, the lights dim, and then a single spotlight on Alba's face. She's still staring at Luci as she slowly starts singing the song 'Because The Night' by Patti Smith.

ALBA

(singing)

Take me now, baby here as I am
Pull me close, try and understand
Desire is the hunger is the fire I breathe

The eyes of Luci and Alba are locked on each other as Alba sings the song.

ALBA

(singing)

Love is the banquet on which we feed,

ALBA (CON'T)
(singing)
Come on now, try and understand
The way I feel when I'm in your hands,
Take my hand come undercover

Luci notices Phillip looking off and follows his eyes to - Otto and Alice acting affectionately at their table.

ALBA
(singing)
They can't hurt you now
They can't hurt you now
They can't hurt you now

Luci struts over to Otto's table and confronts him. Alba watches as she continues singing.

Otto stands to confront Luci, and she slaps his face. He then slaps Luci's face as Phillip steps in to break it up.

Alba watches while she sings.

ALBA
(singing)
Because the night belongs to lovers
Because the night belongs to lust
Because the night belongs to lovers
Because the night belongs to us

As Phillip and Otto argue at the table, Alba watches as Luci turns and quickly exits the club. A couple of the Film Crew Members arrive and step in between Otto and Phillip, preventing the fight from getting out of control.

ALBA
(singing)
Have I doubt when I am alone
Love is a ring on the telephone
Love is an angel disguised as lust
Here in our bed until the morning comes

Alice quietly stands and slithers off as Otto looks over and watches her disappear. He looks over to Alba singing on stage - she's eyeing him. The two hold a hard stare as Phillip and the others step away.

ALBA
(singing)
Come on now try and understand
The way I feel under your command
Take my hands as the sun descends
They can't touch you now
Can't touch you now, can't touch
you now,

Otto continues eyeing Alba as he lifts his drink and drains it. He then turns away and storms out of the club.

ALBA
(singing)
Because the night belongs to lovers
Because the night belongs to lust
Because the night belongs to lovers
Because the night belongs to us

INT. OTTO'S HOTEL ROOM, HOTEL MIRAMAR - NIGHT

Otto sits back on an oversized lounge chair, working a scotch on the rocks as he speaks on the hotel phone.

OTTO
(on the phone)
On the contrary, I think you should come over right now.

BEAT

OTTO
...well, I've been trying to get out of that for the last ten months.

Knock Knock Knock

OTTO
Shit. There's somebody at the door. Let me call you back in a couple of minutes...no, I really want to see you --

Frustrated, Otto hangs up the phone, walks to the door, and opens it.

Phillip comes charging inside Otto's room.

PHILLIP
Luci is missing, and she took Bette with her.

OTTO
Call her.

PHILLIP
She turned her phone off.

Otto smiles.

OTTO
She'll be back in an hour; she always is.

PHILLIP
We're all looking for her, and I think you should join us.

OTTO
Look, I'm busy, and I'm tired.

PHILLIP
But not too tired to leave Alice alone.

OTTO
She's a grown woman.

PHILLIP
And she's already outgrown you. She called her agent.

Phillip turns and heads towards the door.

OTTO
What did she say?

PHILLIP
She said, 'me too'.

Phillip disappears out the door.

EXT. STREETS OF MIRAMAR - EARLY MORNING

The sun is just breaking over the horizon. A 1973 blue-green Citroen 2CV drives through town.

A Man is standing on the corner. PATRICK McAlpin (50) watches the car drive up. The car's horn gives a gentle double honk, and he hesitantly waves. The car pulls over - Patrick opens the rear door and climbs inside.

INT. CITROEN 2CV - EARLY MORNING

Alba is driving the Citroen in the misty early morning of coastal Portugal. Patrick sits in the backseat.

Their eyes communicate via the rearview mirror.

BEAT

PATRICK
(Scottish accent)
I was hoping that Uber would force you to upgrade this piece of junk.

ALBA
(Spanish accent)
They don't know.

BEAT

PATRICK
It's been a while.

ALBA
I never would have accepted this ride if I knew it was you.

PATRICK
If it's a question of money, we could --

ALBA
Not everything is for sale, Patrick.

PATRICK
You'd be surprised.

Alba stops the car in the middle of the road. She turns round in her seat, face-to-face with Patrick.

ALBA
I'm not doing that anymore. With you, or anyone else.

BEAT

PATRICK
You don't need the money.

BEAT

ALBA
Right. Was that a question?

PATRICK
It was not.

BEAT

PATRICK
So, you're still an Uber driver.

ALBA
I'm a singer in a rock band. Was that a ques --

PATRICK
No.

EXT. PRAIA DA LEGUA, BEACH - MORNING

Alba pulls the Citroen onto a dirt pad overlooking the beach.

INT. CITROEN 2CV - MORNING

Alba parks the car, then turns and, again, confronts Patrick face-to-face.

ALBA
Get the fuck out of my car.

Patrick pulls out a folded-up twenty euro note, reaches over, and slides it into Alba's shirt pocket.

PATRICK
Your gratuity. Thank you for the conversation.

Alba watches in frustration as Patrick opens the door, climbs out of the car, and disappears.

Alba reaches down, pulls up a cigarette, puts it into her mouth, and lights it. She gazes off down to the coast as she takes a drag from the smoke.

She spots something on the beach a few hundred meters away and quickly climbs out of the car.

ANGLE ON:

Luci, in the distance, stands barefoot at the water's edge while staring out at the horizon. She's wearing the same red dress she wore at the club the night before. Bette sleeps with a blanket on the sand several meters behind Luci.

CLOSE UP:

Luci stands on the beach. Bette, wrapped in a blanket, sits up. Alba can be seen in the distance by the car, looking down at them.

BACK TO:

Alba's face is euphoric. She climbs back into the car and starts the engine.

EXT. STREET, ELEMENTARY SCHOOL - MORNING

A Boy walks down the sidewalk towards school. The boy is VITOR (11); he walks with a confident gait.

Alba's Citroen pulls up behind him and honks.

Vitor looks over, as Alba calls to him through the open passenger door window.

ALBA
(Portuguese)
Get in!

Vitor shakes his head.

VITOR
(Portuguese)
I'm not going to play your games this morning!

ALBA

It'll just take a few minutes!

VITOR

No!

ALBA

I'll let you drive.

Vitor stops walking and looks over to Alba.

VITOR

What about school?

ALBA

I'll write them another note.

Vitor trots over to the Citroen as Alba slides onto the passenger seat. Vitor jumps into the driver's seat. A couple of other school kids watch with amazement from the sidewalk.

EXT. HOTEL RESTAURANT, VERANDA, HOTEL MIRAMAR - MORNING

Otto is sitting at a table on the veranda overlooking the ocean. He eats his breakfast and sips a Bloody Mary.

He looks up as Phillip and Naomi walk up to his table.

PHILLIP

We haven't heard a thing from her, and she left her purse behind, so she hasn't any money.

Otto takes out a pipe and starts working it.

OTTO

She's in complete control while you idiots scramble around playing hide and seek.

PHILLIP

Otto, Luci doesn't have a car, no money, she's with your five-year-old daughter.

OTTO

Look, it's been over between Luci and me for months now.

NAOMI

If that's true, why did you spend the night in her room three days ago?

OTTO

Well, mostly to be with Bette.

NAOMI

I heard you two making love.

Otto eyes Naomi.

OTTO

What did you think?

BEAT

NAOMI

So so.

Otto smiles as he leans back in his chair and lights his pipe with a wooden matchstick.

ANGLE ON:

A couple of uniformed Policemen walk into the bar, and Phillip waves them over.

PHILLIP

Here they are.

Chief Garcia and Policeman #1 walk over to their table. Phillip stands to greet them.

PHILLIP

Thank you for coming, Chief.

CHIEF GARCIA

You're welcome.

Otto stays seated and watches with mild interest.

PHILLIP

I think you're familiar with everyone here.

Chf. Garcia eyes Otto.

PHILLIP
I was hoping we could have a private conversation.

Chf. Garcia looks over to Policeman #1.

CHIEF GARCIA
(Portuguese)
Wait for me in the lobby.

The Officer nods and walks off.

PHILLIP
Please, sit down.

Chf. Garcia remains standing.

EXT. PRAIADA LEGUA, BEACH - MORNING

Luci and Bette are sitting together on a blanket. They are both looking out at the angry waves and seemingly endless Atlantic Ocean.

BETTE
Where does the water stop?

LUCI
Over three thousand miles away. At New York City.

BETTE
New York?

Luci smiles as Bette who playfully mimes wearing a pair of binoculars with her hands. She pushes her head forward and squints her eyes.

LUCI
Yep.

Vitor steps into the background of the picture frame. He's flying a kite at the shoreline and walks towards them as he focuses on the kite above.

Bette's attention turns to Vitor and his kite.

BETTE
That boy's flying a kite.

LUCI

Look at how high it is.

Vitor smiles at Bette and signals her to come and hold the kite's string spool. Bette looks back at her mother.

BETTE

He's going to let me fly it!

Bette stands, then looks back at Luci.

BETTE

Shall I?

Luci eyes Vitor for a beat and looks back to Bette.

LUCI

I guess so.

Bette smiles as she skips over to Vitor.

Vitor hands Bette the kite's string spool and then points up to the kite.

VITOR

(Portuguese accent)

You have to keep the string tight.
If it becomes too loose, the wind
is gone, and the kite will fail.

Vitor gently takes Bette by the hand that holds the spool and moves it downward - then up - then down, again.

In the distance, Alba can be seen walking towards them along the surf.

VITOR

Can you feel the tension?

BETTE

What's tension?

VITOR

The pull of the kite on the string.

EXT. HOTEL RESTAURANT, VERANDA, HOTEL MIRAMAR - MORNING

Chf. Garcia stands over the table as he converses with Phillip, Otto, and Naomi - all seated.

PHILLIP
Are you familiar with the actor Luci Taylor?

CHIEF GARCIA
Please get to the point, Mr. Hazelton.

Phillip and Otto eye each other.

PHILLIP
Ms. Taylor is missing.

CHIEF GARCIA
Missing?

OTTO
She's kidnapped my daughter, and I want them found immediately!

PHILLIP
Take it easy, Otto.

CHIEF GARCIA
What does he mean?

PHILLIP
Luci and her daughter have left together, and we don't know where they are.

CHIEF GARCIA
The Luci Taylor that I know of is an adult woman.

PHILLIP
Ms. Taylor's daughter, is also Mr. Varga's daughter.

CHIEF GARCIA
It sounds like a private matter between a husband and wife.

OTTO
We're not married.

CHIEF GARCIA
She's too good for you.

OTTO

I beg your pardon!

Chf. Garcia smiles as he looks at Phillip.

CHIEF GARCIA

Gentlemen, what do you want from me?

PHILLIP

We'd like you to, discreetly, help us find Luci Taylor.

CHIEF GARCIA

Do you think she's still in the area?

PHILLIP

She has no money, no car, no change of clothing.

CHIEF GARCIA

Whatever she's doing, as far as we know, it's not illegal. But since there's a child involved, we'll keep our eyes open for her.

PHILLIP

And Chief, could you please keep it quiet? We don't want this to become a media story.

CHIEF GARCIA

I'm sure you don't. Good day, gentlemen.

Phillip and Otto eye each other as Chf. Garcia walks off.

OTTO

(quietly)

What an asshole.

PHILLIP

He's an asshole; you're an asshole. At least we've got the picture in the can.

EXT. PRAIA DA LEGUA, BEACH - MORNING

Luci sits on the sand, watching as Vitor and Bette fly a kite on the edge of the surf.

Her jean bottoms rolled up, a barefoot Alba approaches them.

ALBA
(to Luci)
I'm sorry if my little brother is bothering you with his toys.

VITOR
It's not a toy; besides Alba, she's having fun.

LUCI
It's alright. Kite flying is just another wonderful thing to do at the beach.

VITOR
There is always wind at the shore.

Vitor puts his attention on Bette.

VITOR
(to Bette)
We'll let out more twine and see how high we can take it.

BETTE
Okay.

Alba walks closer to Luci.

LUCI
Your brother has quite a command of the English language.

ALBA
Yes, they start learning English early in school these days. Much earlier than when I was a child.

LUCI
Are you from Miramar?

ALBA

I grew up in Andalucia, and Vitor was born there, too.

LUCI

So, you're Spanish.

ALBA

Where are you from?

LUCI

Liverpool. But I live in Los Angeles now.

ALBA

Are you an actor from that film they're making?

LUCI

How did you guess?

ALBA

You seem familiar, somehow.

LUCI

We just finished shooting yesterday.

ALBA

My name is Alba.

LUCI

Luci Taylor.

The two shake hands with a smile.

ALBA

Did you spend the night here on the beach?

LUCI

Uh...yes. I...I had to get away from the hotel and all the Hollywood bullshit. It was a warm night, so we just slept on a blanket.

ALBA

Vitor and I are going to have some breakfast. Would you like to join us?

LUCI

Sure. Oh, wait. I didn't bring my purse.

ALBA

I have money. Our car is just up the hill.

EXT. SURF'S UP BAR/CAFE - MORNING

Smallish, typical Portuguese white plaster-coated cafe, with a few tables on a deck outside.

INT. SURF'S UP CAFE - MORNING

Inside the cafe, Luci, Bette, Alba, and Vitor enjoy breakfast at a table.

LUCI

Eat your scrambled eggs, Bette.

BETTE

They're not cooked enough; they're raw.

LUCI

Here, try mine.

Luci slides a plate with scrambled eggs over to Bette, and she takes a bite.

LUCI

Alba, it's very nice of you to invite us here, but I'm going to pay you for breakfast.

ALBA

You're my guest. It's nothing.

Vitor addresses Alba.

VITOR
(Portuguese)
Well, I've got better things to do than to hang out with this bitch and her puppy.

Not understanding what he said, Luci and Bette smile at Vitor, and he smiles back at them.

Alba, a bit shocked, smiles at everyone and then responds to Vitor.

ALBA
(Portuguese)
Sweetheart, don't be an asshole. I need you to keep the little one occupied.

VITOR
Why should I? Besides, I've got to go to the library.

Alba, Vitor, Luci, and Bette all smile at each other - Alba chuckles slightly.

Alba notices that some restaurant customers recognize Luci and can't help but stare at her.

ALBA
I think you have a few fans here.

Luci eyes some restaurant customers who recognize her and smiles at them.

LUCI
They probably came by the shoot.

ALBA
Do you want some more orange juice or perhaps a cafe?

LUCI
I think we're okay, thank you.

Alba addresses Vitor.

ALBA
(Portuguese)
Charm the little girl for another hour, and then you can take off.

VITOR
(Portuguese)
Okay, but I want to take photos of the little one's mommy.

ALBA
She's off-limits, Vitor.

VITOR
She's pretty, and I heard what she said about being an actor. They could be worth some money.

ALBA
Don't upset things.

Alba looks back to Luci and softens her manner.

LUCI
Portuguese sounds so lyrical the way you speak it.

Alba smiles at Luci.

ALBA
Yes, and in ways you'll never know.

EXT. CAFE PATIO - MORNING

Luci, Bette, and Vitor step out of the cafe and onto the patio. Luci takes Bette by the hand, strolls over the decking to the railing, and looks out to the ocean.

A BRITISH WOMAN approaches and speaks to Luci.

BRITISH WOMAN
I beg your pardon. I loved your performance in Broken Moon.

LUCI
Thank you very much.

BRITISH WOMAN
May I please get your autograph for my daughter?

LUCI
Of course.

Vitor eyes Luci.

INT. CAFE - MORNING

Alba is standing at the cash register at the end of the bar area as she watches Luci and the British Woman through the window.

WAITRESS
(Portuguese)
Your card has failed.

She hands the card back to Alba.

ALBA
(Portuguese)
What?

Alba pulls out a few euro notes from her jeans pocket.

ALBA
How much was that?

WAITRESS
Eighteen, sixty-four.

Alba lays a five euro note and a few coins on the counter.

Patrick, the man who she gave an Uber ride earlier, walks through the door and stops as he locks eyes with Alba.

PATRICK
Well, good morning, again.

Alba just stares at him as he walks off. Then she remembers.

She reaches inside her shirt pocket, pulls out the twenty euro note Patrick gave her, and hands it to the Waitress.

ALBA
Here.

EXT. CAFE PATIO - LATE MORNING

Alba steps out of the restaurant and onto the patio with the others. She steps up to Luci, who gazes out at the sea.

LUCI

The waves seem so fierce on this side of the Atlantic.

ALBA

Yes. There's a deep trench out there. It forces the water upward, creating enormous, violent waves. Dangerous perhaps, but the surfers love it.

LUCI

I never knew that Portugal was such a popular surfing destination.

ALBA

Now that summer is over, the surfers will rule the beaches.

Luci continues staring out at the ocean - reflecting.

ALBA

What's on your mind?

LUCI

We're kind of stranded.

ALBA

Stranded?

LUCI

I don't want to go back to the hotel. I'm sure they're all talking about me. They know the truth - even more than I do.

ALBA

Come over to my place. You can take a shower and wash the salt and sand away.

LUCI

We've already imposed on you enough.

ALBA

It's right on the beach, with a wonderful view. Very close to here.

Luci looks over to Bette and then to Alba.

LUCI
It wouldn't be too much trouble?

EXT. ALBA'S BEACH HOUSE - DAY

Alba's 1973 Citroen pulls up to the little beach house, which sits next to some stairs that lead down to the beach.

INT. ALBA'S HOUSE - DAY

The front door swings open, and Alba leads Luci, Bette, and Vitor inside.

Luci walks over to a large window that looks out to the sea.

LUCI
Wow. You're practically on the sand here.

ALBA
It belongs to the family of my ex-husband.

LUCI
Oh?

ALBA
They've been trying to move me out, but I have squatter's rights.

BETTE
Mommy, I'm tired.

ALBA
She can take a nap inside Vitor's room.

Vitor's head perks up, and he gives Alba a slight frown.

ALBA
Or maybe my room. It might be better. You can take a shower and clean up. My sister left some clothes here that I think would fit you.

Luci puts her cell phone down on a desk as she smiles at Alba.

LUCI
I don't know.

ALBA
Don't worry; they're not punky looking. She's always been the stylish one.

LUCI
I figured that you were the 'black sheep' type.

Alba smiles as she leads Luci and Bette into her bedroom.

ALBA
The bathroom's right in there. Towels and clothes are in the closet.

LUCI
Thank you, Alba.

ALBA
Would you like hot tea?

LUCI
That would be great.

INT. KITCHEN, ALBA'S HOUSE - DAY

A shower is heard running in the bathroom.

Alba is making some tea.

Vitor steps out from the bedroom area.

Alba looks over to Vitor.

ALBA
(Portuguese)
Where were you?

VITOR
Nowhere.

ANGLE ON:

Vitor sits at a small desk and starts fidgeting with an iPhone.

ALBA
(Portuguese)
What are you doing? Is that Luci's phone?

VITOR
(Portuguese)
Just exploring.

ALBA
How did you get her pin number?

BEAT

VITOR
Trick of the trade.

Alba frowns at him.

ALBA
Put down her phone and get out of here.

VITOR
Why?

Alba walks out of the kitchen area towards Vitor.

ALBA
Take off. Now.

Vitor looks over towards the bathroom, where Luci is taking a shower.

VITOR
What are you going to do?

Alba follows his eyes to the bathroom and then back to Vitor. She shows some mild aggression as she steps over toward Vitor.

ALBA
None of your business.

Vitor stands and raises his hands, surrendering.

VITOR

I'm done here anyway. Will you pick me up later?

ALBA

Remember what we talked about last week?

BEAT

VITOR

Vova?

ALBA

You could start tonight.

VITOR

Your freedom means more to you than I do.

Alba gives Vitor a hard stare. He smiles as he walks towards the front door and opens it.

VITOR

I might be back later.

ALBA

No, Vitor.

Alba walks over to Luci's iPhone and looks down at it as Vitor closes the door behind him.

INT. ALBA'S BEDROOM - DAY

The shower is running as Bette sleeps on top of the bed. The door opens, and Alba quietly steps inside.

Alba takes a few more steps into the room and looks down at Bette - she's sound asleep.

Alba steps over to the bathroom door. It's already ajar, and Alba pulls it open a little more.

She peers through the crack of the opened door, and Luci can be seen taking a shower. The clear glass shower enclosure provides a steamy view of Luci - nude, covered in soap suds. Alba watches as Luci continues to wash herself with a soapy sponge.

Alba is entranced by the sight of Luci in the shower. Her body is semi-obscured by the steam on the glass. Alba looks back down to a sleeping Bette and then back to Luci.

There is a noise outside, and Alba steps over and peers out the bedroom door.

ANGLE ON:

A couple of Surfers. They carry their surfboards as they walk down the stairs next to the house toward the beach below.

Alba turns and steps back to the bathroom door for another look. She shakes nervously as she watches.

Luci rinses off the soap, turns the water off, and opens the shower door.

Alba turns away from the bathroom door.

BETTE

Alba?

Stunned, Alba looks down at Bette, sitting in bed.

BETTE

Where's mommy?

ALBA

(whisper)

She's in the shower, dear.

Alba steps over to Bette and helps her lay her head back on the pillow.

ALBA

(whisper)

Go back to sleep.

Bette obliges and closes her eyes.

Alba turns and steps over to the bedroom door.

LUCI

Wait.

Alba turns to find Luci standing in the bathroom doorway.

LUCI

What were you doing in here?

Alba nervously smiles at Luci.

ALBA

Bette woke up for a moment, and I was putting her back to sleep.

Luci steps over and leans down to attend to Bette.

Alba disappears out the bedroom door as Luci brushes her hand over Bette's hair, comforting her.

INT. LIVING ROOM, ALBA'S HOUSE - DAY

Alba steps out of the kitchen, holding a cup of tea. Luci steps out of the bedroom. She's wearing some of Alba's sister's clothing - they're fashionable, and she looks great.

LUCI

Thank your sister for these clothes. They fit very well.

Alba steps over and hands the tea to Luci.

ALBA

Oh, she hasn't worn that stuff in a while.

There is more noise from Surfers passing down the exterior stairs toward the beach.

EXT. SURF'S UP BAR/CAFE - DAY

A police car pulls up and parks in front of the bar. Chief Garcia climbs out and walks up to the cafe.

INT. SURF'S UP BAR/CAFE - CONTINUOUS

Patrick, Alba's Uber passenger from that morning, is sitting in the back at a table with a couple of SURFERS. The Surfers are drinking beer while Patrick sips a mojito.

PATRICK

...sure, in the world of surfing, you may be well known, but to everyone else, you're just a couple of beach boys searching for the endless summer.

SURFER #1
That'll never change.

SURFER #2
Yeah, they've tried to commercialize surfing several times, but there are already too many sports on television.

SURFER #1
And you can only go so far without TV.

In the background, the bar's front door opens up, and Chf. Garcia steps inside.

Patrick looks over to the Chief as he moves to another table and starts a conversation with some CUSTOMERS.

PATRICK
That's true. However, in the past, they've tried to sell surfing to men. We're going to focus on the women.

SURFER #1
Women?

PATRICK
Studies show that men are more interested in things, and women are more interested in people. Our goal is to make surfing more of a people enterprise.

SURFER #2
Visually, surfing just doesn't translate to television.

PATRICK
These are the days of analytics and social media. There's a lot more to it than just waves and surfboards.

SURFER #1
Like what?

PATRICK
Personalities, fashion, cars, hair -

SURFER #1

Hair?

The two Surfers look at each other and chuckle.

SURFER #2

No surfer worth a damn cares about their hair.

PATRICK

Look, women spend more time on social media than men. And they're more apt to follow a personality because of their appearance than men.

SURFER #1

Most surfers don't give a shit about how they look.

SURFER #2

We get where you're going with this. But surfing is a solitary pursuit. Very intense and, at the same time, very meditative and personal.

SURFER #1

It's hard to explain in words.

PATRICK

As it is with all sports when performed at their highest level.

Chf. Garcia walks over to Patrick's table.

PATRICK

We'll take care of the presentation. You can date high-profile ladies...models.

SURFER #1

I already have a girlfriend.

PATRICK

It's just for marketing.

SURFER #2

Are you going to tell his girlfriend that?

SURFER #1

How are we supposed to meet these ladies?

PATRICK

Gentlemen, that's the easy part.

Chf. Garcia arrives at their table and stares at Patrick.

Patrick looks up to Chf. Garcia.

PATRICK

May I help you with something, Officer?

Garcia looks at the two Surfers and holds eye contact for a beat.

BEAT

CHIEF GARCIA

Do either of you two know where I can purchase some....

Chf. Garcia puts his thumb and index finger together, then up to his lips like he's smoking a joint.

CHIEF GARCIA

...weed?

The two Surfers are dumbfounded, and they continue staring at the Chief with blank faces. Patrick is in shock, too.

Chf. Garcia smiles.

CHIEF GARCIA

I'm just kidding.

The tension at the table breaks as they all smile and take a breath.

INT. ALBA'S HOUSE, LIVING ROOM - DAY

Alba and Luci sit, drinking tea, and talking in the living room. Bette is huddled over the cocktail table, drawing pictures with some markers.

Luci steps up and looks out the window. She watches the Surfers hurry across the sand toward their friends and the waves.

ALBA

Are you returning to Los Angeles now that the film is finished?

LUCI

Bette doesn't start first grade for another year. This could be my last opportunity to take a break.

ALBA

So look for another project in Europe. They might not pay as well, but you could stay busy and enjoy life here.

In the background, through the window, a couple of Surfers are descending the stairs toward the beach.

LUCI

I wouldn't be the first Hollywood actor that took a hiatus in Europe.

ALBA

Look, I've got to run up to Porto for the night. Why don't you and Bette come with me?

LUCI

I've been meaning to get up to Porto.

ALBA

It's the wine capital of Portugal, and it'll give you a little time to figure things out. It's only a few hours' drive.

LUCI

That sounds perfect, Alba. I could probably arrange to get some money through my assistant.

ALBA

Don't worry about money; we won't need much, and I have that.

LUCI

You've been great, Alba.

One of the Surfers using the outside stairs, FRANCISCO (26), stops and looks through the window at Luci. He knocks on the glass.

Luci and Alba turn towards the window.

Alba frowns at him and then gestures to him to move along. Francisco smiles at Luci and waves as if he recognizes her.

LUCI

That boy was one of the workers on the set.

Luci stands and walks over to the window.

ALBA

He's a nobody.

Francisco smiles at Luci.

Luci signals him to walk around to the large sliding door on the deck.

Alba frowns as Bette joins Luci over at the door to meet Francisco. She slides the door open.

BETTE

Hi Francisco!

FRANCISCO

Hello, little one.

Francisco looks inside at Bette and waves to her - she waves back to him.

LUCI

So, you're a surfer?

FRANCISCO

I'm trying to qualify for the MEO Rip Curl surfing tournament in Peniche.

LUCI

Well, you should be careful.

Alba joins them at the door.

FRANCISCO
We do it all the time.

ALBA
Your friends are waiting for you.

FRANCISCO
Come and watch me.

LUCI
I don't know.

FRANCISCO
Please. It would be inspirational to have you there.

Luci eyes a stone-faced Alba and then walks her over away from the door.

LUCI
(whispering)
He's such a sweetheart; I can't deny him a few minutes. Come with us.

ALBA
No, I've got to do some things here.

LUCI
Okay, well, we won't be long.

Luci walks back to Francisco.

LUCI
Shall we watch Francisco go surfing, Bette?

BETTE
Sure!

Bette steps up and takes Luci by the hand. They step out the door, and follow Francisco across the deck and down the short flight of stairs to the sand.

Alba stands at the door and watches them.

INT. SURF'S UP BAR/CAFE - DAY

Patrick and the two Surfers sit at the table. Chf. Garcia stands over their table.

CHIEF GARCIA

There's been a crew shooting a film in Miramar over the last several weeks. And one of their actors is missing.

Chf. Garcia hands a photograph of Luci to Surfer #2, and he eyes it. Patrick leans over to take a look.

SURFER #2

She looks familiar.

SURFER #1

We've seen the crew around town.

PATRICK

Is that Luci Taylor that you're looking for?

CHIEF GARCIA

Have you seen her?

PATRICK

She was here a little while ago. She left with my Uber Driver.

CHIEF GARCIA

Uber Driver?

PATRICK

She drives an old green Citroen 2CV.

SURFER #2

Sure. That woman lives near Praia do Norte. We see her strolling the beach all the time.

SURFER #1

I think she's a singer in a band.

CHIEF GARCIA

A singer?

PATRICK
Her name is Alba Monjardino.

The Surfers and Chf. Garcia eye Patrick.

PATRICK
She was my driver when I was in town a few months back.

EXT. PRAIA DO NORTE, SURFING - DAY

Several Surfers are riding the large waves of Praia do Norte.

ANGLE ON:

Luci and Bette; both smile as they watch Francisco ride the waves.

ANGLE ON:

Francisco surfing a violent wave. He entertains Luci and Bette by doing some tricks on his surfboard.

EXT. PRAIA DO NORTE, ON THE BEACH - DAY

Luci and Bette sit on the sand while watching Francisco maneuver his surfboard out on the waves.

BETTE
Those waves are scary.

LUCI
And dangerous.

BETTE
Look, there are a couple of girl surfers.

ANGLE ON:

A couple of GIRL SURFERS carrying their surfboards. They run into the water and launch into the surf.

BACK TO:

Luci and Bette watching the action.

LUCI
Sure. Girls like surfing just like boys do.

BETTE
I want to surf, too.

LUCI
Maybe one day you can take a lesson from Francisco.

Luci does a quick look back toward Alba's house.

INT. ALBA'S HOUSE, VITOR'S BEDROOM - DAY

Alba walks into Vitor's bedroom. There are posters of Renaldo, the Sex Pistols, and the Portuguese punk rock bands Mata-Ratos and No Time To Waste.

Alba steps over to some shelves. There are several photographs of Vitor and his father. One is of the two hanging out at a rock concert with the band members of Mata-Ratos.

Alba looks at the photos for a moment and then quickly turns them all face down on the shelf - out of view.

There is a metal lockbox safe on another shelf. She opens a cigar box next to it and fishes around, looking for something. She pulls out a half-empty pack of Marlboro cigarettes. She shakes her head in disappointment and tosses the cigarettes onto the shelf.

Alba pulls out a small key and looks it over.

She sticks it into the keyhole of the lockbox and swings open the door. To her amazement, she sticks her hand inside and pulls out a handful of cash - tens and twenties mostly.

ALBA
What the fuck?

Alba takes the stash over to Vitor's bed and empties the lockbox onto the bedspread.

Alba counts several hundred euros, folds them over, and shoves them into her pocket. Then, she pulls out a white envelope and tears it open. It's a credit card. She inspects it with fascination, then shoves that, too, into her pocket.

She closes the lockbox and returns it to the shelf. She drops the key into the cigar box, picks up the Marlboro cigarettes, takes one out, puts it into her mouth, and tosses the pack back into the box.

EXT. PRAIA DO NORTE, SURFING - DAY

Francisco is surfing another big wave. He tries a Rodeo Flip maneuver, where the surfer allows air to get under the surfboard and then flips the board as he jumps into the air.

He's successful on his first try, but the board skids away from him on the second attempt, and he crashes down into the wave.

EXT. ELEMENTARY SCHOOL - DAY

Kids are playing in the schoolyard. Vitor is over near a fence talking to a couple of BOYS (10). Vitor is inspecting the phone of one of the Boys.

VITOR
(Portuguese)
These are pretty good. Who's the girl in the bikini?

BOY #1
(Portuguese)
My next-door neighbor.

Vitor continues flipping through the photos.

VITOR
Now, this is a nice one.

ANGLE ON:

Photo of a Girl in a bikini leaning over - her ass is sticking out towards the camera.

BACK TO:

Vitor hands the cellphone back to Boy #1.

VITOR
Send them to me right now, and then erase them.

Vitor looks to Boy #2.

VITOR
Let me see what you have.

Boy #2 nervously hands Vitor his cell phone, and Vitor starts flipping through some photos.

VITOR

These are shit!

BOY #2

(Portuguese)

I'm sorry, Vitor. I was afraid of getting caught by my father.

Vitor flips through several more and then hurls the cell phone at Boy #2. The phone bounces off Boy #2's chest and onto the ground. He bends over to pick it up, but Vitor blocks it with his foot, grabs Boy #2 by the hair, and pins his head against the fence.

VITOR

All shit!

BOY #2

I'm sorry, Vitor!

VITOR

How much money do you have?

BOY #2

Just a couple of euros!

Vitor lets go of Boy #2 and pushes him back against the fence.

VITOR

Give them to me!

Boy #2 pulls a five-euro note from his pocket.

BOY #2

I need money to take the bus home.

Vitor snatches the money from the Boy's hand.

VITOR

You can walk! And I want better photos by next week. Hear me?

BOY #2

Okay.

Vitor looks at Boy #1.

VITOR

And more from you, too.

BOY #1

Okay.

Vitor turns and walks off.

INT. ALBA'S HOUSE - DAY

Alba finishes packing a few things into a small valise. She closes it and walks over to the large glass door looking out over the deck to the beach. She steps out onto the deck and lights a cigarette.

EXT. PRAIA DO NORTE, ON THE BEACH - DAY

Luci and Bette's heads jerk as they watch Francisco crash. They both quickly stand up on their feet.

BETTE

He fell!

LUCI

I see that. I think he's okay.

Luci points.

LUCI

See him over there? He's alright.

EXT. DECK, ALBA'S HOUSE - DAY

Alba smokes a cigarette while she watches Luci and Bette run up to Francisco as he approaches them, surfboard in hand.

ANGLE ON:

Luci throws a towel over Francisco's shoulders and comforts him. Together with Bette, she hugs him.

INT. ALBA'S HOUSE, LIVING ROOM - DAY

Alba tosses off the cigarette as Luci, Bette, and Francisco walk across the deck. They all enter the house together through the living room.

LUCI

I'd like to make Francisco a hot tea.

ALBA
I'll make him something.

FRANCISCO
I'd prefer an abatanado.

ALBA
Dry yourself off and have a seat on the couch.

Alba disappears into the kitchen as Luci and Francisco follow her. Bette takes her place on some floor pillows in the living room, like before.

LUCI
Cafe, uh?

FRANCISCO
The caffeine helps to stimulate my metabolism and warm me up.

LUCI
Is there a large dry towel or blanket he could wrap around himself?

Alba smiles at Luci.

ALBA
You're a real mother hen, Luci.

LUCI
He really is shaking cold, Alba.

Alba looks over to Francisco.

INT. ALBA'S HOUSE, LIVING ROOM - DAY

Francisco has a blanket wrapped around his shoulders. He sits with Luci on the couch with Bette working on a drawing at the cocktail table.

Alba is standing, leaning against a wall.

LUCI
What did you put in this tea, Alba?

FRANCISCO
Yes, it tastes quite strong.

Alba smiles.

ALBA
Just a little whiskey. That's cannabis tea you're drinking - they go well together.

LUCI
It's delicious.

Francisco considers the taste of the cafe.

FRANCISCO
It doesn't taste like whiskey.

ALBA
What else would it be?

FRANCISCO
(to Luci)
You two should come with me to Neptune Beach tomorrow. I'm giving surfing lessons to a group of teenagers from the UK.

Bette's face lights up.

BETTE
Mommy, can we go with Francisco tomorrow?

LUCI
Sure we can, honey.

Luci looks over at Alba.

BETTE
I'm cold, too.

LUCI
You need a hot bath, dear.

Alba steps over to the closet, pulls down a blanket, and shakes it out.

ALBA

Why don't you get the bath running for Bette. I'll take care of Francisco.

LUCI

That's a great idea.

Luci reaches out and takes Bette by the hand.

LUCI

Sweetheart, let's go into the bathroom and get the water running.

Luci and Bette walk towards Alba's bedroom to the bathroom. Alba looks over to Francisco.

ALBA

I'll make you another cafe. Maybe a little stronger.

FRANCISCO

Thank you, Alba.

INT. ALBA'S HOUSE, KITCHEN - DAY

Alba steps over to a cabinet filled with various household cleaning products. She takes out a small container marked 'Antifreeze' and walks it over to the counter.

ALBA

Would you like another tea or something?

INT. ALBA'S HOUSE, BATHROOM - DAY

Bette is undressed as Luci checks the temperature of the water.

LUCI

(to Alba)

No, Alba. You've been very, very helpful. Thank you.

Luci helps her step over and into the bathtub.

LUCI

Be careful, dear.

BETTE
It's a little hot.

LUCI
Just ease yourself into the water. Slowly.

Bette lowers herself into the water.

BETTE
Is there any bubble bath?

LUCI
No, sweetie.

Luci starts squeezing warm soapy water from a sponge over Bette's shoulders.

LUCI
(to Alba)
We should all go out to dinner and have some nice hot soup.

INT. ALBA'S HOUSE, KITCHEN - DAY

Alba pours some black cafe from a French Press into Francisco's serving cup, and then follows that with several spoonfuls of antifreeze.

Francisco walks into the kitchen behind her - she feels his presence and slips the container of antifreeze under her shirt.

FRANCISCO
I'm feeling a little nauseous.

Alba speaks without turning to look at him.

ALBA
So Francisco, what is your interest in Luci?

FRANCISCO
I could ask you the same question.

ALBA
She's a friend, and I'm helping her through a difficult time.

FRANCISCO
Are you sure that's all?

Alba turns and hands Francisco his cafe.

ALBA
You're a small-town nobody. She would never be interested in you.

Francisco's face grimaces with pain.

FRANCISCO
My stomach is getting worse.

Alba nods to the cafe.

ALBA
Drink up; a little more cafe will fix that.

Francisco's face expresses obvious physical pain. He takes a sip from the cafe.

INT. LIBRARY - DAY

Vitor is sitting at a computer terminal working online. He's got his smartphone hardwired to the computer. He works the mouse and pushes a few buttons on the phone.

ANGLE ON:

With a browser open, Vitor drags several images from his phone to a photo sales site. The photos open when they enter the site.

There are several photographs of a strange woman in her bedroom, putting on a brassiere. One of her breasts is visibly exposed as she raises her arm.

Then another photo of the same woman wearing frumpy-looking panties, bending over.

Vitor's head darts back and forth as he checks to ensure no one is watching.

He opens another photo. This one is of Luci, taking a shower at Alba's house. He opens a couple of other photos of Luci in the shower. None of them show any real nudity. Mostly Luci's back, and body behind the obscured shower glass. Her face and shoulders are visible in a couple of photos.

Vitor laughs to himself and quickly changes websites to hide the photographs. He cautiously looks around the interior of the library again.

INT. ALBA'S HOUSE, BATHROOM - DAY

Luci and Bette at the bathtub. Luci continues working the sponge over Bette's body.

BETTE
When are we going to see Daddy again?

LUCI
I don't know, honey. Do you miss him?

BETTE
Not really.

Luci smiles at Bette and then speaks up to Alba in the other room.

LUCI
(to Alba)
I should contact Phil Hazelton at the hotel. He could send over some money, and I could take us all out for dinner.

INT. ALBA'S HOUSE - DAY

While Francisco sits alone on the couch drinking his cafe, Alba quietly walks over to the area of the house near the front door. She bends over and pulls a rug back, exposing a hatch door built into the floor. She reaches down and opens the hatch door, revealing the crawlspace under the house. She leans the door against the wall - opened.

Alba looks back to Francisco.

INT. LIBRARY - DAY

Vitor continues working at a computer terminal. His smartphone is hardwired to the computer, and he pushes a few buttons on the phone's screen.

He does some quick editing of one of Luci's shower photos. He enlarges it by two hundred percent. Luci's face, neck, and upper part of her breasts are visible, as is her indistinct body behind the shower glass. It looks like a photo of Luci Taylor.

Vitor smiles, appreciating his work.

He saves the new image and then types in THE MOVIE STAR. Vitor drag-and-drops the image into the site's 'for sale' receiving pad. He punches in a sales price of five euros and hits the sell button.

Within seconds it starts generating sales. The sales races up to three hundred and twenty euros, hits a crescendo, and then slows considerably.

Vitor moves the sales proceeds to an onscreen PayPal box, presenting an accounting page. It shows the total transfer amount of 360 euros, the site fee is 64 euros, and the balance transferred to his PayPal account is 2106 euros. Vitor completes the transfer, and his personal PayPal account page is presented. It shows a balance total of over three thousand euros.

Vitor senses the presence of someone and immediately closes the site. A female LIBRARIAN (56) walks past from behind. She glances over to Vitor's computer screen as she passes. Vitor's eyes roll to the side as his head tilts - eyeing the woman.

INT. ABLA'S HOUSE, LIVING ROOM - DAY

Alba is closing the large glass sliding door at the deck. The door closed, she continues looking out over the deck as Luci and a towel-wrapped Bette walk into the room.

Alba turns to Luci.

ALBA

Did you hear that?

LUCI

What?

ALBA

Francisco just left.

Luci takes a few steps towards the glass door and looks out.

LUCI

Left? Why?

ALBA

His wife just stormed up the deck and demanded that he come with her. I think she was jealous.

LUCI

His wife?

ALBA

Sure, I've seen them together before.

LUCI

You knew that he was married?

ALBA

Well, I assumed they were. They've got a little baby.

LUCI

Incredible.

Alba gives Luci a disappointed, quizzical look.

ALBA

Luci, were you interested in him?

Luci dismissively waves her hand.

LUCI

No. Not like that, anyway. Bette liked him.

ALBA

Well, he's just a little boy whose mother came to get him.

LUCI

Yes.

BETTE

Francisco is a little boy?

Luci and Alba chuckle at Bette's question.

ALBA

Where shall we go for dinner?

LUCI
Well. As you said, Porto.

Alba smiles. Luci looks down at Bette.

LUCI
Let's get you dry and hit the road.

BETTE
Okay.

Luci and Bette step into the bedroom as Alba looks over to the floor hatch - it's now closed.

EXT. SURF'S UP CAFE, STREET - DAY

POV across the street from Surf's Up Bar/Cafe. With dusk approaching, the bar's neon lights flash on. Alba's blue-green Citroen whizzes across the highway past the bar.

INT. CITROEN 2CV - DAY

Alba drives, with Luci and Bette in the backseat. All look happy.

LUCI
I've wanted to go to Porto ever since I saw that Anton Yelchin film.

They smile at each other through the rearview mirror.

ALBA
Which hotel shall we stay at?

LUCI
Whichever has the best babysitters.

Alba and Luci chuckle as Bette frowns at her mother.

BETTE
Babysitters?

INT. VOVA'S HOUSE - DAY

The front room of a well-kept, but frumpy old lady's house. There's a dining room table with a protective vinyl tablecloth and a wooden breakfront cabinet with decorative tableware that hasn't been used for years.

The jingle of keys is heard as someone opens the front door. The door opens, and an older, heavy-footed woman steps inside the house.

VOVA (73) steps inside, and she puts a brown paper grocery bag she's holding down on the table as she looks up and startles.

VOVA

Jesus.

She crosses her heart with her right hand.

ANGLE ON:

Vitor sits in the kitchen at a small table, eating a plate of stewy meat and potatoes.

He smiles at Vova.

VITOR

Hello, Vova.

VOVA

How did you get in here?

Vitor waves his hand towards a partially open kitchen window as he eats.

Vova walks into the kitchen and looks at the window.

VOVA

You broke the latch.

VITOR

You shouldn't double-lock it like that.

VOVA

I like it double-locked. It makes me feel secure.

VITOR

This neighborhood is safe, and besides, you never know when I'll show up.

VOVA

Is that my chourico you're eating?

VITOR

I guess so. It's delicious.

VOVA

Yes, that was going to be my dinner.

VITOR

Well, I lied; it's not that good. You look tired - sit down.

Vitor pushes a chair out with his foot.

VOVA

Thank you.

Vova wobbles over to the chair and sits down.

VOVA

Where's your mother?

VITOR

She's with some movie star.

Vitor continues eating the chourico.

VOVA

What?

VITOR

Forget it.

VOVA

At the store, there was talk about an actor from that movie they'd been filming. She and her daughter are missing.

VITOR

Is there a reward?

VOVA

No.

VITOR

Oh.

VOVA

I need some water.

Vova stands, walks over to the sink, and picks up a glass.

She stares at a small jar that's sitting on the counter. She leans over, opens the jar, looks inside, and then turns to Vitor.

VOVA
I had thirty euros in here for the plumber.

VITOR
You have a plumbing problem?

VOVA
Not anymore.

VITOR
Well then, you don't need thirty euros.

VOVA
Where's that money?

VITOR
I don't have it.

VOVA
You took it.

Vitor fishes some cash out of his pocket.

VITOR
If you need some money, I can lend you a little.

He holds out a ten euro note.

Vova looks at it, then to Vitor, and then back to the ten. She reaches over and snaps it out of his hand.

VITOR
I guess I'm spending the night with you.

Vova shoves the ten euros into the jar and closes the top.

VOVA
If you must. But we're watching 'A Loja do Camilo' on television.

The two eye each other for a beat.

BEAT

VITOR

Nope.

EXT. ALBA'S HOUSE - DAY

Chf. Garcia pulls a police car up in front of Alba's house and parks. He and Policeman #1 get out of the car and walk up to the front door.

Chf. Garcia knocks on the door, and they wait for a beat.

BEAT

Policeman #1 looks into the house through a side window near the front door.

A subtle, muffled, nondescript knocking noise is detected from somewhere inside the house.

Chf. Garcia looks to Policeman #1.

CHIEF GARCIA

(Portuguese)

Did you hear that?

POLICEMAN #1

(Portuguese)

Hear what?

CHIEF GARCIA

A noise.

Policeman #1 shakes his head.

Again, Chf. Garcia knocks on the front door. The two men stand quietly, listening for something.

Again, there is a muffled thump detected from somewhere inside the house.

CHIEF GARCIA

There. Did you hear that?

POLICEMAN #1

No. Nothing. What did it sound like?

CHIEF GARCIA

I don't know. Something inside, or underneath.

Chf. Garcia looks down at the bottom of the door.

POLICEMAN #1

Maybe it's the house settling. These beach houses are always shifting in the sand.

The two eye each other for a moment.

CHIEF GARCIA

Let's go.

EXT. PORTO - TWILIGHT

The colorful city of Northern Portugal - the double-deck metal Dom Luis Bridge crosses the River Douro.

EXT. HOTEL, A BRASILEIRA PESTANA - TWILIGHT

The beautiful 'A Brasileira Pestana Hotel' with its Art Nouveau designed ironwork and glass awning around the entrance.

Alba, Luci, and Bette walk up to the entrance carrying a couple of small bags. The DOORMAN opens the door, and a PORTER steps out to help them.

INT. HOTEL, A BRASILEIRA PESTANA - SAME

The trio crosses the lobby to the front desk. Heads turn as several people inside the lobby recognize Luci.

Alba steps up to the DESK CLERK.

ALBA

We'd like a room for the night.

DESK CLERK

That's one night?

ALBA

One, maybe two.

DESK CLERK

One room for three?

Luci and Bette stop at a sitting area in the lobby - Bette sits on the couch while Luci stands.

Alba turns to Luci - they smile at each other.

ALBA

(low voice)

Two rooms. One a suite, with an adjoining door.

DESK CLERK

Suite with an adjoining double room?

The Desk Clerk works the keyboard.

ALBA

Yes.

DESK CLERK

And would you like the key for the adjoining door?

ALBA

(low voice)

Uh...yes.

DESK CLERK

How will you be paying today, Madame?

ALBA

One moment.

Alba turns away from the Desk Clerk. She pulls out the envelope that she found in Vitor's room and pulls out a credit card that reads 'PayPal Visa' on it.

She turns back to the Desk Clerk and hands him the card.

DESK CLERK

Excellent, Madame.

The Desk Clerk goes about processing the credit card. Alba turns and looks back at Luci.

ANGLE ON:

The Hotel MANAGER (55), balding male, wearing a gray suit, steps out of his office and up to the counter, a few meters off from Alba. The Manager notices Luci - the two make eye contact, and smile.

BACK TO:

The Desk Clerk smiles as he holds up the credit card.

DESK CLERK

This card hasn't been activated yet.

ALBA

Activated?

DESK CLERK

Yes. I think you have to call them or go online to activate it. Also, it's in the name of Vitor Monjardino.

ALBA

I'll just pay cash.

DESK CLERK

I'm afraid we don't accept cash at this hotel.

MANAGER

(O.S.)

João.

The Desk Clerk and Alba look over to the Manager, standing at the end of the counter conversing with Luci on the other side.

MANAGER

Please, come here for a moment.

The Desk Clerk steps over to talk to the Manager for a moment and then returns to Alba.

Luci smiles at Alba and waves her over. She then waves Bette over.

LUCI
(to Alba)
I've arranged to pay for the rooms through American Express.

ALBA
But you don't have your purse.

LUCI
The Manager is working it out. It's my treat.

The Porter arrives with a luggage trolley, and they follow him to the elevator.

DESK CLERK
Madame!

Alba steps back over to the Desk Clerk.

BEAT

He holds up a key for her to take.

DESK CLERK
The adjoining door, Madame.

BEAT

Alba nervously takes it.

ALBA
Thank you.

INT. LUCI'S HOTEL ROOM, A BRASILEIRA PESTANA - NIGHT

Luci is dressed up and looking into the bathroom mirror while applying makeup.

Bette sits on the bed in the bedroom, eating a room-service hamburger and french fries.

LUCI
We won't be home that late. But I want you to obey the babysitter and go to bed when she tells you.

BETTE
(disappointed)
Okay.

There's a knock on the door, and Bette jumps off the bed to answer it - Luci joins her in opening the door.

It's TERESA (27), the female babysitter, nice-looking.

TERESA
Good evening, Ms. Taylor. My name is Teresa, the Manager sent me up to watch...Bette, is it?

LUCI
Great, please come in.

She looks down at Bette as she speaks.

TERESA
Are you named after Bette Davis? Because she's one of my favorite actors.

BETTE
Noooo....

LUCI
Yes, she was.

Alba arrives at the open door and steps inside.

ALBA
Good evening.

LUCI
Hello, Alba. I just have to finish my eyes.

Luci rushes back to the mirror to work her eyes.

LUCI
This mascara they brought me absolutely sucks.

EXT. RESTAURANT, VERANDA, HOTEL MIRAMAR - NIGHT

Phillip Hazelton, Naomi, and Otto are sitting at a table talking while having drinks. Chief Garcia approaches in the background.

PHILLIP

Chief Garcia just arrived. I'll tell him our plan.

OTTO

I don't know, Phil. I'm not crazy about running all over Europe searching for Luci Taylor.

Chf. Garcia walks up to their table.

CHIEF GARCIA

Good evening, gentlemen.

PHILLIP

We have a lead on Luci Taylor.

CHIEF GARCIA

Yes?

PHILLIP

American Express tells us she's checked into a hotel in Porto.

CHIEF GARCIA

Porto?

PHILLIP

Otto has agreed to fly up to Porto tomorrow afternoon.

Chf. Garcia eyes Otto. He gives the Chief an unenthusiastic glare.

CHIEF GARCIA

And if you find her, what will you do?

Otto smiles at Phillip and then at Chief.

OTTO

Convince her to return with me.

CHIEF GARCIA

So, you're going to charm her into forgiving you?

Otto smiles.

OTTO
It's been done before.

CHIEF GARCIA
It might not be so easy this time.

OTTO
Why's that?

CHIEF GARCIA
There's another woman involved.

OTTO
Another woman?

Chf. Garcia smiles as Phillip and Otto eye each other.

CHIEF GARCIA
A local woman. Which hotel in Porto?

NAOMI
The Brasileira Pestana.

CHIEF GARCIA
I'm assuming that you've called her.

OTTO
We're counting on the element of surprise.

CHIEF GARCIA
(to Phillip)
Mr. Varga doesn't seem like the kind of man women come back to.

Otto angrily stands at the table.

OTTO
I beg your pardon!

CHIEF GARCIA
(to Phillip)
I have some things to do at the office. Let's talk again in the morning.

Chief Garcia turns and walks off.

PHILLIP

That's fine, Chief.

Phillip eyes Otto.

EXT. STREETS, PORTO - NIGHT

Alba and Luci walk the streets of old Porto. They're walking arm-in-arm, and both are wearing broad smiles.

LUCI

Look at the beautifully tiled buildings.

ALBA

It's called 'azulejo', introduced by the Moors, centuries ago.

Alba points towards the river.

ALBA

Over here.

Alba leads Luci to a vista point overlooking the Douro River. Several bridges cross the river, spaced close to each other. The nearest is a magnificent iron bridge called the Maria Pia Bridge.

ALBA

Porto is known as 'the city of bridges'.

LUCI

They're wonderful.

Alba points off-screen.

ALBA

The closest bridge was designed and built by Gustave Eiffel.

LUCI

Wow, easy to see the similarity.

ALBA

Maybe we'll take a river cruise tomorrow and see all the bridges.

LUCI
Bette would love that.

A vintage tram rumbles over the tracks headed their way.

ALBA
That's our tram. Let's go.

The two skip over the cobblestone street and climb onto the tramcar.

INT. TRAMCAR, PORTO - NIGHT

Alba hands the OPERATOR some cash and then turns back to Luci.

LUCI
It's all so wonderful. Where are we headed?

ALBA
Bela Vista. We'll have a bite, and then go to a wine tasting where I've got my audition.

Luci smiles.

LUCI
Let the show begin.

They smile at each other and then gaze out at the beauty of old Porto.

EXT. BELA VISTA DISTRICT, PORTO - NIGHT

The two women jump off the tramcar and head off, arm in arm, up the street.

EXT. POLICE STATION, MIRAMAR - NIGHT

Chf. Garcia pulls a police car up in front of the station. He climbs out and walks into the front entrance.

INT. RECORDS DESK, POLICE STATION - SAME

Chf. Garcia steps up to a uniformed female officer working the front desk. SERGEANT SILVA (36), pretty, and wears a little facial makeup.

CHIEF GARCIA
Have you ever heard of an Alba Monjardino?

SERGEANT SILVA
Of course.

She turns and disappears into the records shelving.

CHIEF GARCIA
Of course?

SERGEANT SILVA (O.S.)
Interpol was handling the case. They sent it to us to keep on file as general records jurisdiction.

Chief GARCIA
What was Interpol's interest in her?

SERGEANT SILVA
Murder.

Sergeant Silva steps back out and hands Chf. Garcia a three-centimeter thick manila file folder.

CHIEF GARCIA
Murder?

SERGEANT SILVA
Is there an echo in here?

BEAT

CHIEF GARCIA
I'm going to take this to the cafe next door and devour it with a double espresso.

Chf. Garcia walks off.

SERGEANT SILVA
Somebody's working late tonight.

CHIEF GARCIA (O.S.)
Meet me there in an hour.

Sergeant Silva gives a surprised look.

EXT. RESTAURANT, ROOFTOP DINING TERRACE, PORTO - NIGHT

Alba and Luci sit at a table nursing a couple of cocktails while picking at an octopus salad with tiny forks. The colorfully lit city of Porto beneath them.

Alba holds a look at Luci for a moment.

ALBA

When are you going to tell me why you're hiding from everyone?

Luci smiles at Alba.

LUCI

Bette's father is the director of the film that I'm working on, or was working on.

ALBA

The one in Miramar?

Luci nods her head.

LUCI

We finished yesterday - they don't really need me anymore.

ALBA

So....

LUCI

We're not married, and we've been trying to save our relationship. I was hoping that doing this film together would help, but it's only shown how far apart we really are.

ALBA

Sometimes you just have to face reality and move on with your life.

LUCI

I think he's been having an affair with the other actress in the film.

Alba shakes her head.

ALBA

Men are always looking for something else. They're like dogs in the street.

Luci laughs as Alba eyes Luci.

LUCI

Let's go somewhere a little more lively.

Alba smiles.

ALBA

Sure, let's go to that party and kick some ass.

LUCI

Yes!

ALBA

You want to get loaded?

Luci smiles at Alba.

LUCI

What have you got?

ALBA

Magic.

LUCI

Magic?

ALBA

Mushrooms.

LUCI

Hallucinogens?

ALBA

If we're lucky.

Luci smiles wider.

LUCI

Let's see.

INT. CAFÉ NEAR POLICE STATION, MIRAMAR - NIGHT

The clock on the wall reads midnight. Chf. Garcia and Sergeant Silva sit at a table. Alba's file is spread out all over a table. Two empty espresso cups, saucers, and a bottle of Arquardente sit to the side.

Among the papers on the table sits a photocopy of an older Portuguese Newspaper which reads 'TWO LOCALS FALL TO DEATH IN COSTA RICA.'

SERGEANT SILVA
...they conducted a majority of their interviews at our office.

CHIEF GARCIA
Why did they let her leave Costa Rica?

SERGEANT SILVA
They didn't have enough to charge her, but they wanted to continue working the case. Alba Monjardino flew back to Portugal. Interpol issued a Red Notice and brought in an agent from Costa Rica.

Chf. Garcia checks the file.

CHIEF GARCIA
Lieutenant, uh...Raul Rocha.

SERGEANT SILVA
There was no one with Interpol that didn't think she was guilty.

Sergeant Silva looks over and lifts the bottle of Arquardente.

SERGEANT SILVA
This stuff is too sweet. Let's take a step up, shall we?

CHIEF GARCIA
Sure.

Chf. Garcia signals the PROPRIETOR over.

CHIEF GARCIA
(to Sergeant Silva)
What would you like?

SERGEANT SILVA
Some, uh...Scotch, single malt.

PROPRIETOR
I don't have a license to serve alcohol after twelve.

CHIEF GARCIA
Well...can't we serve it?

SERGEANT SILVA
Sure, we can. There's a bottle of Aberlour Drizly on that shelf.

PROPRIETOR
That Scotch is very expensive. Anyway, I should have closed an hour ago.

SERGEANT SILVA
So, drop the bottle and the keys on the table, and go home.

The Proprietor gives Chief Garcia a questioning look.

CHIEF GARCIA
We'll lock the door.

INT. CASTRO WINERY, WINE CAVE, PORTO - NIGHT

A rock band is set up on the stone floor with giant oak barrels and vats behind them. They're cranking out loud music - people dancing and partying.

Seventy well-dressed people are enjoying a Vintage Port tasting party in the fermenting cellar of Castro's Winery.

In the background, the doors swing open - Alba and Luci come crashing inside.

There are tasting tables set up - several Wine Servers wearing black and white uniforms.

ANGLE ON:

Alba and Luci huddle up, and Alba gives Luci the lay of the land.

ALBA
(half-whisper)
Those guys over there are in the Alley Cats. They've been covering the '70s punk scene for thirty-five years.

ANGLE ON:

Three black-threaded rock'n roll burnouts in their late fifties.

ALBA(CONT'D)
They're pretty good musicians and do studio stuff for other artists.

ANGLE ON:

A man, ALFONSO NEGRA (45). He's part of the crowd. Alfonso is wearing a double-breasted tuxedo with an American bolo-style tie.

Alfonso walks out from behind a giant wine vat. He's got a GIRL hanging around his neck.

Alfonso spots Alba and Luci from across the party.

ALFONSO
(to himself)
Interesting.

Alfonso shakes off the Girl and makes his way toward Alba and Luci. They look over at him as he approaches. Alfonso's eyes are fixed on Luci as he arrives.

ALFONSO

Hello.

LUCI

Hi.

Alfonso turns to Alba.

ALFONSO

Bad news.

ALBA

What?

ALFONSO
We've hired Maf Carvalho.

ALBA

Mafalda?

ALFONSO

Somebody was supposed to call you.
I'm sorry.

Alba turns away from Alfonso and Luci. Alfonso eyes Luci as Alba turns back to face him.

ALBA

I'm better than Mafalda, and you
know it.

ALFONSO

Maybe, but Maf has a better
presentation and can hit the high
notes.

ALBA

Presentation?

ALFONSO

She's like a glass of bubbly
champagne, while you're strictly
whiskey and cigarettes.

ALBA

You used to like whiskey and
cigarettes.

ALFONSO

True, but things have changed. And
it didn't help that you slept with
the Castros.

Alba chuckles.

ALBA

Shit, Alfonso. Whatever happened to
sex, drugs, and rock'n roll?

ALFONSO

It died somewhere in the '90s.

Alba looks to Luci. A tear rolls down her cheek.

ALBA

Let's get out of here.

ALFONSO

Wait a minute.

Alfonso wraps his arms around the two women and kisses each of them on the cheek.

ALFONSO

I've got some coke. Let's toot, drink, and dance the night away.

LUCI

I thought it died in the '90s, Alfonso?

ALFONSO

Time for a revival.

Alba takes the drink out of Alfonso's hand and drains the glass - then smashes the glass down on the stone floor.

ALBA

Let's party!

Luci and Alba hug each other.

MONTAGE: Drinking, music, dancing, and partying in the cellars of Castro Winery.

INT. CAFÉ NEAR POLICE STATION, MIRAMAR - NIGHT

The clock on the wall reads 1 am. Chf. Garcia and Sergeant Silva sit at a table with Alba's file spread out.

Glasses and a partially filled bottle of 16-year-old Aberlour Scotch are on the table.

SERGEANT SILVA

...they interviewed Alba's mother six or seven times, and every time she gave a different story.

CHIEF GARCIA

Spanish?

SERGEANT SILVA

Yes, but she was living here.

CHIEF GARCIA

What could she know about it?

SERGEANT SILVA

Probably nothing. But she knew how to wear them out; going on and on about Alba, their family, Andalusia...for hours and hours - she wouldn't let them finish the interview.

Chf. Garcia smiles.

CHIEF GARCIA

She wore them out.

INT. CASTRO WINERY, WINE CAVE, PORTO - NIGHT

People are rocking out to the music.

Alba, Luci, and Alfonso dance and hang on each other. Everyone is dancing and drinking.

Alfonso spoons some coke to the ladies in the bathroom.

Alba watches as Alfonso keeps groping at Luci; attempting to kiss her. She rebuffs him several times, but he's persistent.

Finally, Luci gives in and kisses Alfonso. He tries to drag her behind the wine vats, but Luci resists.

Alba joins Luci and Alfonso in dancing. She hangs on Alfonso and pulls him away when he tries to kiss Luci again. Another MAN pulls Luci over and dances with her. Alfonso pushes Alba off him as he watches Luci dance with the other Man.

Alba aggressively hugs Alfonso and speaks to him (inaudibly) while the two get physical - they wrestle a bit while dancing. Alba pulls Alfonso close to her and holds him there. He can't pull away. His face shows some concern, and a drop of blood trickles out of Alfonso's left nostril as Alba leads him behind the wine vats.

Alba returns to Luci and leads her off so they can dance together.

MONTAGE: Alba and Luci sing with the band. Luci smokes a cigar with a group of MEN.

EXT. HOTEL, A BRASILEIRA PESTANA - NIGHT

A taxi pulls up to the hotel - Alba and Luci are wasted and laugh as they struggle to climb out. Luci stumbles down to one knee, and Alba helps her up. Both continue to laugh as they walk into the hotel.

INT. HOTEL CORRIDOR, A BRASILEIRA PESTANA - NIGHT

Alba and Luci waver down the corridor to their rooms. Alba stops in front of the door to her room as Luci continues to her door.

Luci holds up her hand and watches the hallucinatory trails as she waves it back and forth.

LUCI
(very stoned)
How long do these mushrooms last?

Alba smiles.

ALBA
Hopefully, forever.

LUCI
I'm going to shower and wash the cigar smoke out of my hair.

Alba smiles as Luci opens her door and stumbles inside, leaving the door open.

BEAT

Teresa (babysitter) steps out from Luci's door, and the door closes. Teresa rubs her eyes as if she's just been woken. She looks to Alba.

Alba pulls out a crumpled-up wad of cash and places it atop Teresa's open hand.

TERESA
Thank you.

Alba disappears into her own room and shuts the door.

INT. CAFÉ NEAR POLICE STATION, MIRAMAR - NIGHT

The clock on the wall reads 2:30 am. Chf. Garcia and the Desk Clerk sit at a table with Alba's file spread out all over.

Glasses and a partially filled bottle of 16-year-old Aberlour Scotch are on the table.

CHIEF GARCIA
I'm surprised that Alba didn't return home.

SERGEANT SILVA
For both of them...and the brother, home was Miramar.

Sergeant Silva stares at Chf. Garcia for a beat.

BEAT

CHIEF GARCIA
It's getting late, and I can see tomorrow being a long day.

SERGEANT SILVA
Does this ring home for you?

CHIEF GARCIA
What do you mean?

BEAT

SERGEANT SILVA
Word is, your wife left you for another woman.

BEAT

CHIEF GARCIA
That was one of many reasons.

Chf. Garcia smiles.

CHIEF GARCIA
You and I are going to Porto tomorrow morning.

SERGEANT SILVA
Porto? Why?

CHIEF GARCIA
Because that's where this case has moved.

INT. HOTEL A BRASILEIRA PESTANA - NIGHT

INTERCUT BETWEEN: LUCI'S AND ALBA'S ROOMS

A hot shower runs in Luci's bathroom, and the space is steamy. Luci, nude, stumbles into the shower.

Alba has her face/ear pressed flat against the adjoining door to their rooms. She listens to the sounds from Luci's side.

Luci is in the shower, covered with slippery soap suds and nice warm water.

Alba takes a step back from the door and looks down at the door key in her hand.

Luci is in the shower. In the background, the bathroom door opens, and Alba steps inside - she's nude.

Alba steps inside the shower.

Inside the shower, Luci is rinsing herself. Alba softly puts her hand on Luci's arm and kisses her on the shoulder.

Luci freezes for a moment, then gently turns to face Alba. Luci is reluctant as Alba kisses her on the lips.

INT. LUCI'S ROOM, A BRASILEIRA PESTANA - MORNING

Luci is sleeping in her bed. A sheet is somewhat covering her naked body. The adjoining door is partially open.

Bette wakes up in a small foldout cot and climbs onto Luci's bed. She softly caresses her mother's shoulder as Luci gently wakes and looks up to Bette.

LUCI

Oh. Hi, honey.

Luci looks around the room as memories of the night before come to her.

BETTE

Why are you sleeping so late?

LUCI

I...just needed some rest.

BETTE

You're not wearing any pajamas.

Luci leans up in bed. Bette notices that Luci's left leg is tied to the bottom of the bedpost with a colorful scarf.

BETTE

Why is your leg tied to the bed, Mommy?

Luci thinks for a moment and then offers Bette a fake smile.

LUCI

Oh, I was just playing last night.

BETTE

Playing what?

Alba steps through the adjoining door and into Luci's room.

Bette grabs hold of the scarf that ties her mother.

BETTE

Look at what Mommy was playing last night.

Luci frowns at Alba.

ALBA

Oh, that's funny.

Alba steps over and unties Luci's leg from the bed.

ALBA

(to Luci)

Would you like a cafe?

LUCI

I think we need some privacy right now.

ALBA

What do you mean?

LUCI

Please, leave us alone, and close the door.

Alba and Luci eye each other for a beat, and then Alba steps out of the room and closes the adjoining door behind her.

BETTE
Where is Alba going?

LUCI
Just to her room for a bit.

Luci leans back against her pillows as she remembers the night before and considers the circumstances.

INT. ALBA'S HOUSE - MORNING

Vitor enters the house. He looks around curiously. Cafe and teacups on the kitchen counter. He lifts one of the cups and smells it.

He calls his mother on the phone, but her phone is turned off.

Vitor enters his bedroom and walks over to his metal lockbox.

He eyes the pack of Marlboro cigarettes that sit out on the shelf.

He quickly opens it and pulls out some cash and papers. He scurries over to the bed and empties the lockbox onto it. He quickly picks through the cash, then pulls down the cigar box and dumps that onto the bed.

He thinks for a moment. Then lifts his phone and opens the Tracking App he installed on Luci's phone. He activates it. A map appears with a Blue Dot blinking in Porto. He enlarges the map to see the streets in Porto.

Vitor gathers up the remaining euros from the lockbox, a couple of hundred worth, and puts them into his pocket. He grabs a jacket and disappears out the front door.

INT. HOTEL CAFE, PORTO - MORNING

Teresa sits with Bette at a table. They're both working on some hot chocolate and toast. Bette is wrapped in a yellow sweater while coloring with some crayons on paper.

TERESA
Drink some more hot chocolate,
Bette.

Bette Picks up the hot chocolate and takes a sip.

ANGLE ON:

Alba and Luci are sitting at another table in the cafe.

LUCI
...it's just that I wasn't in any condition to protest last night, and you took advantage of that.

ALBA
Hey, I was just as fucked up as you were. I took more mushrooms than you did.

LUCI
Well, I drank more.

ALBA
That's not true. Anyway, it's not a big deal, Luci.

LUCI
It is to me! I'm very distressed about it.

ALBA
Well, you didn't seem to mind last night.

LUCI
I've never done anything like that before - and I'm not even sure what it is we did.

ALBA
Then, what does it matter?

LUCI
Because, I can sense it. Physically.

BEAT

ALBA
You were a wild woman.

LUCI
Alba, I'm sorry, but I find that hard to believe.

A WAITER steps up to their table.

WAITER
May I help you?

ALBA
Cafe with milk.

LUCI
A screwdriver, please.

The Waiter eyes Alba as he departs.

LUCI
I grew up in a small town and went to a catholic school. Even in a school with all girls, no one ever considered anything like that.

ALBA
Look, Luci --

LUCI
Stop it. You can't make me feel better about this. I feel violated, and...and immoral, somehow.

ALBA
You're overreacting.

LUCI
I need to be cleansed. What's the name of that Cathedral? The one just up north, in Spain?

ALBA
You've got to be kidding...confession?

LUCI
People from all over the world come and make a pilgrimage to that Cathedral.

ALBA
Santiago de Compostela.

LUCI
That's it. I'm taking Bette there.

ALBA

When?

The Waiter drops off their drinks. Alba takes a sip of her cafe.

LUCI

How far is it?

ALBA

A couple of hours by car.

LUCI

Is there a train?

ALBA

No.

LUCI

A bus, then.

ALBA

Look, I'll drive you.

LUCI

Alba, I think we should part ways.

ALBA

It's Sunday, and there are very few buses.

LUCI

I'll figure it out.

ALBA

Luci, I understand what you're going through. Let me help make it better.

LUCI

No.

Luci picks up the screwdriver and takes a couple of gulps.

EXT. HOTEL MIRAMAR, VERANDA RESTAURANT - MORNING

Phillip and Naomi are standing while admiring the view of the Atlantic. Chf. Garcia walks up behind them.

CHIEF GARCIA
Have you heard anything from Ms. Taylor?

They turn to address the Chief.

PHILLIP
We think her phone is turned on, but she's not answering.

CHIEF GARCIA
Some information has come to light. The woman with Luci Taylor could be dangerous.

PHILLIP
Dangerous?

CHIEF GARCIA
Two years ago, she was investigated for the murder of her husband and her sister.

Naomi gasps.

NAOMI
Murder?

CHIEF GARCIA
They fell from a cliff in Costa Rica. There wasn't enough evidence to charge her, so the investigation was dropped. Has Mr. Varga left already?

PHILLIP
Earlier this morning.

CHIEF GARCIA
I'll notify the department up in Porto and head up there immediately.

Chf. Garcia turns and starts walking off, but Phillip grabs his arm.

PHILLIP

Chief, we're going to handle this quietly.

CHIEF GARCIA

This could be kidnapping.

PHILLIP

Mr. Varga will be there shortly.

CHIEF GARCIA

That changes nothing.

PHILLIP

Chief, I forbid you to go there.

Chf. Garcia pushes Phillip off of him.

CHIEF GARCIA

Sir, I'm not asking your permission.

Garcia turns and hurries off.

INT. ALBA'S HOTEL ROOM, A BRASILEIRA PESTANA - DAY

Alba sits by the window. She smokes a cigarette as she stares out to the street below. Her face is rigid. She blows a few smoke rings that float off.

She looks over to the adjoining door that leads to Luci's room and then back out the window.

She puts out the cigarette, stands, and walks over to the adjoining door. She puts her ear against it and listens. She steps back and knocks on the door softly.

ALBA

Luci?

There is no response. She knocks on the door a little harder.

ALBA

Luci?

Nothing.

Alba walks over to her hotel room door, opens it, and steps outside.

INT. HOTEL CORRIDOR, A BRASILEIRA PESTANA - DAY

Alba steps into the corridor to find Luci's door open and a housekeeping DOMESTIC cleaning the room. Alba hurries into Luci's room.

ALBA
(Portuguese)
Where are they? Where is the woman and the little girl?

DOMESTIC
(Portuguese)
This room is vacant, madame.

INT. HOTEL LOBBY, A BRASILEIRA PESTANA - DAY

Alba comes rushing over to the front desk and speaks to the DESK CLERK.

ALBA
Have you seen Luci Taylor, room 414?

DESK CLERK
She checked out a little while ago.

ALBA
Where did she go?

DESK CLERK
I don't know, madame. She rented a car and left.

EXT. AUTOESTRADA, PORTUGAL - DAY

A white Rede Expressos motor coach rolls down the autoestrada. The destination sign on the front reads: PORTO.

INT. REDE EXPRESSOS MOTOR COACH - DAY

Vitor is riding the bus. He looks down at his phone and notices that the Tracking App shows Luci's phone is one hundred kilometers north of Porto, in Spain - and moving further north. Vitor frowns and shakes his head in frustration.

His telephone rings - it's Alba.

VITOR
(Portuguese)
What are you doing in Spain?

ALBA
(Portuguese)
What do you mean?

VITOR
I'm tracking you and your little angel.

ANGLE ON:

Alba is at her car. She tosses her luggage into the backseat, jumps inside, and starts the engine.

ANGLE ON: Alba inside the car.

ALBA
Yes. We're just going for a little drive. We'll be back later today.

VITOR
I'll meet you in Porto. I'm on my way there now.

ALBA
You're coming to Porto?

VITOR
You stole my money, and I want it back.

Alba pulls the Citroen onto the street.

ALBA
I can't talk to you right now, Vitor.

VITOR
I want my money --

Alba turns the telephone off and tosses the phone on the passenger seat as she drives off.

EXT. RESIDENTIAL NEIGHBORHOOD, MIRAMAR - DAY

Chf. Garcia drives a police car down a small residential road.

Typical whitewash-painted houses ascend a small hill.

ANGLE ON:

Vova steps out from the front door of one of the houses and walks across some pavers towards the road.

BACK TO:

Chf. Garcia watches Vova, and she turns and walks up the sidewalk. He pulls the car up to her and rolls down the passenger door window.

CHIEF GARCIA
Good morning, senhora.

Vova looks over to Chf. Garcia and frowns.

CHIEF GARCIA
May I offer you a lift?

VOVA
Thank you, but I don't ride with strangers.

CHIEF GARCIA
Now, who could be safer than the Guarda Nacional?

Vova continues walking as Chf. Garcia slowly follows her in the car.

BEAT

CHIEF GARCIA
Are you Andalusian?

VOVA
I have legal residency. Now, leave me alone.

CHIEF GARCIA
I'd like to talk to you. Give me five minutes.

VOVA
We have nothing to talk about.

CHIEF GARCIA
What about Alba...and Miguel.

Vova stops and eyes Chf. Garcia. She steps over to the open car door window.

VOVA
That girl has already been to hell and back. Leave her alone.

CHIEF GARCIA
Well, she might be in trouble again.

BEAT

CHIEF GARCIA
Five minutes is all I ask.

Vova opens the passenger side door and climbs inside.

VOVA
Drop me off at the market.

Chf. Garcia smiles as he pulls the car forward.

EXT. STREETS OF SANTIAGO DE COMPOSTELA - DAY

Luci drives a two-door Peugeot through the small city - the famous Cathedral towers in the background.

INT. PEUGEOT, STREETS OF SANTIAGO DE COMPOSTELA - CONTINUOUS

Luci drives as she and Bette look up towards the Cathedral.

LUCI
That's where we're going, honey.

BETTE
It looks scary. Are you sure it's not haunted?

LUCI
Pretty sure.

BETTE
Why do we have to go there?

LUCI
Because, mommy has to talk to God.

BETTE

God?

Luci spots something.

LUCI

Here's a parking space.

EXT. HOTEL, A BRASILEIRA PESTANA, PORTO - DAY

A taxi pulls to the curb, and Otto climbs out. He walks into the hotel.

INT. HOTEL, OTTO'S ROOM, PORTO - DAY

Otto lies on the bed while working a whiskey on the rocks. He's on the phone with Phillip.

OTTO

She's gone.

PHILLIP

Where to?

OTTO

Nobody knows, Phil. People don't give their itineraries to hotel clerks.

PHILLIP

We have to find her, Otto. That woman she's with could be dangerous.

OTTO

Luci can take care of herself.

PHILLIP

They think she killed her husband.

OTTO

What?

PHILLIP

Just sit tight; Chief Garcia is on his way, and he's already notified the local police.

OTTO
Well, I'm getting the hell out of here.

PHILLIP
Stay put. You've got to help me put out the fire when Twitter gets a hold of this.

OTTO
When is the next flight out of here?

PHILLIP
Tomorrow morning. By then, they'll have found Luci and Bette, and you can play the hero by bringing them back.

OTTO
I don't want to be a hero!

EXT. SANTIAGO DE COMPOSTELA - DAY

Alba's Citroen 2CV pulls up and parks near the Cathedral. Alba steps out of the car and looks up at the holy edifice.

She pulls out her phone and dials it as she walks the street, peering inside the cars.

Vitor answers.

VITOR
(over phone)
You stole my money to run off with your girlfriend.

ALBA
Where did you get that money, anyway?

VITOR
I'm a businessman. Somebody has to support this family.

Alba spots a rent-a-car sticker on the back bumper of the Peugeot. She hurries over to it and looks inside - Bette's yellow sweater is in the backseat.

ALBA

Vitor, I need your help.

VITOR

Of course, you do. What?

EXT. CATHEDRAL, SANTIAGO DE COMPOSTELA - DAY

Luci holds Bette's hand as they walk up to the cathedral's main entrance.

INT. CATHEDRAL, SANTIAGO DE COMPOSTELA - DAY

Luci and Bette walk down the center aisle of the Grand Cathedral. Luci looks over and spots the confessional booth. There is someone inside. Luci leads Bette over to a pew near the booth and sits her down.

BETTE

This place is scary.

LUCI

(whispering)

Now you be a good girl and be patient for a few minutes.

BETTE

(whispering)

I will, mommy.

A WOMAN steps outside the confessional booth.

LUCI

Okay, it's my turn. Now, don't move from this seat.

Bette grabs hold of her mother's jacket.

BETTE

Mommy, promise to me that you'll tell me what God says.

Luci smiles.

LUCI

I promise.

Luci steps over to the confessional booth hesitantly; she steps inside and takes a seat.

INT. CONFESSIONAL BOOTH, SANTIAGO DE COMPOSTELA - CONTINUOUS

INTERCUT BETWEEN:

Luci and the Priest.

Luci sits in the booth for a moment. She reaches out and slowly, carefully slides the little confessional door open.

She sits silently for a beat.

BEAT

The PRIEST (75) on the other side waits patiently. He leans over and listens to Luci's breathing on the other side.

PRIEST
(whisper)
I'm here for you; there's nothing to be afraid of.

LUCI
(whisper)
Thank you, Father. I'm just not sure how to frame my confession.

PRIEST
How long has it been since you've been to confession, my dear?

LUCI
Many years...too long.

EXT. RESIDENTIAL NEIGHBORHOOD, MIRAMAR - DAY

The police car is parked across the road from a small neighborhood market.

INT. POLICE CAR - DAY

Car parked; Chf. Garcia and Vova sit in the front seat talking.

VOVA

...she was sixteen, and cried all day, every day. She knew that if she had the child, she would be trapped in Jaen forever.

CHIEF GARCIA

Couldn't you help her?

VOVA

The men in our village would kill before they would allow one of our girls to have an abortion. There were no doctors or hospitals where we lived that would help her.

The doctors call themselves 'conscientious objectors'.

CHIEF GARCIA

Did she try to run away?

VOVA

She was forced into marriage with Miguel.

CHIEF GARCIA

He the biological father?

BEAT

VOVA

Yes, and also her cousin.

CHIEF GARCIA

How did they end up in Miramar?

VOVA

Alba rejected the baby as her own. From the beginning, she pushed it away, refusing to breastfeed him. When Vitor was five, Alba fled and found protection here, in Portugal. Miguel found her and brought Vitor to Miramar.

CHIEF GARCIA

What about Alba's sister?

VOVA

Miguel fell in love with her, and she, too, became pregnant. Only fifteen years old.

CHIEF GARCIA

So, you came to help her.

Vova smiles at Chf. Garcia.

VOVA

I've never been brave enough to do the right thing. When Miguel died, I came. You see, I'm not Alba's mother; I'm her aunt. I am the mother of Miguel.

CHIEF GARCIA

In the police report, you're listed as Alba's mother.

VOVA

Yes, that was their mistake. I came here to save Vitor. And I don't know if even that is possible.

INT. CONFESSIONAL BOOTH, SANTIAGO DE COMPOSTELA - DAY

INTERCUT BETWEEN:

Luci and the Priest are sitting inside the confessional booth.

PRIEST

Take a deep breath and try to relax.

Luci takes a deep breath and slowly exhales.

PRIEST

God is very forgiving. Be faithful.

LUCI

I think that I slept with another woman.

The Priest sits up straight - surprised.

PRIEST

When you say slept, what do you mean?

LUCI

Sex. But I didn't agree to it. I'm not sure.

PRIEST

Were you violated?

LUCI

Maybe. I feel like it.

PRIEST

Why do you have so much uncertainty?

LUCI

I had been drinking. We were drinking. And...I can't remember.

PRIEST

Carnal curiosity becomes less inhibited when drinking alcohol.

LUCI

You've heard this before?

PRIEST

Something similar, on occasion. But the feeling that there was a transgression is not so common.

LUCI

I guess it was something that has always intrigued me. But not this way. My young daughter saw me.

PRIEST

Your daughter was there?

LUCI

No. After, in the morning. She didn't understand what she saw.

PRIEST

One always has to consider the children first. Your daughter is safe?

LUCI

(uncertain)

I think so.

Luci leans back and opens the small curtain to check on Bette. The pew is empty; Bette is gone.

Luci's face shows concern as her head darts around - back and forth.

PRIEST

You have to be certain.

Luci becomes more nervous.

LUCI

Please, forgive me, Father. I have to leave.

PRIEST

Of course, you are absolved; God loves you.

There is the clapping of heels on the stone floor of the Cathedral. The Priest pulls away the curtain and looks out.

INT. PEW, CATHEDRAL, SANTIAGO DE COMPOSTELA - DAY

Luci is at the pew where she had left Bette. She searches around frantically.

LUCI

Bette?! Honey?!

EXT. SANTIAGO DE COMPOSTELA - DAY

Luci fumbles with her cell phone as she hurries across the plaza. She looks off and spots Alba's Citroen pulling away on the other side of the plaza. To Luci's horror, the car turns a corner and disappears.

LUCI

No!

Her telephone rings, and she quickly answers it.

LUCI

Hello!

VITOR

(over the phone)

We have Bette.

Luci runs over to where she parked the rent-a-car.

LUCI

Where are you taking her?!

VITOR

She'll be fine, as long as you don't call the police or tell anyone.

LUCI

Please don't hurt her. She's just a little girl.

VITOR

Bette will be in Porto, waiting for you.

LUCI

Porto. Okay, but promise me -

VITOR

I promise. Oh, and you'll have to take a taxi.

Luci arrives at the Peugeot rent-a-car to find all of the tires flat.

LUCI

Oh.

VITOR

We'll call you in a couple of hours.

The phone goes dead.

ANGLE ON:

Vitor hangs up the phone while he strolls around the plaza of the twisted-column at the Porto Cathedral. From the hilltop Cathedral, Vitor stops at the plaza's edge and looks down at the city.

INT. POLICE CAR - DAY

Chief Garcia drives the squad car drives through Miramar. Sergeant Silva sits in the passenger seat.

SERGEANT SILVA
They say you worked homicide in Porto.

CHIEF GARCIA
There's not much homicide in Porto, so there were only a couple of us.

SERGEANT SILVA
Do you ever miss working in the big city?

Chief Garcia smiles.

CHIEF GARCIA
Only in Portugal, is Porto considered a big city.

Chf. Garcia spots something up the road.

CHIEF GARCIA
Look! He can help us.

Sergeant Silva turns to look.

SERGEANT SILVA
Who?

EXT./INT. POLICE CAR - DAY

The police car pulls to the side of the road and up to Patrick, who is walking along the shoulder.

Patrick stops and turns toward the car. Chf. Garcia leans over and speaks to him through the passenger-side door window.

CHIEF GARCIA
We need your help.

PATRICK

Help?

Patrick leans over to the window and smiles as he eyes the two Police Officers.

PATRICK

Oh, Alba Monjardino.

INT. TAXI - DAY

Luci is in the backseat of the taxi as it cruises the autoestrada. The Taxi Driver eyes her through the rearview mirror as her eyes nervously dart around the highway - looking at every car they come across.

LUCI

Please hurry.

TAXI DRIVER

(while driving)

I'm going as fast as I can. There are police on this route, and I'm not even licensed to drive in Portugal.

Her phone rings, and she answers it.

LUCI

Hello!

NAOMI

Luci? Are you okay?

LUCI

Oh. Hello...yes.

NAOMI

We've been looking all over for you. Otto flew into Porto this morning.

LUCI

Otto? In Porto?

NAOMI

And Luci, that woman you're with - she's suspected of murder.

LUCI

What?

NAOMI

Last year, in Costa Rica. Her husband and sister died suspiciously.

LUCI

Where's Otto?

NAOMI

He'll be at the Hotel Brasileira. Are you safe? Where are you?

LUCI

I'm fine. I'll call you back.

Luci hangs up the phone and just stares out the window in a daze.

EXT. PORTO CATHEDRAL - DAY

Vitor is sitting on the ledge of the plaza overlooking the city. He's with a couple of boys. Vitor is shuffling through a cell phone.

VITOR

(Portuguese)

I can use this one, too.

BOY #4

(Portuguese)

What do you do with these photos? Those are his cousins there.

VITOR

People like to look at them. They buy them from me.

BOY #3

(Portuguese)

So, that's three euros.

Vitor finishes with the cell phone and hands it back to Boy #3. He pulls some money out of his pocket and hands some to each of the two Boys.

VITOR

That's one euro, and three for you.

Alba walks up - she holds hands with Bette.

ALBA

Vitor.

Vitor looks over and smiles at her and then waves the Boys off.

VITOR

(to the Boys)

Send them to me now. I might be back here tomorrow. You know what I want.

BOY #3

Okay. See you.

Boy #4 eyes Vitor suspiciously as he walks off with Boy #3.

Vitor looks up to Alba approaching with Bette.

ALBA

(Portuguese)

What were you doing with those boys?

VITOR

What do you care?

ALBA

You're eleven years old, Vitor.

VITOR

So?

ALBA

Act like an eleven-year-old.

Vitor stares at Bette and then his mother for a beat.

BEAT

VITOR

Why did you hate my father so much?

ALBA

I didn't hate --

VITOR

You did!

BEAT

VITOR

What happened in Costa Rica?

ALBA

Why do you keep asking me that?

VITOR

Because I don't believe you.

ALBA

Where is she?

BEAT

Vitor looks down at Bette and smiles.

VITOR

It's nice to see you again. Bette.

Vitor pulls out his cell phone and checks it.

VITOR

She just arrived at a hotel.

Vitor holds out the phone, and Alba leans over to take a look.

INT. HOTEL, A BRASILEIRA PESTANA - DAY

Luci struts through the hotel's lobby and up to the Hotel Manager. The Taxi Driver follows her.

LUCI
(to Hotel Manager)
Is Otto Varga staying here?

HOTEL MANAGER

Room 424.

LUCI

Please pay this Taxi Driver and charge it to his room.

HOTEL MANAGER
Yes, madame.

Luci hurries off as the Taxi Driver steps up to the Hotel Manager.

HOTEL MANAGER
(to Taxi Driver)
What's the charge for the taxi?

TAXI DRIVER
Three hundred and forty euros.

HOTEL MANAGER
What?!

INT. HOTEL CORRIDOR - DAY

Luci stands in front of a hotel room door. The door opens to Otto.

OTTO
Luci.

Luci gives Otto a frantic look.

LUCI
She's got, Bette!

OTTO
Who?

Luci charges into Otto's hotel room.

LUCI
That evil, fucking bitch I was with!

INT. OTTO'S ROOM, HOTEL - DAY

It's a suite; Otto sits on the couch as Luci paces nervously with a whiskey in her hand. A half-filled bottle of whiskey sits on the cocktail table.

LUCI
(very angry)
Well, one good thing about this bloody experience is that it's

LUCI (CON'T)
really awakened me to how pathetic my life has been the past few years!

OTTO
I'm sorry you had to see it the way you did --

LUCI
Don't be. You're an asshole. Why should I see it any other way?!

OTTO
I think we should get the police --

LUCI
No! I'm not going to let you fuck this up, too. She'll show up, alright. I'm her bait.

OTTO
Okay. Just take it easy.

LUCI
Do you have any valium?

BEAT

OTTO
They're on the counter in the bathroom.

Luci walks towards the bathroom and through the bedroom.

OTTO
I don't think it's a good idea to take Valium while you're drinking liquor.

LUCI
Fuck you, Otto.

INT. POLICE CAR, HIGHWAY - DAY

Chief Garcia drives the squad car along the highway. Sergeant Silva sits in the passenger seat, and Patrick in the back.

PATRICK

...It's a little cliffside shack just north of the city. Alba uses it as a hideaway when she feels the world is closing in on her.

CHIEF GARCIA

Does that happen often?

PATRICK

Too often for my taste.

Chf. Garcia and Sergeant Silva eye each other.

SERGEANT SILVA

You might have tried to help her.

PATRICK

I have my own demons to preoccupy me.

INT. BATHROOM, OTTO'S HOTEL ROOM - DAY

The door closed, Luci leans over the countertop as she tries to gather herself together. She opens the pill bottle from the counter and pops one in her mouth. She follows with a few swallows from a glass of water.

Luci leans towards the mirror and inspects her tired, haggard face.

The sound of the doorbell is heard O.S. - Luci turns her head slightly with curiosity.

She lifts the glass and takes another swallow of water.

Suddenly, there is the loud sound of crashing glass in the other room.

Luci opens the bathroom door and steps outside.

LUCI

Otto!

There is another loud crashing sound from the living room. Luci hurries over to the bedroom door and opens it.

ANGLE ON:

Otto crashes into the furniture as he reels around the living room in desperation. He holds his neck while being strangled by s black leather bondage sex choker with a locking ratchet. He can't speak, and he can't breathe.

Luci watches in horror as Otto falls to the floor, twisting and kicking as he's dying of cerebral ischemia and asphyxia.

In complete shock, Luci looks beyond Otto to find Alba standing on the other side of the room, staring at her.

ALBA

I did it for you, Luci.

Alba leans over to the cocktail table, lifts the whiskey bottle by the neck, and crashes it over the cocktail table. She holds up the jagged-edged bottle as she walks over toward Luci.

Luci, still in desperate shock, looks around the room frantically. She looks back at Alba.

LUCI

Bette!?

BEAT

ALBA

Vitor.

LUCI

No!

INT. POLICE CAR - DAY

Chf. Garcia drives through the streets of Porto. Sergeant Silva and Patrick with him.

CHIEF GARCIA

We'll start here.

EXT. HOTEL, A BRASILEIRA PESTANA - DAY

Chf. Garcia pulls his cruiser over to the curb in front of the hotel.

CHIEF GARCIA

Luci Taylor's husband is supposed to be staying here. I'm going to check it out. Wait for me.

SERGEANT SILVA

Okay.

INT. HOTEL, A BRASILEIRA PESTANA - DAY

Chf. Garcia walks up to the front desk and speaks to the CLERK.

CHIEF GARCIA

Is Otto Varga staying here?

DESK CLERK

Yes, he is.

CHIEF GARCIA

Is Luci Taylor with him?

DESK CLERK

She walked out of the hotel a couple of minutes ago.

CHIEF GARCIA

Really?

DESK CLERK

She was with the woman she was staying with last night.

CHIEF GARCIA

Alba Monjardino?

DESK CLERK

Yes, that's the one.

CHIEF GARCIA

Where did they go? Were they driving?

DESK CLERK

I didn't notice; I'm sorry. But Ms. Taylor did look very upset.

CHIEF GARCIA

Go check Varga's room.

DESK CLERK

Why?

CHIEF GARCIA

Just do it!

Chf. Garcia rushes out the front entrance.

EXT. HOTEL, A BRASILEIRA PESTANA - DAY

Chf. Garcia rushes out of the hotel and over to Sergeant Silva and Patrick, outside leaning against the police car.

CHIEF GARCIA

(to Sergeant Silva)

You're driving.

SERGEANT SILVA

Okay, Chief.

Sergeant Silva goes to the driver's side, and they all jump inside the car.

INT. POLICE CAR - DAY

Sergeant Silva pulls the cruiser out onto the street.

SERGEANT SILVA

Where to?

Chf. Garcia turns and eyes Patrick.

CHIEF GARCIA

You heard the Sergeant.

Patrick smiles.

PATRICK

Make a right up here, and head north up the coastal route.

EXT. CLIFFS, NORTH OF PORTO - DAY

The Citroen 2CV cruises a coastal route along the shore.

INT. CITROEN 2CV - LATE AFTERNOON

Eleven-year-old Vitor is driving the car. Luci is in the front passenger seat, while Alba and Bette are in the backseat.

Luci looks down at the jagged-edged whiskey bottle Alba is holding in her hand. The city of Porto is in the background.

LUCI
Where are you taking us?

ALBA
There's a little cove up ahead.

LUCI
Alba, please. Let us go - everything will be fine.

ALBA
Sure, fine for you.

Vitor eyes his mother in the rearview mirror.

ALBA
(to Vitor)
Turn off the road up here.

LUCI
Vitor, you're not even a teenager. Don't destroy your future --

ALBA
You've lived your pretty little movie star life. The life of a princess. You're too good for people like us.

LUCI
That's not true. We became friends; that must mean something to you.

ALBA
You would never accept me...not the way I wanted you to.

BETTE
Mommy!

ALBA

We're stopping, dear. Right here, Vitor. Pull over.

Vitor pulls the car over.

EXT. COASTAL CLIFFS, PORTUGAL - LATE AFTERNOON

They all get out of the car just down the hill from a little wooden shack. They're at the edge of a steep cliff. Alba pushes Luci off to the side.

ALBA

We could have loved each other.

LUCI

Loved each other?

ALBA

Does that sound shocking to you?

Luci watches as Vitor takes Bette by the hand and leads her around a small cliff shelf that disappears around a point.

LUCI

Vitor! No!

Alba threatens Luci with the broken bottle, forcing her towards the cliff's edge. Luci looks down to the beach - it's thirty-five meters down to some rocks.

LUCI

Tell Vitor to stay here!

Alba looks back at Vitor and Bette as they disappear around a point, out of view.

ALBA

Vitor!

Luci takes a step to follow Vitor, but Alba threatens her again with the jagged bottle.

ANGLE ON:

Vitor and Bette, alone on a cliff shelf.

Vitor takes out his cell phone.

VITOR

Shall we play a game of fashion model?

BETTE

Fashion model?

VITOR

I'm the photographer, and you're a famous international fashion model. I'll take your picture while you pose for me.

Bette looks back to her mother, but she's out of sight. Vitor reaches over and tears Bette's blouse off of her.

INT. POLICE CAR - LATE AFTERNOON

They're driving along the coast. Patrick is giving directions.

PATRICK

Turn here, and drive along the coast. Alba finds comfort along the shore.

EXT. COASTAL CLIFFS, PORTUGAL - LATE AFTERNOON

INTERCUT BETWEEN: Luci and Alba, Vitor and Bette.

ANGLE ON:

ALBA

Why did you run from me? Does making love with me seem so horrid?

LUCI

Making love? Is that what you think we did?

ANGLE ON:

Vitor and Bette. Bette is undressed, wearing nothing but some panties. With his cell phone, Vitor photographs a crying and frightened Bette. She's posing for him - tears running down her cheeks.

VITOR

Now, pull down your panties a little bit more.

BETTE

No!

Vitor smiles as he takes photos. She starts to pull her panties down lower.

VITOR

That's it, now further.

BACK TO:

Alba, with the jagged bottle, slashes out at Luci.

LUCI

Stop, Alba! You don't know what you're doing!

ALBA

I do know!

LUCI

We'll find help for you!

INT./EXT. POLICE CAR - LATE AFTERNOON

The three are driving along the coast. Patrick directs Sergeant Silva, who's driving.

PATRICK

Pull over! Here!

SERGEANT SILVA

Where?

PATRICK

Right here.

Chf. Garcia jumps out of the car and rushes over to the cliff's edge. Chf. Garcia searches down at the coast. He looks over the cliffs and spots a distant Luci and Alba wrestling near the Citroen at the cliff's edge, about two hundred meters off.

Chf. Garcia points.

CHIEF GARCIA

There!

Sergeant Silva looks over and spots them.

ANGLE ON:

Luci pushes Alba as she tries to get to Bette.

LUCI

What is he doing with her? Stop him!

Alba cuts Luci's chin with the jagged glass bottle and immediately shows remorse.

ALBA

I'm sorry, Luci.

Blood dripping from her chin, Luci lifts a rock to help fight Alba, but Alba knocks it out of her hand and slashes the jagged glass across Luci's shoulder.

BACK TO:

Chief Garcia and Sergeant Silva.

CHIEF GARCIA

Take out your gun!

Sergeant Silva pulls her revolver out of its holster - she looks to Garcia.

CHIEF GARCIA

Fire it in the air!

Sergeant Silva looks at Chf. Garcia, confused.

CHIEF GARCIA

Do it!

Sergeant Silva raises his pistol in the air and fires a shot.

BACK TO:

Alba steps back from Luci and looks off toward the gunshot.

Alba looks back to Luci, then to the police, and then to Luci again.

ALBA
I'm sorry, Luci. I love you.

Alba steps over to the cliff.

LUCI
No, Alba!

Alba lunges off of the cliff.

BACK TO:

Chf. Garcia, Sergeant Silva, and Patrick watch as Alba falls thirty-five meters to the rocks below.

BACK TO:

Luci stumbles back, leaning against the Citroen for support. She's breathing heavily. She looks over to find Vitor rushing out from behind the rocks. He stops and stares at Luci for a beat.

BEAT

Bette, wearing nothing but her torn panties, comes out crying. She rushes over to her mother, and they hug each other.

Vitor looks down, over the cliff, to his fallen mother.

The police car pulls up, all quickly climb out, and hurry over to Luci.

CHIEF GARCIA
Are you alright?

LUCI
I think so.

Chf. Garcia looks down at the undressed Bette and then over to Vitor, who stands there in shock.

Chf. Garcia pulls off his jacket, wraps it around Bette's shoulders, and then walks over to Vitor.

CHIEF GARCIA
Give me that!

Vitor raises his hand and presents his cell phone to the Chief. Garcia takes it and then turns to Sergeant Silva.

CHIEF GARCIA
Cuff him, and put him in back.

EXT. COASTAL CLIFFS, PORTUGAL - LATE AFTERNOON

POV: drone shot slowly pulling away from the Group standing on the cliffs. Sergeant Silva leads Vitor to the back door of the police cruiser. Chf. Garcia stands and looks at Luci and Bette as they comfort each other.

The drone turns away from the Group and flies down the coastal cliffs of Northern Portugal.

THE END

First draft was written while living in a lake house near Bellingham, Washington - winter 2012/13.

THE KARMIC KHROMOSOME

Written by
Paul Charles Bailly

2013

EXT. LONDON SKYSCRAPER, ROOFTOP - DAY

Thirty people arranged in a grid are doing yoga high above the city. They make a colorful abstract as an undulating mass of loose-fitting yoga wear - mostly Thai pants and leotards.

The class is led by LISA WHITE (38), who has short blonde hair atop a firm, fit body. Assisting Lisa at the front of the class is James 'KARMIC' PRESTON (22), with slightly swelled almond-shaped eyes, and a flattened nose with a roundish face. The common physical features of Down Syndrome.

Lisa instructs the class through the yogic exercise of 'sun salutations.'

Karmic's body is twisted in an extremely contorted yoga posture as his iPhone rings. He quickly lifts it for a look and then gives Lisa a glance, she nods, and he unwraps his intertwined limbs and scampers off.

INT. BEVERLY HILLS HOME, GUEST HOUSE - DAY

JOHN BOSS (42) and CAMILLA DUNNE (55) are nude and in the process of heated intercourse. They stand leaning against the wall at a large front window of a second-story guesthouse.

They each moan excessively as John bounces Camilla against the wall.

Camilla cranes her neck and looks out the window.

In the background downstairs, JENNIFER WHITMAN (20), her mother, LESLIE WHITMAN (44), and her father, CHARLES WHITMAN (50), are all walking across the backyard towards the guesthouse.

CAMILLA

Oh, fuck me.

John accelerates his motion - pumps harder, faster.

EXT. BEVERLY HILLS HOME, BACK YARD - DAY

Jennifer, Leslie, and Charles stop walking.

JENNIFER

I'd put a pool right here. I mean, Dad, every house in Beverly Hills should have a pool.

CHARLES
The realtor says that I wouldn't get the money out of it, and I'd never use it.

LESLIE
How much would it cost?

CHARLES
About one fifty.

JENNIFER
Umm....

INT. GUEST HOUSE - DAY

John is still working Camilla against the wall as she watches out the window.

CAMILLA
Fuck me.

Again, John picks up the pace of slamming her aggressively.

JOHN
I am fucking you!

Camilla looks back at him.

CAMILLA
No, I mean. Fuck me. I forgot that I invited these people over to see the damn house.

John keeps up the motion as he looks out the window.

EXT. BEVERLY HILLS HOME, BACK YARD - DAY

JENNIFER
One hundred and fifty thousand? Well, I'd be here more often.

John can be heard reaching his climax from the upstairs guesthouse.

JOHN (O.S.)
Uhhhh!

They all look up towards the guesthouse for a moment.

They see nothing.

CHARLES
The house groaned when it heard
that price.

LESLIE
I don't think so, dear.

JENNIFER
This is Beverly Hills. One hundred
and fifty thousand is not enough to
make a house groan.

CHARLES
But still, it's money, and
complicated in terms of building
permits and grading this area.

JENNIFER
Our house wouldn't groan for under
three hundred thousand.

INT. GUEST HOUSE - DAY

John and Camilla are hurriedly getting dressed.

JOHN
Who are they?

CAMILLA
He's a film director. He's got his
ex-wife and daughter with him. I
wanted to introduce you two.

JOHN
The daughter?

CAMILLA
Ex-wife. They just got divorced,
and she's got a bundle.

John steps over and looks out the window. He lifts Camilla's purse and fishes out some Black Russian cigarettes.

CAMILLA

Hey, those are twenty dollars a pack.

John pops a cigarette in his mouth and stuffs a couple more into his shirt pocket.

JOHN

Fleeced her husband?

CAMILLA

Nope. She's old money.

JOHN

Let's go down and meet her.

CAMILLA

Not like this. You're going out the window.

Camilla stops getting dressed and glares at John as he steps over to the window.

JOHN

What?

CAMILLA

With her, you'd have to pay for dinner once in a while.

INT. BEVERLY HILLS HOME, BACK YARD - DAY

The backyard group continues its tour of the estate.

JENNIFER

Let's see if the back door is unlocked.

The downstairs door of the guesthouse opens, and Camilla stumbles out.

CAMILLA

Hello, all.

Camilla stops for a beat to adjust her shoe.

LESLIE
Camilla. Was that you making all that noise upstairs?

CAMILLA
I was rearranging some furniture and didn't notice that you had arrived.

Camilla walks up to the group and shakes hands with Jennifer.

LESLIE
Sounded like some heavy lifting.

JENNIFER
Mother.

CAMILLA
It's okay, honey. Your mother has been throwing knives at me for years.

CUT TO:

In the back alley, John lowers himself out of the back window and drops down to the alley below. He quickly hustles into his silver Rolls Royce Phantom. He starts the engine and drives off.

BACK TO:

Camilla and Leslie lean forward and kiss each other's cheeks.

JENNIFER
I'm surprised we haven't met before.

CAMILLA
The nouveau riche. We don't fit in everywhere.

JENNIFER
Well, as long as you're, riche. That's what's important.

Charles steps forward, hand extended.

CHARLES
Charles Whitman. Thanks for inviting us to see your house.

CAMILLA

Nice to meet you, Charles. I'll show you around.

INT. HOSPITAL ROOM, LONDON - NIGHT

The lights are dim. The sound of the respirator gently puffs in the background. CYNTHIA PRESTON, (44) is lying unconscious in bed connected to life support. Several LED monitors illuminate her present condition. She seems stable.

Karmic sits in the lotus position on the other bed in the room. He quietly watches her as he leans over and grabs a can of Cheez-Whiz. He squirts the number '21' on a circular water cracker, then consumes it in one bite.

Karmic's snack is suddenly interrupted as a loud buzzer breaks the silence. Horizontal lines appear on the monitors. Several hospital staff rush into the room and hurriedly try to revive Cynthia.

EXT. BEVERLY HILLS, RODEO DRIVE - DAY

John is traversing his Rolls Royce through the gaudy canals of Beverly Hills.

His iPhone rings, and he answers it.

JOHN

What's up?

John pulls up to a stop light. He peers out the car window and locks eyes with DARLING (27), one of the seemingly ubiquitous beauties standing on the street corner.

JOHN

An attorney from London? I don't know him. If he calls again, tell him I don't work there anymore.

John smiles and signals for Darling to come over and get into the car. She returns the smile and hustles over as the light is changing.

JOHN

Look, I know about the hearing Tuesday. I'll be in the office shortly.

John hangs up the phone as Darling slides into the front seat. He kisses her hand as he greets her.

JOHN
John Boss.

DARLING
Darling Apropos.

John smiles.

JOHN
Apropos? Yes, it is, darling.

INT. HOSPITAL ROOM, LONDON - NIGHT

Hospital personnel go about getting Cynthia's body wrapped up and onto a gurney for transport.

Seated, Karmic stares off as Lisa stands over him.

LISA
(British accent)
Jeremy Middleton will be over tomorrow to explain the plans that your mother made for you.

KARMIC
(British accent)
I wonder how she'll come back?

LISA
I'll be staying with you until things get worked out.

KARMIC
She always loved peacocks, but the males are the colorful ones.

LISA
You won't be alone, Karmic. I promise, there will always be someone there for you.

KARMIC
She could come back as a male peacock.

LISA

Yes.

KARMIC

She hated men, you know.

LISA

She and me, both.

INT. REAL ESTATE OFFICE, BEVERLY HILLS - DAY

John hurries around the office while his assistant, TODD (27), reads him his telephone messages.

TODD

Mrs. Dunne called, and she wants to see you at her house tonight at six.

JOHN

I just left there.

TODD

The bank called, and your account is overdrawn by over eleven thousand dollars. They need a deposit pronto, or you start bouncing.

Todd turns and looks at John.

TODD

A bill collector called regarding the Rolls - they say you're behind two months and want --

Todd eyes a note he's holding.

TODD

-- your car payments are thirty-four hundred dollars a month?

JOHN

Hey! I don't get into your personal shit.

TODD

That's because my personal shit isn't nearly stressful enough for you.

John and Todd lock eyes for a beat.

TODD

American Express called, and they say you're now three months overdue. The Department of Real Estate called, and your hearing is next Tuesday.

JOHN

I got that one.

TODD

-- and if you don't show up again, your license will be suspended immediately - with possible revocation.

JOHN

Fuckers. They'd be doing me a favor.

RON HOLLYWOOD (55), walks into John's office.

RON

We need to talk.

JOHN

What's up?

RON

Minnie says that she never got that escrow deposit for the Newman's closing.

JOHN

Yeah, I don't know how it happened, but that money got deposited into my trust account by mistake.

Ron walks over and closes the door for privacy.

RON

That's commingling. It's illegal.

JOHN

I know, I know. I'm fixing it and sending the cash over.

RON

When?

JOHN

I'm working on it - I'll call Minnie.

Todd continues reading the telephone messages.

TODD

Someone named Gino called and said; the Lakers by four and a half.

Ron gives John a very concerned look.

John walks up to Todd and snatches all the messages from his hand.

RON

Look, real estate agents don't ask their clients to co-sign an automobile loan or to borrow their lake house in Tahoe.

JOHN

Can I help it if they all love me?

RON

You burnt half the house down!

JOHN

It wasn't my fault.

Frustrated, Ron leaves the office.

TODD

And, oh, the bank called again to say that it's your trust account that's overdrawn.

John looks off as Todd glares at him.

TODD

How can your trust account be overdrawn if the Newman's money is there?

INT. LUXURY APARTMENT/LIVING ROOM, LONDON - DAY

JEREMY MIDDLETON (67), and Lisa are sitting on the couch in a high-end, well-furnished contemporary apartment overlooking the city. Jeremy is a gray-haired three-piece suit attorney.

JEREMY

(British accent)

The trust is really quite explicit, Lisa. Cynthia wanted Mr. Boss to be given the opportunity to spend some time with his son.

LISA

From what I've heard, the bloke's a complete fraud.

JEREMY

None of that matters.

They both look off-screen.

ANGLE ON:

Karmic, eyes shut, is sitting quietly in lotus position while meditating. He's wearing a colorful robe. There are candles lit and incense burning.

LISA

I just wish there was a better way.

JEREMY

We're looking for his father now. He's a real estate agent in Beverly Hills.

LISA

Really? That figures.

INT. NIGHTCLUB, SUNSET STRIP - NIGHT

John is sitting at the bar counter with Darling. His shirt is unbuttoned, and his tie loosely hanging around his neck.

JOHN
We'll have a drink and then go up to my place.

DARLING
Okay, but I'd like to get paid before we leave.

JOHN
Paid?

DARLING
Twelve hundred dollars for the night.

John leans back in his stool and lights a Black Russian cigarette he stole from Camilla.

JOHN
You're a pro.

DARLING
Fully licensed.

JOHN
They give licenses for --

DARLING
As a masseuse.

Suddenly a big, tough, black DUDE pounces on him. He pins John against the wall and pushes his face right up into John's.

DUDE
You bet on the Lakers and lost last night. You were supposed to pay up today.

JOHN
Uh, yeah. I was going to call later.

DUDE
Later doesn't work in this business, asshole.

John pushes the Dude back. The Dude snatches John's cigarette out of his mouth, gives it a queer look, and puts it in his own mouth.

John looks over to a couple of other TOUGHS eyeing him.

JOHN

Are they with you?

Dude jerks John back against the wall.

DUDE

They want a piece of you. How much should I give them?

John pulls out a wad of cash, and the Dude takes it from him.

JOHN

Hey, that's not all yours. That's over thirty grand.

DUDE

Okay.

The Dude counts out twenty-five thousand.

DUDE

That's twenty-five.

He counts out two more.

DUDE

Finder's fee.

JOHN

Finder's fee?

DUDE

Had to find you.

The Dude stuffs the few bills left into John's pocket, turns, signals to his friends, and they all disappear.

Dazed, John looks over to see a well-dressed prep school type standing in front of him. He's a PROCESS SERVER.

PROCESS SERVER

Are you John Boss?

JOHN

Yeah.

Process Server hands John a white envelope.

PROCESS SERVER

This is a legal summons delivery. Coldwell Banker is suing you.

JOHN

I work for Coldwell Banker.

PROCESS SERVER

Not anymore. Also, they've contacted the police department, and there's a warrant out for your arrest, so you might stay away from home tonight.

JOHN

Thanks. I think.

The Process Server walks off as John's phone rings.

He answers it.

JOHN

Hello.

LESLIE

Is this John Boss?

JOHN

Yes.

LESLIE

I'm Leslie Whitman. Camilla Dunne thought that you and I should meet each other.

JOHN

Right. Well, what are you doing tonight?

Leslie laughs for a moment.

LESLIE

I wasn't thinking of tonight. Or even the near future. You see, I'm taking my daughter to Monte Carlo for most of the spring, and we're leaving in a couple of days.

JOHN
The Cote d'Azur. I love it.

LESLIE
Have you been there?

JOHN
Of course.

LESLIE
Where do you usually stay?

JOHN
Oh...I, uh --

LESLIE
We're at the Hotel De Paris.

JOHN
What room number?

LESLIE
Uh...why, I don't know.

JOHN
I might be there myself. I love the Riviera.

LESLIE
John, you are funny.

JOHN
Really. Why not?

LESLIE
Well, don't come on my account - I mean - I just wanted to touch bases before I left, so it was easier to talk the next time.

JOHN
Well, thank you for calling Leslie. I look forward to seeing you.

LESLIE
Okay, then. Bye.

JOHN

Good-bye.

John hangs up the phone and stares off in thought.

DARLING

Hey.

John turns and looks at her.

INT. LUXURY APARTMENT, LONDON - DAY

Karmic watches over a dozen or so Hippies spread out around the open living room of the apartment. They're all meditating in the lotus position.

Incense burning and Indian sitar music create a peaceful ambiance.

The doorbell rings, and Karmic walks over and answers it.

It's a DELIVERY MAN with several cardboard boxes stacked on a hand trolly.

DELIVERY MAN

I've got several cases of Dr. Pepper and Cheez Whiz for this address.

KARMIC

Great. Come on in.

Karmic turns to the meditating group.

KARMIC

Lunch is here!

INT. BEL AIR HOUSE - MORNING

The house is entirely empty - void of furniture.

The soft, ubiquitous ringtone of an iPhone can be heard.

Shirtless, but wearing pants, John sleeps on the carpeted floor of the living room. His head rests on Darling's stomach like a pillow - she's completely nude.

John's eyes flutter open. He looks around and then struggles to his feet. He's obviously very hung over.

The iPhone continues to ring from a distance.

John stumbles off, searching for his phone, leaving Darling sleeping on the floor.

In the bar area, he finds his suit jacket and fishes his phone out from a pocket.

JOHN

Hello.

TODD (O.S.)

Where the hell have you been?

JOHN

I'm...uh...it doesn't really matter, does it?

REAL ESTATE OFFICE, BEVERLY HILLS - SAME

Todd sits at his desk on the telephone as he peers through a clear glass wall panel at a couple of MEN on the other side.

TODD

As we speak, there are two FBI agents sitting in the lobby waiting for you.

BACK TO:

INT. BEL AIR HOUSE - MORNING

John is casually getting dressed while listening to Todd on the speakerphone of his cell.

JOHN

They fired me last night.

TODD (O.S.)

Uh, I thought that was supposed to happen today.

JOHN

Really?

TODD

Yeah. Oh, I've got that British attorney on the other line, and he's very anxious to speak to you.

JOHN

No, Todd. I don't --

JEREMY

(British accent)

Hello. Mr. Boss?

JOHN

Yes.

INTERCUT: Between John and Jeremy.

JEREMY

Mr. Boss, this is Jeremy Middleton, I'm the attorney for Cynthia Preston. Do you know who she is?

JOHN

I recall the name.

JEREMY

Mr. Boss. Cynthia has died. She's left you some money and an allowance predicated on some conditions regarding your son, James.

Lifting his shoes, John quietly makes his way to a large front window.

JOHN

Cynthia is dead?

JEREMY

Yes.

JOHN

How did she die?

JEREMY

Leukemia. She passed away Tuesday.

John looks out the front window to find a real estate broker and three clients walking up the drive of the house. They've come for a showing.

John slips on his shoes, hurries to the side door, and steps outside.

JOHN

You said something about money. How much?

JEREMY

Three hundred thousand pounds to start. And a monthly stipend of forty thousand. That is as long as you're taking care of James.

John struts past the group there to view the house, walking up the driveway. He acknowledges them with a smile and a nod.

JOHN

(to house viewing group)

Good morning.

(back to Jeremy)

I have to say, that I'm disappointed.

JEREMY

Disappointed?

JOHN

I thought that Cynthia was rich. I mean, rich, rich.

JEREMY

After three years, you get another twenty million. And Karmic inherits two hundred million when he turns twenty-five.

JOHN

Oh.

JEREMY

If you were here in London, I could give it to you today.

JOHN

Write the check, Jeremy. I'm on my way.

EXT. HEATHROW AIRPORT, LONDON - DAY

A British Airways 747-400 descends and skirts a slight rubber burn as it lands on the tarmac.

INT. LAWYER'S OFFICE, LONDON - DAY

Trust attorney Jeremy Middleton is sitting behind a large, dark wooden desk. Lisa is there in a chair opposite the desk. Karmic is seated on the bench at an upright piano against the wall in the background. He's playing with the keys, seemingly in an awkward, non-musical way.

JEREMY

I spoke to the agency he works for in Beverly Hills, and the indication is that he's not welcome back.

LISA

Well, there's another bridge burned. Jeremy, I have to reiterate, leaving Karmic with this man concerns me.

JEREMY

It's not up to us, Lisa. Cynthia gave this considerable thought. I know, because I was advising her against this idea - we all were. Anyway --

A loud buzzer interrupts the conversation. Jeremy lifts the receiver on the phone.

JEREMY

Yes? Please, send him in.

Jeremy hangs up the phone and smiles at Lisa.

JEREMY

Well, you're about to meet him.

LISA

Wonderful.

The office door swings open, and in walks, John, followed by a taxi DRIVER.

Jeremy steps from around his desk and walks towards the door.

JEREMY

Mr. Boss. I'm Jeremy Middleton, and this is a dear friend of Cynthia's, Lisa White.

John focuses on Lisa as she extends her hand.

LISA

Hello.

John takes Lisa by the hand and gives her a wide smile.

JOHN

Very nice to meet you, Lisa.

LISA

Right.

John holds onto Lisa's hand a bit longer than necessary, and she breaks their grasp with a slight jerk.

John smiles at Lisa and then turns to Jeremy.

JEREMY

Thank you for coming.

DRIVER

Beg your pardon, gentlemen.

They all turn to the driver.

DRIVER

That's seventy-three pounds.

Jeremy looks over to John. John smiles.

JEREMY

I'll get it.

Jeremy pulls out some cash and pays the Driver.

JEREMY

Right, then.

DRIVER

Thanks.

The Driver leaves, and they all sit down.

John twists his head around and eyes Karmic who's still tinkering with the piano.

JOHN

So. Let's get the show on the road.

JEREMY

Fine. As I told you yesterday by telephone, Cynthia has left you a substantial sum correlated to the amount of energy you dedicate to your son's life.

JOHN

You were talking one hundred thousand pounds to start.

JEREMY

Yes.

JOHN

Well, I've started.

LISA

Precisely what are your intentions, Mr. Boss?

JOHN

At this moment, I intend to fulfill whatever obligation necessary to collect the three hundred thousand pounds.

There is silence as Jeremy and Lisa stare at John for a moment.

JEREMY

Very well.

Jeremy opens a large checkbook sitting on the desk in front of him.

JEREMY

You're due one hundred thousand if you accept the responsibility as Karmic's legal guardian. Do you accept this responsibility?

JOHN

I do.

Jeremy pushes a document and a pen across the table.

JEREMY

Sign this.

Jeremy writes a cheque.

John signs the document.

Jeremy tears the cheque out and hands it over the desk to John.

JEREMY

You are also due fifty thousand pounds per month as living expenses for you both.

JOHN

I'll take it.

Jeremy goes about writing another cheque.

LISA

You must feel like you're in Las Vegas, Mr. Boss.

John smiles.

JOHN

I wish Vegas were this easy.

JEREMY

If you remain with Karmic, you'll receive an additional two million pounds every year starting one year from today.

JOHN

What is the total value of the trust?

JEREMY

That is something I cannot discuss with you, Mr. Boss.

Jeremy slides another cheque across the desk.

JOHN
Okay. Well, I think I'll take James home now.

Noticeably, Karmic stops tinkering with the piano. The three look over at him.

LISA
It isn't legal, but James goes by the name of Karmic now.

JOHN
Karmic? What kind of a name is that?

Karmic turns and looks at John.

KARMIC
It's a denominal adjective.

INT. LUXURY APARTMENT, LONDON - DAY

John, Karmic, and Lisa enter the apartment. John drops his bags on the floor as he smiles. He likes what he sees.

JOHN
Very nice.

He turns to Karmic.

JOHN
Contemporary. I like it.

KARMIC
It's loosely based on the style of Mies van der Rohe.

John looks over to Karmic.

JOHN
Oh.

LISA
There's a third bedroom off the kitchen you might be comfortable in.

JOHN

Where did Cynthia sleep?

LISA

In the master bedroom.

JOHN

That'll work.

Startled, both Karmic and Lisa eye John as he looks over some framed photos on the bookshelves.

JOHN

Lisa, I'm going to need some help getting rid of Cynthia's things.

LISA

She kept a storage facility near the airport.

JOHN

Great.

ANGLE ON:

There is a photo of Karmic dressed in a saffron-colored robe and standing with the Dalai Lama and several Tibetan monks on a shelf.

JOHN

Where was this taken?

KARMIC

Katmandu.

JOHN

Katmandu?

KARMIC

Nepal.

JOHN

Right.

ANGLE ON:

Another photo. This one of Karmic and several brown-skinned young men - all wearing tight, diving speedos.

JOHN

And this one is --

KARMIC

A few years ago, mother took me cliff diving in Acapulco.

JOHN

You look a little gay in that speedo, James.

John turns and looks over to Karmic.

JOHN

Is there something I don't know about you?

Lisa steps up to them.

LISA

I thought I'd make us some tea.

JOHN

Lisa, I really appreciate your help, but I think it's time you left James and me alone.

LISA

I thought I'd show you the flat and go over Karmic's routine.

JOHN

That's okay. We can work it out.

LISA

Well --

JOHN

Really. I just want to spend some time with...Karmic.

Lisa gathers her things and steps towards the door.

LISA

I'm leaving my card on the table. Please don't hesitate to call me if you have any questions.

JOHN

Thank you.

Lisa gives Karmic a look of equal parts concern and sympathy as she steps out the door.

LISA

Karmic, you know how to reach me.

KARMIC

Goodbye, Lisa.

As the door shuts, John turns to Karmic.

JOHN

I'm going to take a shower, and then I want you to accompany me to the bank. Twenty minutes, okay?

Karmic just stares at John as he walks off.

INT. LONDON BANK - DAY

John politely holds the door open for Karmic, and the two enter the large bank lobby. The interior is of an old school, old money motif of dark wood and brass trim.

Karmic is wearing a Manchester United football jersey, number twenty-one (21).

A good-looking female TELLER (30), walks up to them.

John extends his hand to the woman.

TELLER

May I help you?

JOHN

I'd like to open a new account with your bank.

TELLER

Please...

As with Lisa, John extends his grip on the Teller's hand until she uncomfortably jerks it away.

TELLER

...follow me.

INT. OFFICE CUBICAL AT LONDON BANK - CONTINUOUS

The Teller, John, and Karmic sit at her desk.

John slides the cheques Jeremy gave him in front of her.

She lifts the cheques for inspection.

TELLER
Jeremy Middleton, Esquire.

JOHN
Also, I want to close my son's account. As you see, I'm his legal guardian.

TELLER
Certainly.

She starts typing on her keyboard.

Karmic's attention drifts off to a couple of YOUNG WOMEN smiling and chatting several feet away - at first, they don't notice him.

JOHN
When will cash be available?

TELLER
Immediately, sir.

Karmic continues his stare, and the giggly Young Women notices it. They return his gaze with nervous laughter.

Who's this freak watching them? How dare he?

JOHN
I'll need a debit card ASAP.

TELLER
We should have it here in twenty-four hours.

Karmic's expression is blank as the Young Women are incensed, and they scowl at Karmic as they strut away in a huff.

The Teller finished typing and printing, puts a couple of documents in front of John for a signature.

TELLER
If the two of you will sign here.

JOHN

I'll sign for Karmic.

John leans across the desk.

JOHN

(half whisper)

He's a bit, funny.

John stands as the Teller looks to Karmic. He's still staring off to where the Young Women were standing moments earlier.

TELLER

I see.

John turns and walks off.

Karmic looks over to the Teller, making eye contact for the first time, and throws her a confident wink. He stands and walks off.

The Teller stands, watching him. Stupefied.

INT. KARMIC'S BEDROOM, APARTMENT, LONDON - MORNING

A sleeping Karmic wakes up to muffled talking outside his bedroom door. Curious, he climbs out of bed and walks over to the door. Opening it, he steps out.

INT. LIVING ROOM OF APARTMENT, LONDON - CONTINUOUS

Karmic steps into the living room just as John is bidding several people goodbye at the front door.

JOHN

I'm sure you'll love it here.
Thanks for coming. Bye.

John closes the door and turns towards Karmic.

JOHN

Good morning.

KARMIC

Who were those people?

JOHN

Our tenants.

KARMIC

Tenants?

John walks over to the dining room table and lifts a multi-page document for Karmic to see.

JOHN

They just signed a six-month lease for this apartment. We're out of here tomorrow.

KARMIC

What?

JOHN

Yep. You better get packing. We're headed to Bangkok.

They hold a stare for a moment.

JOHN

We're just doing a little traveling.

EXT. BANGKOK INTERNATIONAL AIRPORT - DAY

A Thai Airlines 747 lands on the tarmac.

INT. DOCTOR'S OFFICE, BANGKOK - DAY

Karmic is undressed to his briefs - standing in front of a full-length mirror. He's a little on the short side, and squatty. All the classic Down syndrome attributes are present. John and a Thai DOCTOR stand off to the side, staring at Karmic - inspecting him.

JOHN

For sure. It's a project, but it can be done.

While speaking, John maneuvers around Karmic, pointing and calling attention to different areas of his body where he wants work done with a thick blue felt marker.

JOHN

We pull up the jowls, round the eyes...liposuct the fuck out of his waist, ass, and thighs. Make him as thin as possible.

DOCTOR
(Thai accent,
broken English)
Too extensive.

JOHN
What does that even mean? Look, he's a healthy, active kid. Hell, he's only twenty years old.

KARMIC
Twenty-two.

JOHN
Didn't think you could count that high.

The Doctor walks around Karmic, inspecting him - marking him with his own blue marker. Karmic looks like the diagram of a beef steer - choice cuts highlighted in blue.

The Doctor opens Karmic's mouth to look at his teeth.

Disappointed, he looks back to John.

JOHN
A little whitening.

DOCTOR
I don't do that --

JOHN
I'm not asking you to.

The Doctor continues shaking his head while circling Karmic.

DOCTOR
I can maybe do the face in one session and pump out the fat the same week.

JOHN
There you go.

KARMIC
(Thai language)
Can you make me look like Gene Kelly?

DOCTOR
(Thai language)
Can you dance?

KARMIC
No.

DOCTOR
Then what's the point?

The Doctor turns to John, who looks on in shock.

DOCTOR
Everything. Twenty-five thousand.

The two men stare at each other.

JOHN
Fifteen.

DOCTOR
I need anesthesiologist, a professional.

JOHN
Do it without one.

Karmic gives John a concerned look.

DOCTOR
This is a big job.

The Doctor continues walking around Karmic with a concerned look. He suddenly stops.

DOCTOR
Twenty thousand dollars.

JOHN
Fifteen.

DOCTOR
Get out!

The Doctor pushes John and a half-naked Karmic towards the door.

JOHN
No! Wait!

INT. TAILOR'S SHOP, BANGKOK - DAY

John is standing in the center of the fitting room while a couple of assistant tailors measure him for a suit.

JOHN

No better value than Thai silk.

Karmic steps out from a curtain.

He is a couple of weeks post-surgery and looks very handsome - the Thai surgeon did a magnificent job. Gone are the most physical signs of Down syndrome. Karmic is a handsome young man.

Karmic wears a stunning velvet smoking jacket.

The WORKERS react with amazement to his entrance.

WORKERS

Ohhhhhhhh.

John is stunned. He stands there, shaking his head in disbelief.

JOHN

There's no such thing as overdressing.

EXT. NICE INTERNATIONAL AIRPORT, FRANCE - DAY

An Air France Airbus 320 lands on the tarmac.

INT. NICE INTERNATIONAL AIRPORT - DAY

Karmic and John are at the front of a long line of people waiting to pass through Immigration.

Signaled, they walk over to an Immigration kiosk.

John hands their passports to the Immigration Officer - he opens one of them.

IMMIGRATION OFFICER

(French)

Bonjour.

JOHN

Hello.

IMMIGRATION OFFICER

You're coming from Bangkok?

JOHN

Yes.

The Immigration Officer stamps the passport and opens the other.

It is Karmic's passport and has an older, pre-Bangkok photo of Karmic.

The Immigration Officer does a double take at Karmic and then smiles.

IMMIGRATION OFFICER

Close enough.

He hands the passports back to John.

IMMIGRATION OFFICER

Merci.

John takes the passports and walks off. Karmic and the Immigration Officer hold a look as Karmic walks off.

EXT. HOTEL DE PARIS, MONTE CARLO, MONACO - DAY

A white Rolls Royce limousine pulls up in front of the prestigious one-hundred-and-fifty-year-old hotel. The CHAUFFEUR exits and works the luggage out of the trunk as John and Karmic step out from the back of the car.

Karmic is wearing an off-white two-piece suit, a hand-woven Panama fedora, and sunglasses. He looks both beauteous and elegant. John is also quite dashing.

DOORMAN

(French)

Good afternoon, gentlemen.

The Doorman swings the door open, and both enter the hotel, followed by a PORTER and luggage trolley.

INT. HOTEL DE PARIS LOBBY, MONTE CARLO, MONACO - CONTINUOUS

Heads turn as John and Karmic walk through the lobby. John steps up to the registration counter.

REGISTRATION CLERK
Hello.

JOHN
I've got a reservation.

REGISTRATION CLERK
Your name, please.

JOHN
John Boss.

REGISTRATION CLERK
Thank you. That's John and James Boss?

JOHN
Yes.

REGISTRATION CLERK
Very good. I have you together in one of our Exclusive Two Bedroom Suites. With a view of the Mediterranean.

JOHN
And that's at the monthly rate?

REGISTRATION CLERK
Yes, sir. May I have both of your passports, please?

John pulls out their passports and puts them on the counter.

Karmic stands there - sunglasses still on - looking perfect.

REGISTRATION CLERK
Very good. Bruno will be your Porter, and he will escort you up to your room.

JOHN
Thank you.

John turns and acknowledges BRUNO.

EXT. HOTEL DE PARIS, MONTE CARLO, MONACO - DAY

A group of WOMEN is gathered in a large gazebo. They are taking a Japanese calligraphy class outside with the beach as a backdrop.

Each stands in front of an easel while pecking away at a work-in-progress. The INSTRUCTOR, a Japanese woman, strolls about helping the women/students with their work.

Two of the Women are Leslie and Jennifer Whitman - both wearing the loose, light-colored clothes you'd expect to see in the summer on the Riviera.

JENNIFER

You really should have invested a few more dollars in developing your daughter's artistic aptitude.

LESLIE

Or lack thereof.

JENNIFER

I beg your pardon.

Karmic notices the class as he walks past the gazebo. He smiles as he walks up to view Jennifer's work. She speaks to Karmic.

JENNIFER

This is the second class, so cut me some slack.

KARMIC

Don't be afraid.

Karmic takes her brush hand in his and, with a couple of quick strokes, creates an orchid in a bed of reeds.

JENNIFER

Well. Clearly, you've done this before.

The Instructor walks up behind them and takes a look.

INSTRUCTOR

We're painting bamboo today.

Still holding Jennifer's hand, Karmic applies a few more strokes, and in an instant, a bush of bamboo surrounds the orchid.

John steps out of the hotel in the background and looks around for Karmic.

Karmic spots John in the distance. He releases Jennifer's hand.

KARMIC
Don't be afraid.

JENNIFER
Afraid?

Karmic waves his hand over the painting.

KARMIC
To stroke.

Karmic turns and walks off.

The Instructor, Leslie, and Jennifer - all three Women watch him with fascination.

An African man, DIDIER (35), leans against a post while watching Karmic as he walks by.

DIDIER
I like your style, man. Very nice.

Karmic smiles back as he struts past.

INT. ROOM 714, HOTEL DE PARIS - DAY

Bruno leads John and Karmic into the room - another Porter follows with the luggage cart.

Bruno walks over to a bottle of Champagne in a bucket on the living room table.

BRUNO
(French accent)
Shall I, sir?

JOHN
Go ahead.

Bruno speaks while opening the bottle of Champagne.

BRUNO
This is a splendid room. You get the sun almost all day, and the weather should be magnificent this week.

He pops the cork out of the bottle, starts pouring, and hands a glass to each John and Karmic.

John eyes Karmic curiously as he takes the glass of wine and sips it.

Bruno draws open the curtains and the French doors on the balcony.

BRUNO

Full breakfast is included with your room - either downstairs in the Cote Jardin or here in your place if you prefer.

JOHN

What time is dinner?

John walks over to the bar area and pulls up a valise. He opens it and unpacks several bottles of liquor. A bottle of Skyy vodka, a bottle of Johnny Walker Black, and a bottle of Bombay Sapphire Gin.

BRUNO

You have your choice of Le Louis XV or La Salle Empire - both are open at eight.

JOHN

Would you make reservations for us at Louis XV for nine o'clock, please?

BRUNO

Excellent, sir.

John leads Bruno over to the door and opens it.

JOHN

Also, is there a Mrs. Leslie Whitman staying in the hotel?

BRUNO

I'm not sure, sir. I can find out.

John pulls out a bill and hands it to Bruno.

JOHN

Do that. And I'd like to know with whom she's been spending time.

BRUNO

Sir?

John pulls out another bill and hands it to Bruno.

BRUNO

Excellent, sir.

Bruno and the other Porter exit.

John turns to Karmic.

JOHN

I thought, for now, we would skip the expense of lunch, so fill yourself up at breakfast.

KARMIC

Can we have breakfast now?

JOHN

It's three thirty.

KARMIC

Oh.

JOHN

There are going to be a lot of very sophisticated women here, so let me do the talking. I don't want you opening your mouth and fucking things up.

KARMIC

Okay.

JOHN

Also. White tuxedos tonight. First impression is everything.

INT. CASINO HOTEL DE PARIS - NIGHT

The casino is in full swing. Everyone is dressed up for the evening. Not black-tie formal, but high-end tasteful. It's an international crowd - very exotic. Asia, India, Africa, and the Middle East are all represented.

Jennifer sits at a crowded roulette table. She reaches over and puts a small stack of chips on the six black square.

Jennifer looks up, and something catches her attention.

Karmic steps out from the crowd. He's decked out in an off-white tuxedo jacket, and black bow tie.

CROUPIER spins the wheel.

CROUPIER
(French accent)
And here we go.

Karmic looks around, and the curiosity of the commotion lures him to the roulette table.

Leaning up against the rail, he attracts the Croupier's attention.

CROUPIER
Place a bet, sir. Call a number.

Confused, Karmic stares at the Croupier - frozen.

The Croupier signals Karmic with his wooden rake.

CROUPIER
A number, sir.

Karmic looks down at the board.

KARMIC
Twenty-one.

CROUPIER
Twenty-one. Vingt-et-un.

Nobody is paying him much attention as the other players are shuffling about placing their bets.

The Croupier sees that Karmic is confused and keeps riding him as he spins the wheel.

CROUPIER
Place a bet, sir?

Karmic lifts his hands to show that he has no chips with which to bet. A RUSSIAN man (50) steps forward and leans over the table.

RUSSIAN
(Russian accent)
I've got it.

The Russian places a small stack of chips on the ‘red 21’ square.

CROUPIER

No more bets, ladies and gentlemen. No more bets.

Jennifer eyes Karmic as he watches the little ball bounce around the wheel with fascination.

The ball settles in twenty-one.

CROUPIER

Twenty-one, red.

The Russian laughs as he slaps Karmic on the back.

RUSSIAN

Well done, friend! Well done!

CROUPIER

Vingt-et-un, rouge. Vingt-et-un, rouge, is the winner.

Wooden rake in hand, the Croupier shuffles chips in and out to the winners and losers.

Again, he looks over to Karmic.

CROUPIER

Sir. It is your call.

Karmic is still a bit uncomfortable. He looks around and locks eyes with Jennifer.

She smiles at him as he gives her a look of confusion.

CROUPIER

Place a wager, sir?

KARMIC

Twenty-one.

CROUPIER

Vingt-et-un. You are quite confident, uh?

KARMIC

Twenty-one, red.

RUSSIAN
He said twenty-one.

The Russian pushes a towering stack of chips onto the 'red 21' square. Several others eagerly follow him.

The Croupier spins the wheel again.

A few more people push their chips onto the 'red 21' square.

MAN #2
I'm on twenty-one also.

CROUPIER
Yes, you are, sir. Yes, you are. Everybody wants twenty-one red!

OTHERS
Twenty-one! Red!

The Croupier rolls his eyes.

The ball bounces around and lands on...'red 21'.

The Croupier is shocked.

CROUPIER
Vingt-et-un, rouge. Vingt-et-un.

The Croupier looks over to the PIT BOSS, and the two share a 'what the fuck?' look, as again he shuffles chips around the board.

Karmic turns and walks off as the Russian gathers his winnings and follows him.

INT. CASINO, COMMON AREA - NIGHT

Jennifer approaches Karmic.

JENNIFER
Well, that was remarkable.

KARMIC
It's just a ball bouncing around.

JENNIFER
I mean your luck...kismet.

KARMIC

No, I'm Karmic.

JENNIFER

Exactly.

Jennifer puts her hand out to shake.

JENNIFER

My name is Jennifer Whitman, and I just wanted to shake your hand, Mr.? --

KARMIC

(James Bond imitation)

Boss. James Boss.

Stunned by his response, Jennifer stands there in silence and watches as Karmic walks off without shaking her hand.

The Russian catches up to Karmic.

RUSSIAN

Hey! Where are you going?

KARMIC

We're having dinner.

RUSSIAN

We're on a roll. I mean, you are.

KARMIC

Excuse me.

Karmic turns and walks off.

The Russian holds out some chips and continues to follow him.

RUSSIAN

I wanted to give you some of this.

KARMIC

Why?

SAUDI MAN (48), approaches Karmic. He's Middle Eastern, well-dressed, and wearing the headdress of the Saudi royal family. He is flanked by his son, SAUDI SON (18).

SAUDI MAN

Excuse me, sir.

Karmic turns towards Saudi Man.

SAUDI MAN

I wonder if you would play cards with me.

KARMIC

We're having dinner.

Karmic turns and walks off. The Saudi and Russian continue to follow him.

SAUDI MAN

I just witnessed your success at the roulette table, and I wanted to prove to my son that there is no such thing as luck. There is only God's will.

KARMIC

What if God wished to 'will' luck to a man? Don't you think that's possible?

SAUDI MAN

Yes. But not here - to you.

Karmic continues walking as the men continue to follow him.

SAUDI MAN

Please. I only ask for a moment of your time.

Karmic stops and stares at the Saudi Man.

KARMIC

Where?

SAUDI MAN

Over here.

INT. BACCARAT SALON - NIGHT

The Saudi Man leads the small group into a semi-private room - set off from the main casino lobby.

There is a dealer's shoe filled with cards on a table.

Another PIT BOSS approaches them and speaks to the Saudi Man.

PIT BOSS
Excuse me, sir.

SAUDI MAN
Please, Gonzalo. Give us some privacy here.

Gonzalo, the Pit Boss, reaches out to stop the Russian as he backs off.

PIT BOSS
This is a private game, sir.

The Russian shakes off Gonzalo as he gestures to Karmic.

RUSSIAN
I'm with him.

Gonzalo backs off, as they all step inside the room.

The Saudi gestures to Karmic.

SAUDI MAN
Please, have a seat.

Karmic sits down, and the Saudi Man sits across the table in front of the dealer's shoe. He pulls the card-holding the shoe towards him.

SAUDI MAN
Baccarat?

KARMIC
What does that mean?

SAUDI MAN
Of course. You're British. You play Black Jack. Right?

Jennifer arrives at the door and leans against the jamb as she watches the events from the background.

The Saudi pushes a small stack of chips out to the center of the table.

SAUDI MAN
One thousand Euros.

KARMIC
I don't have any --

The Russian steps forward and puts some chips on the table.

RUSSIAN
I'm his underwriter.

The Saudi Man looks up at him.

SAUDI MAN
Yes, I saw you two together.

The Saudi deals two cards to Karmic and two to himself.

SAUDI MAN
Okay. It's your call.

Karmic looks down at the cards sitting face down on the table. He looks up to the Saudi Man.

KARMIC
Twenty-one, red.

SAUDI MAN
What?

KARMIC
Twenty-one --

SAUDI MAN
But you haven't looked at your cards.

Karmic just stares at the Saudi.

KARMIC
Twenty-one, red.

The Saudi's son steps forward and reaches for Karmic's cards.

SAUDI SON
Let's see.

SAUDI MAN
No.

The Saudi Man puts his hand over Karmic's cards.

SAUDI MAN
You never question a man's word. If he says he has twenty-one, I will believe him.

All watch in fascination as the Saudi Man pushes the played cards to the side and pushes out another stack of chips.

RUSSIAN
Black Jack pays double.

The Saudi eyes the Russian as he pushes another stack of chips forward. The Russian eagerly pulls in the winnings.

SAUDI MAN
Five thousand.

The Russian steps forward and increases his stack.

RUSSIAN
Five thousand.

The Saudi deals another round of cards.

Karmic lifts the two cards and inspects them before placing them back on the table.

KARMIC
Twenty-one, red.

SAUDI MAN
What?

SAUDI SON
That's impossible. I don't believe him, father.

RUSSIAN
That's ten thousand.

The Saudi Man stares at Karmic for a moment.

SAUDI MAN
I believe him.

SAUDI SON
Father?!

Frustrated, the Saudi brushes the cards to the side.

The Russian leans over and pulls in their winnings.

SAUDI MAN

Another.

The Saudi Son pushes forward two large stacks of chips as his father deals another round of blackjack, two cards each.

RUSSIAN

Twenty thousand?

The Russian slides the chips to the center of the table.

The Saudi Son leans over to take a look, as his father lifts his cards for a peek.

Karmic lifts his cards and then quickly returns them to the table. Face down.

The Saudi Man and Karmic stare at each other for a moment.

SAUDI MAN

Well?

KARMIC

Yes?

SAUDI MAN

Would you like another card?

Karmic smiles at him, a bit confused.

KARMIC

Sure.

The Saudi flips a card down in front of Karmic, face up - it's a five of hearts.

Karmic looks down at the card and then back to the Saudi.

SAUDI MAN

Well?

KARMIC

Yes?

SAUDI MAN

Would you like another card?

Again, Karmic smiles at the Saudi.

KARMIC

Sure.

The Saudi flips out another card - it's a two of hearts.

The Russian eyes Karmic with concern.

Gonzalo, the Pit Boss, eyes Karmic with concern.

Jennifer, at the doorway, eyes Karmic with concern.

Karmic looks down at the card and then up at the Saudi.

SAUDI MAN

Well?

KARMIC

Yes?

SAUDI MAN

Friend, I am afraid to ask.

KARMIC

Go ahead.

SAUDI MAN

Would you like another card?

Karmic smiles.

KARMIC

Please.

The Saudi peels off another card and places it on the table in front of Karmic.

KARMIC

It's really very kind of you.

It's a three of hearts.

Karmic looks down at the card and then back to the Saudi.

SAUDI MAN

Well?

All stare at Karmic.

RUSSIAN

Christ, man. What do you have?

Karmic looks at the Russian.

KARMIC

Twenty-one, red.

RUSSIAN

Wooo hooo!

The Russian reaches over and starts pulling the chips over. The Saudi Man blocks him with his arm.

SAUDI MAN

Wait!

There is silence at the table.

SAUDI MAN

Forgive me, but I'm afraid that I will need to see your cards.

The Russian counts the cards facing upward as he arranges them.

RUSSIAN

Two and three are five, and five is ten.

Then he flips one of the down cards over - it's a ten of hearts.

SAUDI SON

That's twenty.

The Russian flips over the other down card - it's an ace of hearts.

RUSSIAN

Twenty-one!

Karmic stands up as all at the table respond in disbelief.

RUSSIAN

All hearts. Red.

KARMIC

May I go now?

SAUDI MAN

Please.

SAUDI SON

He already had Black Jack!

In shock, all watch as Karmic walks out of the room. The Russian goes about gathering up the winnings.

SAUDI MAN

He's just toying with us.

ANGLE ON:

Karmic and Jennifer share a smile as he leaves the room.

JENNIFER

Hello again.

KARMIC

Hi.

She looks back to the table as the Russian finishes gathering up the winnings and eagerly follows Karmic out of the room.

RUSSIAN

My friend!

INT. HOTEL RESTAURANT, LOUIS XV - NIGHT

The restaurant is classically elegant - columns and white linen.

John sits at the table, drinking a martini. He looks up as Karmic arrives.

JOHN

Well, it's about time.

KARMIC

Sorry.

JOHN

Where have you been?

Karmic sits.

KARMIC

Black Jack.

JOHN

Gambling?

The Russian walks up to the table.

RUSSIAN

Excuse me, but I wanted to give you your share.

He puts a couple of stacks of chips onto the table in front of Karmic.

JOHN

What is this?

RUSSIAN

I was backing your friend at the tables and --

JOHN

Those are his winnings?

Karmic gives the Russian a distressed look as he pushes the chips away.

KARMIC

I don't want any of these.

John reaches over to Karmic.

JOHN

Leave them.

John looks up at the Russian.

JOHN

Thank you. Now, please go away.

ANGLE ON:

Jennifer and her mother, Leslie, sitting at a dining table.

Leslie sits at a table across the room from John and Karmic.

Jennifer walks up to a table and slides into a chair. She's still preoccupied with Karmic as she does so.

Leslie looks up from her iPad.

LESLIE

Your father thinks he's going to be nominated for another Golden Globe.

JENNIFER

Really? God, I'd love to fuck George Clooney.

LESLIE

No. I'm going to fuck George Clooney.

JENNIFER

Mother. Isn't that guy over there an architect in Beverly Hills?

Jennifer lifts a small pair of opera glasses from the table and peers through them as Leslie looks over toward John's table.

LESLIE

Yes. I mean, no. His name is John Boss - he's a real estate broker. I thought he might show up.

JENNIFER

Who's his friend?

LESLIE

I do not know.

BACK TO:

John snatches the arm of the Maitre D', as he passes.

JOHN

Yves, please take these chips to the front desk and have them credited toward our bill.

Yves gathers up the chips and walks off.

John gives Karmic a hard stare.

JOHN

I don't know what kind of crazy life you had with your mother, but we can't afford to gamble.

KARMIC

My mother --

JOHN

Everything with me is calculated. I leave nothing to chance.

John looks over to the ladies' table to find them both gawking at him and Karmic.

JOHN

I know I'm asking the impossible, but if you could make that girl over there interested in you, it would be a monumental step.

Karmic joins John and looks over to their table.

ANGLE ON:

Jennifer is still looking through the mini binoculars.

JENNIFER

I think I'm in love.

LESLIE

What's that on their table - an aperitif?

POV: through the opera glasses.

Jennifer focuses on the object sitting on the table.

JENNIFER

No, it's a --

ANGLE ON:

A can of Cheez-Whiz sits on the table. John snatches it off the table and makes it disappear.

BACK TO:

Jennifer looks up from the glasses - perplexed.

John and Karmic look over at them and smile. John is holding up a martini as a salutation.

LESLIE

Raise your glass, dear.

Jennifer and Leslie raise their glasses and smile at the gentlemen.

LESLIE

He sent me a note earlier. He's a player and a little pushy, but he's cute.

JENNIFER

He's staying here?

LESLIE

Yes.

JENNIFER

Let's invite them over.

LESLIE

Be a little reserved, dear. They're not going anywhere.

INT. HOTEL DE PARIS LOBBY - LATER

John leads Karmic to the elevator.

JOHN

When people engage you in conversation, don't feel pressure to be overly talkative. A taciturn person is a mysterious person, and a little mystery will create intrigue and help you stay out of trouble.

Jennifer pops out from around the corner.

JENNIFER

Hello.

JOHN

Good evening.

JENNIFER

I'm Jennifer Whitman.

My mother is --

JOHN

I know your mother, Jennifer. I'm John Boss, and this is James.

Karmic just stares at Jennifer.

JENNIFER

Where are you two headed?

JOHN

I have some reading to do before the market opens.

JENNIFER

New York is six hours back. NYSE doesn't open until tomorrow afternoon.

JOHN

I was referring to the markets in Hong Kong.

JENNIFER

Oh.

She reaches down and grabs hold of Karmic's hand.

JENNIFER

I feel like dancing...take me?

KARMIC

I don't dance.

Jennifer lifts her arms up and shakes her hips like an Egyptian seductress.

Amused, Karmic gives her a wide grin.

JENNIFER

Fine, I'll do the dancing, and you lay the hundred dollar bills over the rail.

KARMIC

I have no money.

JENNIFER

The club is in the hotel. We sign for everything.

John gives the situation a concerned look but loosens up with a half-smile.

JOHN

Go ahead, Karmic.

He looks at Jennifer.

JOHN

Karmic doesn't drink. And please, don't keep him out too late.

Jennifer smiles.

JENNIFER

You sound like you're his dad.

JOHN

I am.

JENNIFER

Oh.

The elevator door opens and John steps inside.

JOHN

Good night.

JENNIFER

'Night.

Karmic watches John disappear with mild concern.

Jennifer pulls Karmic's arm.

JENNIFER

Let's go.

INT. NIGHTCLUB - NIGHT

The joint is jumping - spinning lights and loud techno dance music.

Jennifer leads Karmic through the club and over to the bar.

She leans over to the BARTENDER.

JENNIFER
Two shots of Ketel One and a...
(to Karmic)
What do you want?

KARMIC
Dr. Pepper.

JENNIFER
(to the Bartender)
Rum and coke.

JENNIFER
(to Karmic)
My mother knows your father from Beverly Hills, but we've never seen you around town.

KARMIC
I'm from London.

JENNIFER
Really?

KARMIC
London is in England.

JENNIFER
Yeah, I heard about that. Where did you go to school?

KARMIC
Many schools, all over the world.

The Bartender puts the drinks on the counter. Jennifer hands Karmic his rum and coke.

JENNIFER
Here, drink this.

Karmic takes a swallow and then gives the glass a confused look.

JENNIFER
You like that, uh?

KARMIC
It's a bit weird.

Jennifer lifts a shot glass and 'clinks' cheers with Karmic's glass.

Jennifer drains her shot glass as Karmic takes another swallow.

The music turns to an Afro-Caribbean drum-based beat.

Jennifer starts getting into the music and does a little dance as she speaks to Karmic.

JENNIFER
You like gambling?

KARMIC
Gambling?

JENNIFER
Don't kid with me. I saw you earlier. You looked pretty smooth at that table.

KARMIC
Was that with the little ball or those weird cards?

Jennifer laughs.

JENNIFER
Obviously, you've had some practice.

Jennifer gets more into the music.

JENNIFER
Take another swallow.

Hesitant, Karmic takes another tough gulp. Jennifer lifts the drink from his hand and hands it to a passing WAITRESS.

She grabs Karmic's hand and leads him onto the dance floor.

JENNIFER
Let's go, James. Loosen up a bit.

KARMIC
Actually, I'm called Karmic.

JENNIFER
What kind of name is that?

KARMIC

It's a denominal adjective.

Jennifer gives him a queer look as she starts letting it go and dances around Karmic, who just stands there watching her.

Karmic awkwardly stumbles around the dance floor, dancing the best he can.

He looks over and spots Didier, the African guy he saw on the beach earlier. Didier is dancing with two GIRLS. He's dancing in a methodical, rhythmic tribal kind of dance that looks impressive.

Karmic makes an attempt to mimic the dancing of the Didier. He looks awkward as he steps forward and then back again while twirling his arms and shaking his head to the music.

Jennifer smiles as she realizes what Karmic is up to. She, too, copies the rhythmic sequence and bodily movements of Didier.

After several repetitions, both Karmic and Jennifer find the 'step' and become pretty fluid in their dance.

Several others on the dance floor notice what they're doing and follow suit until most of the dancers on the floor are doing the same dance in total synchronization.

They all form two lines facing each other in unison, stepping forward and then back...twirling their arms and bobbing their heads to the beat.

Didier dances through the center of the two lines leaning his body way back in a 'limbo' fashion. Karmic follows him and does so with surprisingly fluid agility.

As the music winds down to a conclusion, the crowd of dancers all erupt in celebration.

Jennifer leaps over to Karmic and hugs him affectionately. Karmic is slightly shocked but enchanted by her actions.

Didier pats Karmic on the shoulder as he passes.

DIDIER

You have the rhythm of the tribe,
my friend. You are a natural.

Didier walks off as Jennifer pulls Karmic towards her.

She lights a cigarette.

JENNIFER
Do you smoke?

KARMIC
I should be getting back.

JENNIFER
I'll only let you go if you promise to spend the day with me tomorrow.

KARMIC
I'll have to talk to John and see what he thinks.

Jennifer sticks the cigarette into Karmic's mouth.

JENNIFER
Do you always ask your dad's permission to see a girl?

KARMIC
That was mother's department.

JENNIFER
Yeah? Well, she's not here. Is she?

INT. HOTEL ROOM 714 - NIGHT

The front doorbell rings, and John, dressed in his robe, walks over and opens the door.

Karmic is standing there - black bow tie loose, hair mussed, and a cigarette dangling in his mouth.

He smiles at John.

JOHN
Get in here.

John pulls Karmic inside the door and shuts it.

JOHN
I'm concerned about you being on your own.

KARMIC
I wasn't alone. I was with Jennifer.

JOHN

I mean without me.

John snatches the cigarette out of Karmic's mouth.

KARMIC

She made me promise to see her again tomorrow.

JOHN

Did she? We'll make it a foursome. I'll rent a car, and we'll take them for a drive in the country.

John turns and walks off.

JOHN

Now, go to bed. We've got a big day tomorrow.

INT. HOTEL CORRIDOR, ROOM 714 - MORNING

A Porter is delivering the morning newspapers at the foot of the doors as Karmic quietly sneaks out of the front door of the room.

INT. HOTEL LOBBY - MORNING

Lloyd (35), a stunning woman, sits on the chaise in the lobby of the hotel. She's smartly dressed and sips a cup of tea as she reads a magazine.

Karmic walks into the lobby and looks over. Spotting her, he seems astonished. Hesitantly, Karmic walks over to her.

As he approaches, Lloyd turns to him and smiles wonderfully.

LLOYD

Hello, Karmic.

KARMIC

Hello.

Lloyd stands.

LLOYD

I have a room for us.

Karmic smiles.

KARMIC

Great.

EXT. VALET STAND, HOTEL DE PARIS - MORNING

Leslie, wearing a large sun hat, walks out of the hotel. Jennifer, also dressed for the sun, approaches her.

JENNIFER

I thought you hated that hat?

LESLIE

I do, but it cost me so much money I've got to get a couple of days' use out of it.

EXT. MONTE CARLO, STREETS - DAY

John is driving a blue 1965 Mercedes 250se convertible - top down. Karmic sits in the passenger seat.

JOHN

Well, don't get too enthralled with her. Beverly Hills girls can be really capricious - they go from one guy to another.

KARMIC

What does capricious mean?

JOHN

It means Jennifer could be a complicated little fucking minx. That's what.

KARMIC

Isn't there an animal called minx?

JOHN

That's a mink, and if you get serious with this chick, you'll learn about that too, soon enough.

John spots something up ahead.

JOHN

Here we go.

EXT. HOTEL DE PARIS - DAY

Jennifer and Leslie are standing in the valet area in front of the hotel. The Mercedes convertible pulls up to the curb in front of them.

Karmic gets out and then jumps into the backseat. Jennifer follows him with Leslie in the front.

EXT. MONTE CARLO, STREETS - DAY

The four rumble out of town into the French countryside.

JOHN

I learned to drive in a car like this.

LESLIE

Really?

JOHN

My father had one. My sister and I used to fight over who got to borrow his car on weekends.

LESLIE

Really, that's so cute. My father drove a Ferrari and wouldn't let anybody near it. We learned how to drive in the family station wagon.

BACKSEAT:

Jennifer stares at Karmic like a girl wholly infatuated.

JENNIFER

How did you sleep last night?

KARMIC

I usually sleep on my stomach. I've got a septum issue that causes snoring.

JENNIFER

Thanks for the warning.

FRONT SEAT:

JOHN

I thought we'd drive out to a little vineyard I know of and then have an early supper in St. Paul de Vence.

LESLIE

Sounds lovely, John.

EXT. FRENCH VINEYARD - DAY

The group is taking a walking tour around the grounds of the vineyard. They walk among the vines, with the winery buildings in the background.

They're being led by SANDRINE (27), a pretty young French woman who works at the vineyard.

SANDRINE

The Provence is the warmest wine region in France and has been influenced by many cultures over the years.

Sandrine looks over to Karmic.

SANDRINE

They've been growing wine in this area for over twenty-five hundred years.

Karmic and Sandrine share a smile.

JOHN

What are these grapes here?

John bends over and lifts a handful of the dark earth.

SANDRINE

These are Grenache; it's a fruit that grows very well here.

John smells the soil.

JOHN

Is there limestone in this soil?

SANDRINE

Yes, there is. Grenache is a variety that ripens late and is helped by the hot, dry climate in the south.

JOHN

So wine produced here would have higher alcohol content, but less acid and tannin.

Leslie and Jennifer give each other a look of being surprisingly impressed by John's knowledge.

SANDRINE

Exactly. We often blend it with other wines to help balance it.

Again, Sandrine locks eyes with Karmic.

LESLIE

I'm getting thirsty. Shall we try a little?

SANDRINE

Of course. Please follow me.

Sandrine leads the group toward the winery buildings.

Jennifer holds Karmic's arm as they fall back a little.

JENNIFER

I think she has a crush on you.

KARMIC

What do you mean?

JENNIFER

The way you two were staring at each other.

KARMIC

Yes, she's quite charming.

JENNIFER

She's a bit 'earthy' for your taste? I mean, she doesn't wear makeup, and I bet she doesn't even shave her legs.

KARMIC

Why would she shave her legs?

Jennifer laughs.

JENNIFER

Karmic, stop playing with me. I'm a very jealous woman.

KARMIC

Do you shave your legs?

JENNIFER

No, I wax.

She leans closer to him.

JENNIFER

I've got a delicious Brazilian.

KARMIC

I've eaten Brazilian.

JENNIFER

Yeah?

Karmic gives Jennifer a wide smile.

KARMIC

Plantains...delicious.

Jennifer gives Karmic a jealous look.

INT. WINERY - DAY

The four sit around a small round table in the corner of the cafe. Glasses of wine, cheeses, and bread are on the table in front of them.

John holds up his glass of wine for inspection.

JOHN

Excellent color.

Monsieur OLIVIER, the proprietor of the winery, approaches their table.

OLIVIER

That is a Grenache blended with Cinsault.

JOHN

That would explain the softness and unusual, but very pleasant bouquet.

OLIVIER

Exactly. It's something we've only been doing for a few years.

John turns to Leslie.

JOHN

It's a hearty grape - very dark with thick skin.

OLIVIER

We're happy with the results.

KARMIC

Do you have any Dr. Pepper?

Jennifer and Leslie laugh as Monsieur eyes the full glass on the table in front of Karmic.

JENNIFER

Stop joking, Karmic.

OLIVIER

You don't like our wine, Monsieur?

JOHN

He's not really a wine drinker.

OLIVIER

Oh, there must be something here you would like. What is your favorite wine?

KARMIC

I'm sorry, but --

OLIVIER

Please. Name a wine. Name a year -- any year.

There is complete silence for a moment as all stare at Karmic.

KARMIC
Twenty-one.

JOHN
What?

JENNIFER
Karmic, come on.

OLIVIER
No, no. What did you say?

KARMIC
Twenty-one, red.

BEAT:

OLIVIER
Who told you about that?

Karmic and Monsieur Olivier lock eyes for a moment.

JOHN
I'm sorry, Monsieur. He's just kidding around.

OLIVIER
He's referring to my Chateau Margaux 1921. It's not well known, but I own several cases and keep them here. As he said, it's a red.

Monsieur Olivier calls a WAITER over and speaks to him in French.

OLIVIER
(in French)
Bring me a bottle of the Margaux 1921 - quickly.

The Waiter disappears.

Olivier looks over to Karmic.

OLIVIER
How did you know about my collection?

JOHN

It's fine, Monsieur. Really, the wine is perfect.

LESLIE

It's delicious.

OLIVIER

No, no. It is my pleasure. This gentleman obviously has something in mind. As the proprietor, I am obligated to satisfy his taste.

The Waiter arrives with the wine and hands the bottle to Monsieur Olivier.

OLIVIER

(to the Waiter)

A fresh glass.

Olivier pushes a screw through the cork and works the bottle.

He speaks as he does this - directing his words to Karmic.

OLIVIER

It's an extraordinary wine from the Bordeaux region. Mostly made from Cabernet Sauvignon with Merlot, Cabernet Franc, and Petit Verdot.

The Cork pops out from the bottle.

OLIVIER

But then you knew that, uh?

Karmic smiles at Monsieur Olivier.

The Waiter arrives with a glass and hands it to Olivier. It's an oversized wine glass.

Olivier pours the wine into the glass.

OLIVIER

This is not the correct type of glass, but I know you Americans like quantity.

KARMIC

British.

OLIVIER

God save the Queen.

He places the full glass on the table in front of Karmic.

OLIVIER

Please, try that.

Karmic reaches over, lifts the glass to his lips, and takes a swallow. And another swallow.

Karmic chug-a-lugs from the glass until it is completely drained. Six swallows.

With the satisfaction of meeting a challenge, he slams the empty glass onto the table.

All just stare at Karmic with amazement.

He burps.

EXT. ST. PAUL DE VENCE - TWILIGHT

The fortified, medieval town of St. Paul de Vence sits up on the hill - nothing has changed here in over five hundred years. The sun is setting into the Mediterranean.

The blue Mercedes convertible winds up an ancient cobbled road into the town.

EXT. RESTAURANT TERRACE - TWILIGHT

John, Leslie, Karmic, and Jennifer follow the WAITER across the large stone terrace and sit at a table on the viewing edge.

EXT. RESTAURANT TERRACE TABLE - LATER

The four sit at the table. Empty glasses and finished plates tell the tale of the last few hours.

KARMIC

...I spent two years in Asia studying Buddhism.

JENNIFER

Where exactly?

KARMIC
India, Thailand, and Japan.

LESLIE
Why Buddhism?

KARMIC
Well --

JOHN
I thought it was a fitting way for Karmic to experience cultural and religious diversity.

Karmic gives John a hard stare.

JENNIFER
Did you ever meet the Dalai Lama?

KARMIC
He gave me my name.

JENNIFER
What?

Jennifer laughs.

KARMIC
He said that I possessed enough positive karma for three lifetimes.

TIME MONTAGE:

The foursome eating at restaurants all over Europe.

EXT. CAFE LES DEUX MAGOTS, PARIS - DAY

The four at a table at the famous cafe in Saint Germain des Pres.

KARMIC
...sure, I've played polo with Prince William several times.

All look on with amazement.

LESLIE
That's just fantastic!

KARMIC

I have to say. The Prince is considerably overrated…riding a pony.

They all break out in laughter.

EXT. RESTAURANT TRE SCALINI, PIAZZA NAVONA, ROME - DAY

Fountain and Egyptian obelisk in the background - the four sit at a table.

JENNIFER

...the Pope?

KARMIC

Yes, we had dinner in the Belvedere.

JOHN

What's the Belvedere?

LESLIE

The building that houses the Vatican apartments and Museum.

JENNIFER

Who designed the Belvedere?

LESLIE

I don't know.

All look over to Karmic.

KARMIC

Why, Bramante, of course.

EXT. RESTAURANT LA TABLE D'EDGARD, LAUSANNE - DAY

John, Karmic, and Jennifer are sitting at the table on the terrace - Lake Geneva sits in the background.

Leslie comes walking up to the table carrying a smallish decorative shopping bag.

JENNIFER

Where were you, mother?

LESLIE

I'd ordered something for the boys that I wanted to pick up.

Leslie hands John and Karmic each a small gift-wrapped box.

JOHN

Leslie. You shouldn't have.

LESLIE

(to Jennifer)

I didn't get you anything this time, dear, sorry.

JENNIFER

It's okay.

The two men stare at the boxes on the table in front of them.

LESLIE

Go ahead and open them.

They proceed to open the boxes. Jennifer helps Karmic as he struggles a bit with the ribbon.

John opens his box, revealing a gold Rolex watch.

JOHN

A watch.

LESLIE

I couldn't help but notice that neither of you had a wristwatch.

JOHN

Leslie, they're beautiful.

LESLIE

Try them on. They're Rolexes.

John looks over to Karmic and gives him a tactful wink.

EXT. BEACH, MONTE CARLO - DAY

INTERCUT: Between all at the beach and water.

John and Leslie are lying on chaise lounges reading and taking in the sun. Iced cocktails sit on the small table that sits between them.

Karmic is swimming out in the water near the floating platform. He's wearing a scuba mask and holding an underwater knife. He places some abalone onto the corner of the floating platform and then dives down under the water for more.

Jennifer is walking along the strand. She looks stunning in a stylish summer hat, swimsuit cover-up dress, and is carrying a beach bag.

FLORIO (27), a handsome young Italian man dressed for the beach himself, comes running up to Jennifer.

FLORIO
Hello, Miss America.

JENNIFER
I beg your pardon.

FLORIO
I think you are beautiful.

JENNIFER
Well, thank you.

FLORIO
I also think you have come here to meet me.

JENNIFER
I don't think so.

FLORIO
You are here for romance, am I correct?

A bit frustrated, Jennifer stops to give Florio her attention.

FLORIO
My name is Florio Sforza. I am from Milan. Have you ever been there?

JENNIFER
(in Italian)
Yes. And I don't go looking for romance signore Sforza. When romance needs a friend, it knows where I am.

FLORIO
(in Italian)
I knew it. You are a romantic American - and you speak Italian.

JENNIFER
There are a few of us.

FLORIO
(English)
Will you have dinner with me?

JENNIFER
I'll say that your invitations are tempting. But I'm afraid that I already have a crush this trip. Maybe next time, bye.

Jennifer walks off, and Florio follows her.

FLORIO
You mean with James Boss? That cannot be.

JENNIFER
Yes, he would be my boyfriend.

Florio stops as Jennifer continues walking.

FLORIO
James Boss is a playboy. I've seen him with several women around the hotel.

JENNIFER
I beg your pardon.

FLORIO
It's true. He doesn't love you the way you wish.

JENNIFER
What do you know about it?

FLORIO
I only know what I see.

Jennifer pushes Florio away and walks off.

JENNIFER
(Italian)
Enjoy your stay, ciao.

FLORIO
Ciao.

Jennifer walks up to John and Leslie, both still sunbathing. She places her bag on an adjacent lounge and starts undressing.

JENNIFER
Where is Karmic?

LESLIE
He said he was going to round up some snacks.

JENNIFER
The bar?

LESLIE
The platform.

Jennifer turns and looks out to the water. She smiles and runs to join Karmic.

Karmic surfaces with another abalone as Jennifer arrives.

JENNIFER
Hi. What are you up to?

KARMIC
I've located a cluster of abalone on the bottom.

Jennifer swims up to Karmic and grabs him around the neck. He looks at her uncomfortably.

JENNIFER
You've lived in Japan.
(half whisper)
Do they taste like abalone?

KARMIC
(confused)
They?

Jennifer nods her head.

JENNIFER
You know - the women.

KARMIC
Women? Well, I --

JENNIFER
You don't like to talk about sex, do you?

Karmic looks at Jennifer with nervous silence.

KARMIC
I'm not sure.

FLORIO (O.S.)
I like it.

Florio swims up to Jennifer with a big smile on his face.

FLORIO
I said --

JENNIFER
I heard you. Anyway, I'm sure you misunderstood me.

FLORIO
I don't think so.

JENNIFER
Well, you couldn't possibly have discerned the nuance of our conversation. I mean you just arrived and -

FLORIO
I understood you perfectly. You said --

JENNIFER
I know what I said, Florio.

KARMIC
I think he understood you, Jennifer.

JENNIFER
Karmic, please.

FLORIO
(in Italian)
I wanted to invite you to come sailing with me.

JENNIFER
(in Italian)
I beg your pardon, but I'm with my boyfriend right now.

FLORIO
(in Italian)
He's not your boyfriend.

Jennifer looks over to Karmic and then back to Florio.

JENNIFER
(in Italian)
He most certainly is my boyfriend.

FLORIO
(in Italian)
So, bring him. There's enough room for everybody.

JENNIFER
Please don't speak Italian. It really is quite rude.

FLORIO
(in Italian)
The marina - eleven tomorrow morning. It's the schooner - wooden hull, named Belle Belle.

JENNIFER
We'll see.

FLORIO
(in Italian)
A schooner is a double mast --

JENNIFER
I know what a schooner is.

FLORIO
(in Italian)
You are beautiful, Jennifer.

Florio directs his words to Karmic as he swims off.

FLORIO
Tomorrow, James. We'll all go sailing.

KARMIC
Okay, Florio. And please, call me Karmic.

FLORIO
What kind of name is Karmic?

JENNIFER
(frustrated)
It's a denominal adjective.

BEAT:

FLORIO
Well, see you tomorrow.

KARMIC
Bye.

Florio swims off.

Jennifer turns to Karmic.

JENNIFER
Really, Karmic. You could have helped me out a little better than that.

KARMIC
He seems nice.

JENNIFER
I'm going back. See you later.

Frustrated, Jennifer swims off.

INT. HOTEL DE PARIS LOBBY, MONTE CARLO, MONACO - DAY

John and Karmic walk into the Hotel from the beach. Karmic spots something O.S. - he freezes.

ANGLE ON:

SAMANTHA (25), dark hair, a little chubby and homely. She's a uniformed hotel worker carrying some beach towels.

She's watching SEBASTIAN (27), the son of some wealthy guests. Sebastian uncomfortably returns her gaze as he stands with his parents.

Karmic recognizes that something is going on between the two.

Samantha looks over to Karmic, the voyeur. He smiles at her and waves slightly.

John breaks the silence.

JOHN

The elevator's here.

Karmic stares at Samantha as he walks over to the elevator and steps inside.

INT. ELEVATOR - CONTINUOUS

John looks at Karmic as the doors slide closed.

JOHN

What's up with that?

Abruptly, Karmic steps out of the elevator.

KARMIC

See you later.

JOHN

Hey!

EXT. CAFE, STREET - DAY

Karmic and April are sitting street-side at a small cafe. They seem happy and animated in their talk as they drink espresso.

Florio stands against the counter of the cafe - wearing sunglasses with espresso in hand. He watches Karmic and April with interest.

EXT. MARINA, MONTE CARLO - MORNING

Jennifer and Karmic weave their way around the wooden planks of the marina. Jennifer carries a decorative paper shopping bag with handles.

The place bustles with the morning yachting crowd.

Karmic is looking good, dressed in a snappy sailing outfit, which includes a classic white captain's cap.

JENNIFER

I hope no one's intimidated by that outfit.

KARMIC

No such thing as overdressing.

FLORIO (O.S.)

Hey! Over here!

Florio stands on the deck of the beautiful schooner. Teak-slatted hull and masts stand elegantly over the azure blue backdrop of the Mediterranean sky.

FLORIO

Karmic, you look very sophisticated - quite the part.

JENNIFER

What about me?

FLORIO

Yes, you look nice too.

JENNIFER

Well. I guess that's a compliment.

Jennifer and Karmic climb aboard the handsome sailing yacht.

JENNIFER

Here you go.

She hands Florio the shopping bag.

FLORIO

What is this?

JENNIFER

Karmic had the hotel make us abalone sandwiches.

Florio leans over and smells the food.

Florio smiles.

FLORIO

Okay! Let's push her off!

LUCA, the first mate, jumps off of the boat onto the dock and starts unhitching the ropes.

EXT. SCHOONER BELLE BELLE, OUT TO SEA - DAY

Florio mans the helm with one hand and holds a bottle of beer in the other.

Jennifer and Karmic sit and enjoy the sun, the sea air, and the ride.

FLORIO

When I was a boy, my father and I raced these waters.

JENNIFER

Your father liked sailing too?

FLORIO

He still does. As we speak, he's somewhere in the Indian Ocean returning from Perth.

JENNIFER

Seems so romantic.

FLORIO

(in Italian)

It is romantic, Jennifer. Perhaps one day you and I will be far out to sea.

Jennifer looks to Karmic and then back to Florio.

JENNIFER

(in Italian)

Don't say that. Even in Italian.

She looks back to Karmic to find he's gone.

She turns around to find him over at the main mast, pulling off his shirt and kicking off his shoes.

JENNIFER

Karmic?

Karmic starts climbing the main mast.

Florio signals to Luca to help him slow the boat down.

JENNIFER

Karmic, what are you doing?

FLORIO

(in Italian)

Easy, Karmic. Easy now!

Florio smiles gleefully as he stands. Jennifer shows concern as Karmic continues climbing up the mast.

The boat slows to a crawl as Karmic reaches the top of the mast and balances himself on the small rigging platform.

FLORIO

(in Italian)

This guy is absolutely crazy.

Atop the platform, Karmic unbuttons and pulls off his pants - he is now completely nude.

JENNIFER

My God. Karmic, please be careful!

Karmic positions himself at the edge of the platform and concentrates as if he's about to dive.

Jennifer and Florio look at each other. Luca crosses his heart.

LUCA

(in Italian)

Holy Mother of God.

Karmic dives.

From high above the water, and in top form, Karmic glides through the air in a perfect swan dive that barely causes a ripple as he disappears into the water.

INT. LOBBY, HOTEL DE PARIS LOBBY - DAY

Jennifer huddles around Karmic, who has an Ace bandage covering his right shoulder and is wrapped in a blanket. Florio follows them.

A hotel porter approaches Jennifer.

PORTER

Do you need any help, Madame?

JENNIFER

He sprained his shoulder. And he's a little shaky.

PORTER

Is there something I can bring you?

JENNIFER

Yes, a pot of hot tea up to his room.

(to Karmic)

What room number are you in?

KARMIC

Seven fourteen.

JENNIFER

And please hurry.

Arm around Karmic, Jennifer leads him to the elevator as the doors open and a couple of people exit.

FLORIO

Jennifer, I want to talk to you.

Jennifer and Karmic enter the elevator.

JENNIFER

Not now, Florio.

FLORIO

But I must!

JENNIFER

Later.

Karmic smiles at Florio - he's happy and cozy, wrapped in Jennifer's arms as the elevator doors close.

INT. HOTEL ROOM 714 - DAY

Partially covered with a blanket, Karmic is dressed in fancy silver pajamas as he lies on the sofa drinking Dr. Pepper.

Jennifer and John sit with him.

JENNIFER

...I'm telling you, if it were the Olympics, he would have gotten a ten from every judge. It was flawless.

KARMIC

I've done it from higher many times.

JENNIFER

What is with you, Karmic? You can't just randomly decide to pull a stunt like that. There are other people to think about.

KARMIC

Like Florio?

JENNIFER

Like me.

JOHN

You were out at sea, Karmic, miles from any help.

Jennifer gets up and starts putting on her sweater to leave.

KARMIC

Where are you going?

JENNIFER

I'm just leaving here. It doesn't matter where I'm going.

KARMIC

Hey, I think I'm catching a cold.

JENNIFER

You'll live.

John follows Jennifer to the door.

JOHN

He'll be fine. We'll meet you downstairs for dinner at eight.

JENNIFER

I think I'm going to take the night off.

John opens the door for her.

JOHN

Don't be mad, Jennifer. In many ways, he's very young at heart.

JENNIFER

Yeah, well, young at heart works for some people, but not everyone.

She turns and walks off down the corridor.

John closes the door and turns to Karmic.

JOHN

That's just fucking great.

John walks over to Karmic.

KARMIC

I've dived from cliffs in Acapulco.

JOHN

Yeah? Have you ever dived on a girl before?

KARMIC

What do you mean?

JOHN

You know what I mean. Oh, yeah. You know.

John crouches down to get closer to Karmic.

JOHN

I know you want her, too. I can see it in your eyes.

BEAT

KARMIC

I love her.

JOHN

The stakes are big here, James.
Maybe, too big for you.

Karmic glares at John as he stands up and walks off.

INT. HOTEL ROOM 714 - MORNING

Dressed in his robe, Karmic stands on the balcony and looks out to the beach.

He spots Jennifer walking up the strand.

She meets with Florio, and the two kiss cheeks and walk off together.

Karmic turns and steps off of the balcony into his room.

EXT. BEACH - DAY

Out of uniform, Samantha sits alone on the beach. She's awkward among all the tan, beautiful people who stroll along the shore and swim in the water.

Carrying a couple of bottles of Dr. Pepper, Karmic comes walking up behind her. He sits on the sand and hands Samantha one of the bottles.

KARMIC

Dr. Pepper?

She takes it from him.

SAMANTHA

(French accent)

Thank you.

They each take a swallow from their bottles.

KARMIC

What part of France are you from?

SAMANTHA

A small village, near the Pyrenees.

KARMIC
Do you miss your family?

SAMANTHA
A little. But this is the best a young girl from my village can hope for.

KARMIC
I know what it's like to feel...that life is not fair.

SAMANTHA
I don't think so.

KARMIC
He likes you. I can tell.

SAMANTHA
Who?

KARMIC
You know.

SAMANTHA
How do you know?

KARMIC
Because, like you, I've spent my entire life watching people, from the outside.

SAMANTHA
I've seen you with that pretty girl.

KARMIC
Yeah, but I'm a Cinderella story.

SAMANTHA
Stop kidding.

KARMIC
Trust me, my situation is way freakier than you could ever imagine.

Karmic looks over to John, who's standing on the strand watching him.

John is not happy and gives Karmic a signal to join him.

KARMIC
Let's take a drive.

SAMANTHA
Where to?

KARMIC
Does it matter?

Karmic holds out his hand.

KARMIC
I'm Karmic.

SAMANTHA
Samantha, but they call me Sam.

KARMIC
Nice to meet you, Sam. Meet me out front in fifteen minutes.

SAMANTHA
Okay.

Karmic gets up and walks off.

EXT. BEACH STRAND - DAY

John confronts Karmic as he steps up onto the strand.

JOHN
I can't decide if you're trying to circumvent my efforts or if you're actually more stupid than I had thought - I mean, if that's even possible.

The two men stare at each other for a beat.

KARMIC
I'm going out for the morning.

JOHN
Where?

KARMIC
None of your business.

Karmic walks off.

EXT. CAR AGENCY - DAY

Karmic and a rental AGENT stand in the lot filled with fancy expensive automobiles.

KARMIC
What do you recommend?

AGENT
If you don't know what you want, then just pick a number.

Karmic turns and looks out over the assortment of cars.

CLOSE UP:

A red Ferrari convertible with a license plate reading '21'.

The roar of the engine.

Karmic, behind the steering wheel, guns the engine and burns rubber by spinning the tires. He whips the car in circles, doing 'doughnuts' around the lot, barely in control.

The Agent watches in horror as, after several complete rotations, the car finally comes to rest - the engine stalled.

INTERCUT: BETWEEN LIMOUSINE AND CAFE - DAY

In the back of a Chauffeured Bentley limousine, Karmic and Samantha motor through the streets of Monte Carlo.

Samantha leans over and pushes her face against the window.

SAMANTHA
Amazing how different the streets look from a limousine.

KARMIC
Look at this.

Karmic flips down a vanity mirror.

Samantha frowns at her own reflection.

KARMIC

Now, let your hair down and try some of this.

He hands her some lipstick.

KARMIC

It's called --

Karmic pulls out a torn page from a magazine and reads from it.

KARMIC

Absolute Rouge.

She turns the lipstick and rolls it out.

SAMANTHA

I'm afraid to get in trouble with the hotel.

KARMIC

The Dalai Lama once told me that if it's not worth the risk, it's...uh?

SAMANTHA

Yes?

KARMIC

I can't remember the rest. Just do it.

She leans forward, unpins and shakes out her hair, and applies the lipstick.

CUT TO:

At the same street-side cafe, Jennifer is sitting with Florio at one table - Sebastian is seated with his parents at another.

JENNIFER

I just don't believe it.

FLORIO

It is true. Two different women in two days. And both are very pretty.

JENNIFER

I know that Karmic loves me very much. He wouldn't look at another woman.

BACK TO:

Samantha laughs uncomfortably as she can't get over how pretty she looks.

Sunroof open, she holds her hand up to shield the sun.

KARMIC
Here, these came with the car.

Karmic pulls out a pair of chic sunglasses and hands them to Samantha.

SAMANTHA
Prada.

She puts them on.

The limousine cruises through the quaint cobbled streets.

CUT TO:

Both Jennifer and Sebastian spot Karmic and Samantha standing up through the sunroof of the limousine as they drive by. They both raise themselves slightly out of their chairs to get a better view as the limo passes.

ANGLE ON:

Karmic and 'pretty' Samantha are laughing as they drive by.

The heads of Jennifer and Sebastian turn as they watch the car pass. Then, the two notice each other eyeing the car and hold a common stare for a moment as they re-seat themselves.

FLORIO
What are you doing?

JENNIFER
I just saw him.

FLORIO
Who?

JENNIFER
Karmic, of course. He was with a woman.

FLORIO

I told you he's a playboy. Everyone knows it but you.

EXT. HILLSIDE OVERLOOKING THE BEACH, MONTE CARLO - DAY

High on a rocky precipice overlooking the Mediterranean, Karmic is seated in a meditative lotus position - legs crossed and eyes closed, he faces the water.

Samantha is also seated on a large rock in the meditative lotus position - as is the Chauffeur - all are quiet and serene.

EXT. MONTE CARLO, STREETS - DAY

Jennifer and Florio are walking the streets together. Jennifer is deep in thought. Florio tries to put his arm around her, but she rebuffs - shakes her head.

INT. FASHION BOUTIQUE, MONTE CARLO - LATER

Karmic and Samantha walk into the shop. Karmic pulls swimsuits, hats, and other clothes off the shelves and pushes them at Samantha playfully.

Karmic steps up to the shopkeeper and hands her the Hotel's card.

KARMIC

She wants to dress beautifully. Can you help us?

SHOP KEEPER

(French)

Oui, avec plaisir.

EXT. RESTAURANT TERRACE, MONTE CARLO - NIGHT

John and Leslie are seated at a candle-lit table. Glasses of wine sit in front of them. The soft sound of the surf can be heard in the background.

JOHN

If you bought the apartment in Paris, you could put it in my name. That way, no one would know about it.

LESLIE

That could work. I'd have to talk to my attorney here and see what the options are in terms of holding title.

JOHN

And you could deduct my commission from the sales price.

LESLIE

It's still three million dollars. That's a lot of money in a soft market.

JOHN

Commission on three million could be one hundred thousand.

LESLIE

What's with Karmic lately? He's been aloof lately, and Jennifer seems a little dismayed.

Leslie looks up to find Jennifer walking into the restaurant.

JOHN

I'll have a talk with him.

LESLIE

Please, do that.

Jennifer walks up to the table and seats herself.

JOHN

Are you alone?

JENNIFER

I'm meeting Florio in the piano bar after dinner.

JOHN

Oh.

Leslie eyes John.

EXT. BEACH STRAND, MONTE CARLO - NIGHT

Didier is huddled up with a young couple on the walk.

The Man lights a cigarette for him. He smiles, thanks the Man, and walks off.

EXT. BEACH CAFE - NIGHT

Karmic is sitting with Sebastian at a table at the beach cafe. A WAITER walks up and puts an ice bucket with a bottle of Champagne and four fluted glasses on the table in front of him.

WAITER #3

Comme vous avez demande, Monsieur.

KARMIC

Is this the best you have?

The Waiter pours Karmic a glass.

Karmic hands the glass to Sebastian, and he tastes the wine.

WAITER #3

Within reason. It's Pol Roger. Of course, it's debatable, but for my taste, it doesn't get much better.

The Waiter pours another glass.

SEBASTIAN

It's wonderful.

KARMIC

(to the Waiter)

Thank you.

The Waiter walks off.

Karmic lifts the glass and looks it over. He sniffs it, then takes a swallow.

His face cringes as he coughs lightly.

Karmic smiles as Samantha walks up to the table. Dressed up, she is elegant and beautiful.

Surprised, Sebastian stands to greet her.

KARMIC
Good evening, Samantha.

SAMANTHA
Hello.

Karmic pours some Champagne and hands the glass to Samantha.

KARMIC
Sebastian, this is my friend Samantha. Samantha, Sebastian.

SEBASTIAN
Very nice to meet you.

SAMANTHA
Hello, Sebastian.

Karmic looks over to Didier walking the strand.

He pours Sebastian a little more.

KARMIC
I feel intense chemistry between the two of you.

Karmic holds up his right hand and shakes it short and quick - like a vibration.

KARMIC
It’s electric. And that's why I thought you two should meet.

EXT. BEACH STRAND - NIGHT

A couple of SECURITY GUARDS from the Hotel come walking up to Didier.

SECURITY #1
(in French)
The Hotel doesn’t like loitering around the beach.

DIDIER
I’m not loitering, friend.

SECURITY #1

They don't like people bothering the guests.

SECURITY #2

We don't like that either.

DIDIER

That gentleman offered me a cigarette.

SECURITY #2

Where are you from?

DIDIER

Does that matter?

SECURITY #2

It does to me.

KARMIC

May I help?

The two Security Guards turn to find Karmic standing there.

SECURITY #1

No, sir. This man doesn't belong here and --

KARMIC

Where does he belong?

SECURITY #1

That's not for us to decide.

KARMIC

What about my table?

SECURITY #2

Did you invite him?

Karmic gestures towards the bar area as he addresses Didier.

KARMIC

Please, join us.

DIDIER

I'd love to, man.

KARMIC
Thank you for finding him for me, Gentlemen.

Karmic nods to both the Security.

SECURITY #1
No problem.

SECURITY #2
Certainly.

Karmic and Didier walk over to Sebastian and Samantha at the table.

DIDIER
So, you are like a white knight.

KARMIC
A white knight?

DIDIER
Yes, you...you are so perfect. Handsome, wealthy. You came to save me, uh? I don't belong?

KARMIC
If there is an imposter among us - it would be me.

DIDIER
So beautiful. Shakespeare?

Didier looks back towards the two Security Guards - now distant.

DIDIER
It's impossible that you could ever know what it's like to be considered unexceptional among the exceptional.

Karmic smiles at Didier as he hands him a glass of Champagne.

KARMIC
I used to feel sorry for myself. Now, I feel sorry for everyone else.

He turns to Samantha and Sebastian.

KARMIC
Be thankful. The dark clouded future that you feared has opened to a brilliant sun.

Karmic takes Samantha's hand and places it with Sebastian's hand.

They all raise their glasses.

KARMIC
Unexceptional. A state of mind.

DIDIER
Solute.

SEBASTIAN
Cheers.

SAMANTHA
Beautiful.

Karmic looks over and spots Lloyd waiting for him near the hotel.

INT. LOBBY, HOTEL DE PARIS - NIGHT

John, Leslie, and Jennifer are walking across the hotel lobby as Karmic steps out of one of the private offices with Lloyd.

They stop and watch Lloyd lean over to kiss Karmic on the cheek, then she turns and walks off.

John walks over to Karmic.

JOHN
What's going on?

KARMIC
Nothing that concerns you.

JOHN
Hey, I'm your legal guardian - if it concerns you, it concerns me.

Leslie turns to Karmic.

LESLIE
Karmic, people that play with other people's emotions always end up alone. My daughter means a lot to me --

JENNIFER
Mother. Leave it alone.

KARMIC
She means a lot to me too.

LESLIE
Well, not enough, apparently.

KARMIC
Enough?

LESLIE
I'm her mother, and if I say it's not enough, then it's not enough.

Karmic smiles at both of them.

KARMIC
I love her.

Jennifer eyes Karmic as she's led away by her mother.

INT. PIANO BAR, HOTEL DE PARIS - LATER

A smallish horseshoe bar and a PIANO PLAYER is tickling the keys near the center of the room.

Jennifer, Florio, Leslie, and John are sitting together at a banquette table having cocktails.

FLORIO
Anyway, the French Riviera is for old money. Boring.

LESLIE
Old money, new money. Either you have it, or you don't.

JENNIFER
Mother.

FLORIO
(to Leslie)
I'm sailing for Mallorca in a couple of days, and I want your daughter to join me.

LESLIE
What about us?

FLORIO
Of course, you can come as well. It's the best beach of the Mediterranean.

A couple of Italian GIRLS walk by their table. A pretty BRUNETTE stops and looks at Florio.

BRUNETTE
(in Italian)
Florio. Are we still going to Mallorca this Saturday?

The other Girls stop and turn around.

FLORIO
(in Italian)
Uh? Yes, I am hoping to be leaving.

Karmic walks inside the room wearing a stunning burgundy silk velvet smoking jacket.

BRUNETTE #2
(in Italian)
Tell Luca that I'll bring his favorite sandwiches.

FLORIO
(in Italian)
I'll call you tomorrow.

ALL THE GIRLS
(in Italian)
Ciao, Florio. Bye. Kisses.

Florio smiles while looking away from Jennifer - avoiding eye contact.

Jennifer and Leslie hold a look for a moment.

Karmic walks over to the piano and hands the Piano Player a glass of cognac as he slides onto the stool and starts playing the piano.

Karmic plays the instrumental of the Billy Joel song She's Always a Woman.

JENNIFER
(in Italian)
Things are going to be a little crowded on that schooner.

FLORIO
(in Italian)
I don't think they're coming.

Softly, Karmic starts singing the song while playing the piano.

KARMIC
(singing)
She can thrill with a smile
She can sooth with her eyes
She can renew your faith with her casual lies
And she only reveals what she wants you to see
She hides like a child,
But she's always a woman to me

Karmic looks over to Jennifer, and the two lock eyes as he sings.

KARMIC
She can lead you to love
She can take you or leave you
She can ask for the truth
But she'll never believe you
And she can't be convicted
She's earned her degree
And the most she will do
Is throw shadows at you
But she's always a woman to me

Jennifer stands and walks over to Karmic at the piano. She sits next to him.

KARMIC
Oh--she takes care of herself
She can wait if she wants
She's ahead of her time
Oh--and she never gives out
And she never gives in
She just changes her mind

KARMIC (CON'T)

She is frequently kind
And she's suddenly cruel
She can do as she pleases
She's nobody's fool
But she'll bring out the best
And the worst you can be
Blame it all on yourself
Cause she's always a woman to me

Karmic leans over and kisses Jennifer.

Florio watches them uncomfortably. Leslie smiles at John.

EXT. BEACH, MONTE CARLO - NIGHT

Deep into the night, Karmic and Jennifer are kneeling chest high in the water holding each other - kissing each other.

Their clothes are on the sand. The lights of the hotel flicker in the background.

A half-filled bottle of Champagne and glasses sit on the sand.

KARMIC

I'll never be an investment banker or an engineer. But I'll be a good husband...loyal and thoughtful.

JENNIFER

I believe you, Karmic.

KARMIC

I'll be a good father too. Patient...spiritually enlightened.

JENNIFER

What more could a girl ask for?

KARMIC

Oh, and I've got a trust fund worth over eighty million pounds.

JENNIFER

Well, I guess a girl could ask for that, but you've already got it.

They embrace in another long kiss.

INT. HOTEL BEDROOM - MORNING

The phone rings, waking Karmic and Jennifer, who are sleeping in a bed layered with white cotton sheets.

Jennifer answers the phone.

JENNIFER

Hello? Yes, hold on.

She hands the phone to Karmic.

KARMIC

Hello. Yes. Okay, I'll be right down - oh, could you contact my father and ask him to join us, please? Thank you, goodbye.

Karmic cradles the phone and slides out of bed.

JENNIFER

What's going on?

KARMIC

I've got a little business meeting this morning.

Karmic starts getting dressed.

JENNIFER

Business meeting?

KARMIC

It shouldn't take long.

Karmic leans over and kisses Jennifer.

KARMIC

I'll be down at breakfast.

JENNIFER

I'll join you in a bit.

KARMIC

Sure.

INT. HOTEL CAFE - MORNING

Karmic is sitting at a table having breakfast with April and Lloyd - the two ladies we saw him with earlier.

The can of Cheez Whiz sits in front of Karmic on the table.

John comes walking up to the table.

JOHN

What's going on here, James?

KARMIC

Please have a seat.

John eyes Karmic as he sits down.

A Waiter arrives.

WAITER #4

May I get you something, sir?

JOHN

Coffee, please.

WAITER #4

Very good, sir.

JOHN

James, where were you last night? I don't want you staying out without talking to me.

KARMIC

I stayed with Jennifer.

JOHN

I'm confident that Leslie wouldn't appreciate your sleeping with her daughter, either.

KARMIC

It's not her decision. Or yours.

JOHN

Aren't you a...I would have thought that you were a virgin, James.

KARMIC

And you would have been correct.

JOHN

I have to insist that you --

KARMIC

I'd like to introduce you to April Smythe, Esquire. April is a solicitor in Jeremy Middleton's office. They're in charge of administering my trust.

JOHN

Yes, I know Jeremy.

APRIL

Mr. Boss, Karmic has asked us to represent him in a legal action to liberate him from outside guardianship as a legal requirement.

JOHN

Well, I'll fight it. There's no way --

APRIL

Mr. Boss, it has already been done.

She shuffles some court documents across the table for John to view.

APRIL

As of this morning, Karmic enjoys the freedom of any other adult British citizen.

JOHN

He doesn't have the mental capacity to manage himself. He needs me.

APRIL

Mr. Boss, this is Dr. Lloyd the court-appointed psychologist.

Lloyd, the other woman at the table, speaks up.

LLOYD

Yes, I've been working with Mr. Boss for several days, and after conducting a standard capability assessment yesterday, I've concluded that he is indeed psychologically capable of being a lawfully independent person.

Lloyd pushes some documentation over to John. In near shock, John looks it over.

KARMIC

Don't worry, John. We'll work things out for you financially. I'm very grateful to you.

John looks over to Karmic with a blank stare.

Karmic stumbles through pronouncing his next line.

KARMIC

In...advertent...ly, you made all of this possible.

JOHN

I did?

KARMIC

You're still my father, and I'm happy for that.

Jennifer and Leslie come walking up to the table.

JENNIFER

May we join you?

KARMIC

Of course. Please have a seat.

Waiters shuffle about the table.

Karmic eyes April and getting the message, she cues Lloyd that it's time for them to make their exit.

APRIL

If there's anything else you require, please contact me.

April puts her business card down in front of John.

April and Lloyd walk off as Florio approaches, flanked by the four Italian Girls he spoke to the night before.

FLORIO

I just wanted to bid you all farewell.

KARMIC

(Italian)

Florio, are you still planning on sailing to Mallorca?

Not realizing he spoke Italian, Jennifer, and Florio give Karmic a perplexed look.

FLORIO

(Italian)

I depart...or, we depart this afternoon.

KARMIC

Would it be an intrusion if we joined you?

FLORIO

(English)

You want to come with me?

KARMIC

If we're welcome.

FLORIO

Of course, but I don't have room on my boat.

KARMIC

I've made arrangements for another schooner.

FLORIO

In that case, it would be fantastic.

Karmic eyes Jennifer and Leslie.

KARMIC

How does the beach at Mallorca sound to you?

JENNIFER

Fine.

LESLIE

Wonderful.

Karmic looks at John.

KARMIC

Dad? Are you up for it?

Still a bit in shock, John hesitates for a moment.

JOHN

Yeah, sure.

KARMIC

Great. Let's finish breakfast.

Karmic turns towards a Waiter and hands him the can of Cheez Whiz.

KARMIC

Please get rid of this for me.

The Waiter takes the can.

WAITER #4

Anything else?

KARMIC

A bottle of Champagne. Florio, have a seat. I'm buying everyone breakfast.

FLORIO

Thank you.

Karmic stands and gestures to Florio's women.

KARMIC

(Italian)

Ladies, please.

EXT. OPEN WATER, MEDITERRANEAN SEA - DAY

Sails trim, Florio's schooner glides across the water. Florio and the three topless WOMEN sunbathing on the deck.

Behind them is another sailing vessel, a ketch. A bit smaller, but it, too, is a beauty. It cuts through the wake of the lead boat.

John and Leslie are at the bow enjoying the sun.

Samantha and Sebastian are sitting under the rear mast.

Karmic and Jennifer are at the stern - Karmic is at the helm.

Jennifer throws her arms around Karmic and hugs him - she kisses his cheek - both smile at each other.

THE END

First draft written in Anchorage, Alaska 2008.

Written as a lark, but still based on real experiences in Rishikesh, Varanasi, and other travels that included India and Nepal with a band of very wise Buddhist backpackers between 2005 - 2008.

THE DHARMA KINGS

Written by
Paul Charles Bailly

2008

FADE IN:

INT. OFFICE - DAY

Sitting behind a desk is a woman wearing a white turban, a white long-sleeved new-age smock with an off-white vest, eyeglasses, and no make-up. She's a stereotypical New-Age-Golden-Temple type.

She speaks directly to the camera.

NEW AGE WOMAN

This film should never have been made. Not only is it sacrilegious and profane. It's an insult to spiritual people of every faith. It pretends to represent an accurate Western attitude towards Eastern philosophies when, in fact, it mocks those very beliefs. It's not only completely absurd; it's insulting. Like we in the West are incapable of really getting it, just because we're of another culture and in another hemisphere. I mean, hey, I've been to India...and anyway, you sit down and watch this thing for almost two hours and...and...and it's not even funny --

SMASH CUT TO:

EXT. RISHIKESH, INDIA - DAY

A panoramic sweep of a small Indian village on the Ganges River. As this is the Himalayan foothills - the rushing river is clear blue - the lush green jungle hillside sits behind the many ashrams and traditional buildings that make up this holy vestige.

SUPERIMPOSE: RISHIKESH, INDIA

EXT. RISHIKESH VILLAGE STREET - DAY

Two American men stroll a narrow pedestrian passageway. MARCELLO (37) and COSMIC (24), both dressed in casual, modern Western attire. They walk among the many villagers, street hawkers, and shops. This is a small town, but there is a hectic bustle that projects the ambiance of a much larger place.

COSMIC
Suffering has a cause. We're constantly suffering to survive.

MARCELLO
Yes, but the cause of suffering can be ended.

COSMIC
It takes on so many forms. I can't see how anyone could -

MARCELLO
We have to release the suffering by abandoning our expectations.

COSMIC
The moment you start possessing, is the moment you are owned.

MARCELLO
Exactly. And possession is extended to one's ego.

COSMIC
The ego.

MARCELLO
To be identified with one's ego is to be enslaved.

EXT. NEW DELHI AIRPORT - DAY

An Air India Boeing 747 skids as it lands on the tarmac.

INT. TAXI, NEW DELHI AIRPORT - DAY

POV: From the backseat

An Indian TAXI DRIVER sits behind the wheel of his cab. He looks into the rearview mirror as JACK BOGART (O.S.), climbs into the back and shuts the door.

JACK (O.S.)
Do you know where this is?

Jack hands a piece of paper over the seat to the Taxi Driver. He eyes the paper.

TAXI DRIVER
Yes, but it is very far from here.

JACK (O.S.)
That's okay; just go there.

INTERCUT: BETWEEN TAXI AND MARCELLO/COSMIC - DAY

Marcello and Cosmic walk along the sandy shore of the Ganges River while talking.

COSMIC
So...desire, frustration, suffering, one's ego...can all be eliminated?

MARCELLO
Of course, they can. We can accomplish anything if we're dedicated enough.

CUT TO:

POV: Taxi Driver through the windshield.

The taxi is driving at high speed on a small country road. It stops for nothing. All in its path, hurry out of the way. People on the road dive to safety - sheep scramble out of the way - another car is forced off the road.

BACK TO:

Marcello and Cosmic sit in a meditative posture under a bodhi tree while black-faced white monkeys wander about in the background.

COSMIC
How do we do it?

MARCELLO
That's what we have to find out. I can tell you this. It's not going to be easy. We will have to give up some things that are very important to us and change how we perceive ourselves.

CUT TO:

POV: Taxi Driver through the windshield.

A man on a bicycle is forced into an ox cart - a band of monkeys shrieks as they bound out of the way - a family backs off as they watch in horror.

BACK TO:

Marcello and Cosmic are seated while overlooking the Ganges from the rooftop of a restaurant.

COSMIC

So, desires for success, admiration...even sex can all be eliminated.

MARCELLO

Exactly.

COSMIC

Nirvana.

MARCELLO

Yes. Enlightenment.

CUT TO:

POV: Taxi Driver through the windshield.

Another car is forced off the road - the taxi plows through a group of goats and chickens. A chicken bounces off the windshield - children dive out of the way.

JACK (O.S.)

That's what I'm talking about. Now we're making time.

BACK TO:

Marcello and Cosmic are lying on their backs, eyes closed, while enjoying a reiki massage applied to them by two beautiful young Indian women.

COSMIC

Do you really think that Jack Bogart is capable of doing this? I mean, a Hollywood actor?

MARCELLO

Don't underestimate Jack.

Marcello and Cosmic hold a look at each other.

MARCELLO

On the other hand, don't overestimate him either.

COSMIC

Forty-two days in detox.

MARCELLO

He'd been taking Valium for nineteen years. Besides, he thinks he's doing me a favor.

COSMIC

Wow, Jack Bogart, in Rishikesh.

EXT. RISHIKESH - DAY

The taxi screeches to a halt at a small but animated transportation depot. Motorcycles, motor-rickshaws, and tiny vans overstuffed with people are moving in every direction.

EXT. RISHIKESH PEDESTRIAN STREET - DAY

JACK BOGART (46) walking in slow motion. He glides down the street - lean build, sandy blond hair, and sunglasses. Jack's groomed like the Hollywood legend he is. His unbuttoned, untucked blue silk dress shirt blows open, exposing a sleeveless white silk t-shirt. The LOCALS turn to watch him as he floats past them.

EXT. VED NIKETAN ASHRAM, RISHIKESH - DAY

Marcello and Cosmic stand at the anterior of the wide two-story galleries that make up the Ved Niketan Ashram. Jack comes walking up, followed by a wooden luggage trolley Attendant toting several large trunks.

Several townspeople have joined his procession through Rishikesh. Jack walks up to Marcello and Cosmic and stops.

JACK
Couldn't we just have become enlightened in L.A.?

MARCELLO
No, Jack. Nobody can become enlightened in Los Angeles. Just like nobody can make a film in Rishikesh.

JACK
Who'd want to?

Jack looks over to an eagerly awaiting Cosmic, staring up at him.

JACK
Who's this, your house boy?

MARCELLO
No. This is Cosmic. He's a graduate student at the Colorado Institute of Clairvoyant and Integral Studies near Boulder. He's going to be taking this journey with us.

JACK
Clairvoyant and Integral Studies?

COSMIC
Yeah, I plan on opening a clinic that does everything from life energy conservation and spiritual radiation therapy to shadow reading.

JACK
Shadow reading. Now that's important.

An excited Cosmic eagerly hands Jack an autograph book.

COSMIC
Would you mind, Mr. Bogart?

JACK
An autograph? Not at all, Cosmic.

Jack takes the book from Cosmic and continues speaking while he fingers through it.

JACK

So, how long is this enlightenment thing going to take? I've got a meeting in L.A. with Marty late next week.

MARCELLO

Jack, this is not some Robert Redford film festival in Provo -

JACK

That's Sundance, Marcello...Park City.

MARCELLO

Whatever. It's going to take as long as it takes.

Jack scowls at the autograph book.

JACK

Who the hell is this?

COSMIC

Justin Timberlake. He's my favorite singer.

Jack tears the page out of the book, crumples it up, and tosses it to the ground. Cosmic's mouth hangs open in shock as he watches Jack sign the book.

JACK

(to Marcello)

I just wanted you to know, in case we could speed things up.

Jack shoves the autograph book back to Cosmic without looking at him.

MARCELLO

This way.

Marcello leads Jack into the registration office of the ashram.

INT. ASHRAM REGISTRATION OFFICE - DAY

An Indian DESK CLERK and his ASSISTANT are seated behind a desk. They're wearing traditional dress; kurtas, turbans, and sandals.

Marcello, Jack, and Cosmic enter.

MARCELLO
This is the guest I was telling you about.

DESK CLERK
You look familiar. Have you been here before?

JACK
No. But perhaps you've seen the film -

MARCELLO
It's his first time in India.

Jack pulls out a pack of Dunhill cigarettes and lights one as a PORTER steps up.

PORTER
Sir, there is no smoking on the premises of the ashram.

JACK
I'm not smoking this.

Jack takes a drag and blows the smoke in the Porter's face.

COSMIC
He's wearing it.

Jack eyes Cosmic and smiles.

The Porter's hand flashes over and snaps the cigarette out of Jack's mouth.

DESK CLERK
We won't tolerate misbehavior in the ashram.

JACK
Fuck you. Where's my room?

DESK CLERK
You must register first. Your passport, please.

Jack turns to Marcello in frustration.

JACK

Marcello, I told you to find me a place that -

MARCELLO

It's okay, don't worry about it, Jack.

Marcello fleeces Jack's pockets, pulls out his passport, and hands it to Cosmic.

MARCELLO

Take care of things here, would you?

COSMIC

Sure.

Marcello leads Jack out of the room.

EXT. ASHRAM GALLERY - DAY

Marcello and Jack step out of the office. Several porters stand with Jack's luggage, waiting for instructions.

MARCELLO

You're upstairs in one of the larger suites.

JACK

Now, that's what I'm talking about.

INT. JACK'S SUITE, ASHRAM - DAY

Marcello opens a pair of doors bringing light into Jack's suite. It's sparse on furniture, on the dark side, and not very comfortable looking. They're followed by several Indian porters that are carrying Jack's luggage. Jack walks through the place - his face showing disappointment.

JACK

Great. These are about the worst accommodations I've ever had in my fucking life.

MARCELLO

You should see our rooms.

JACK

Is there an interior decorator in town?

Marcello stares at Jack.

JACK

Right. Well, I've got enough shit in these trunks to bring this place to life.

Just then, an enraged brown monkey crashes onto the back door's metal security bars. It shakes the bars violently as it shrieks. Jack turns to one of the men carrying the trunks.

JACK

You and your friends better plan on staying here for a while.

An Indian man walks up to Marcello and hands him some white, folded Indian clothes.

JACK

And could you have someone - preferably Cosmic, kill that monkey?

MARCELLO

Of course, Jack.

(hands Jack the clothes)

Here are some things you need to wear tomorrow.

Jack gives Marcello a suspicious look as he takes them.

Cosmic walks into the room. He presents Jack's passport, and Marcello snatches it and leads Cosmic back out of Jack's room.

MARCELLO

We're having dinner at seven tonight.

JACK

I'll eat in. Besides, I'm going to be busy setting this place up.

MARCELLO

Alright, tomorrow morning at eight, then. Get a good night's sleep.

JACK

Right.

EXT. ASHRAM FRONT COURTYARD - MORNING

Loud, techno sounds from a ghetto blaster are heard around the courtyard. A group of thirty Indian children dressed in colorful attire are dancing to the music.

Cosmic is standing behind the music player, vocalizing what appears to be multiple techno-sound effects into a microphone. Marcello stands near Cosmic - encouraging him by bobbing his head and swaying in place.

ANGLE ON:

Jack opens his door upstairs just as the music suddenly cuts off. He steps out and peers down to the courtyard. All is silent as the animated rainbow of children disperses into the yard. Jack looks down.

In the courtyard, Cosmic and Marcello look up at Jack.

MARCELLO

Ready?

JACK

Uh...yeah.

EXT. VED NIKETAN ASHRAM - MORNING

The three gather in front of the ashram and walk the narrow road that parallels the river. They're dressed identically - white cotton kurtas and draw-string pants.

MARCELLO

All settled in, Jack?

JACK

Yeah, but I was up till midnight directing my team. Is there a place in this town where I can buy a new mattress? My back is killing me.

COSMIC

You should take a class in reiki massage while you're here, Mr. Bogart.

JACK

I have a masseuse in Los Angeles - I don't see how learning massage could possibly benefit me.

The three look over to find a Jesus Christ look-a-like humbly walking by them. He is slightly built, long hair, bearded with loose hanging clothes - he totally looks like an authentic image of Jesus Christ.

EXT. RISHIKESH, PEDESTRIAN STREET - DAY

Cloaked in their white kurtas, Marcello, Jack, and Cosmic walk the street. Heads turn as some of the Western women recognize Jack.

COSMIC

Wow, Mr. Bogart. I feel like I'm walking with a deity.

JACK

I know what you mean, son.

COSMIC

If you don't mind my asking, Mr. Bogart - how old are you?

Jack rolls his eyes at Marcello, then turns to Cosmic.

JACK

Forty-five.

COSMIC

Wow.

Jack gives Marcello another look. Marcello spots a food stall and directs them over to it.

MARCELLO

We'd better get something in our stomachs before it gets too late.

JACK

It's not that I'm old, Cosmic - just a little closer to death.

MARCELLO

What do you think death is, Jack?

JACK

I don't know, but I'm hoping it's like anything going on at the Playboy Mansion.

Marcello steps up to a man working the shop.

MARCELLO

Namaste. Three lassis and three apple samosas, please.

COSMIC

If I'm reincarnated, I want to come back as a Toxoplasma gondii, the mind-altering parasite.

JACK

Well, that's ambitious of you, Cosmic. Why not come back as colon cancer?

The three sit at a table as a WAITER delivers their drinks and food.

COSMIC

You don't understand; it's a good parasite -

JACK

So, Marcello, when do we get this enlightenment thing rolling? I'm on kind of a timeline.

MARCELLO

This morning. Right after breakfast.

Jack raises his lassi to the others.

JACK

To the next fucking life, and hopefully a better fucking life.

EXT. HILLSIDE CAVE - DAY

Marcello, Jack, and Cosmic arrive at the entrance to a small cave - all a bit winded from the hike. The cave entrance is partially covered with a simple Indian cloth. The trio walks up to the entrance and stands for a moment, eyeing the mouth of the cave. Marcello reaches over, opens the cave's cover, and peers inside.

Suddenly, a man comes charging out. His name is OLIVER (55), and he is brandishing a walking stick and has a wild expression on his face. He is waif-thin and shivers like a hard-up heroin junky.

OLIVER
(British accent)
Get out of here, you unholy Buddhist demons.

MARCELLO
Relax, friend.

COSMIC
We're not demons.

JACK
Speak for yourself.

Oliver shakes as he speaks.

OLIVER
I apologize, but I'm a schizophrenic!

JACK
Really? So am I.

Oliver, puzzled, looks over to Jack.

OLIVER
I'm sorry that you're schizophrenic.

JACK
I'm not.

Jack looks over to Cosmic.

JACK
You wouldn't believe the female libido in L.A.

OLIVER

You are a demon!

Oliver swings his stick at Jack - he steps back, avoiding it.

MARCELLO

Jack, please.

Marcello holds up his hands, giving Oliver a calming presence.

MARCELLO

Oliver. It's said that you once pursued enlightenment.

OLIVER

Enlightenment! Uh!

COSMIC

What happened?

OLIVER

I was emotionally stripped and then forced to look at things I didn't want to see. Things nobody would like to see in themselves.

MARCELLO

So, you couldn't handle the personal introspection?

OLIVER

No, I got through that alright.

COSMIC

Your ego, you struggled with dissolving your ego?

OLIVER

No, no. Everything was going fine. Even wonderfully. That is, until they showed up.

He nods toward Jack.

MARCELLO

They?

OLIVER

The Californians. They ruined everything. It all became a trendy, soy, chai, latte-drinking fashion show.

Oliver, Marcello, and Cosmic look over to Jack.

JACK

Hey, since when is practicing spirituality and looking good doing it a paradox?

OLIVER

To them, Buddhist ideas are like herbal remedies one picks up at an over-priced ayurvedic boutique.

MARCELLO

They reject Buddhism on its own terms?

OLIVER

Exactly. It's not Buddhism. It's 'what Buddhism means to me!'

MARCELLO

So the trendoids have a skewed perception.

OLIVER

Eastern ideas float about like little self-esteem life preservers - clung to by inflating egos.

MARCELLO

We want to follow the path to enlightenment.

OLIVER

My advice is to head north. Find the great tree and meditate there for 49 days - it all flows through the tree.

COSMIC

Kashmir.

OLIVER

Kashmir.

Oliver leans over to Marcello and nods towards Jack.

OLIVER

Los Angeles.

BEAT

MARCELLO

Yeah.

Oliver darts behind the cloth and back into his cave. Marcello and Cosmic look over to Jack.

JACK

Hey, just say the word, and I'm out of here.

MARCELLO

Let's go.

They turn and walk down the hill.

JACK

(distant)

I was born in Minneapolis, if it makes you feel any better.

EXT. RISHIKESH, NARROW ALLEYWAY - DAY

The three walk down the alleyway. Still in discussion.

JACK

Well, that was helpful. Any more psychos before we get this thing started?

MARCELLO

Jack. This thing has already started.

A WESTERN WOMAN runs up to Jack out of nowhere, kisses him on the lips, and disappears. Jack laughs as Cosmic watches in awe as she runs off.

COSMIC

Wow!

JACK

It's nothing, really.

COSMIC

How many women have you slept with, Mr. Bogart?

JACK

Thousands.

MAMA LOVE (58) walks by them. She is a big-haired blonde with big fake tits wrapped in a tight-fitting gold spandex and faux leopard skin suit. She eyes Jack as they pass.

MAMA LOVE

Look out, Buddha; Hollywood's arrived.

Jack lights a cigarette as he and Cosmic turn to watch her walk off.

JACK

Who the fuck was that?

COSMIC

Mama Love.

JACK

Mama Love?

MARCELLO

She's from the Bay Area. Claims to be a love guru.

JACK

(shaking his head)

Frisco. They hate us in L.A.

COSMIC

What's the difference?

JACK

In San Francisco they do opera. In L.A., we do...ecstasy.

Cosmic turns to look back at Mama Love one more time.

COSMIC

Would you sleep with her, Mr.
Bogart?

JACK

(shaking his head)

Older women have too much baggage -
I should know, it's guys like me
that gave it to them.

COSMIC

Not even with a bag over her head?

Jack looks over to Marcello and then to Cosmic.

JACK

Maybe with a bag over my head.
Cosmic, the first thing I consider
when sizing up a chick is if I'd go
down on her. Sure, I'd fuck almost
anyone...but how many would I go
down on? That's what makes the
difference.

Cosmic is listening to Jack intensely as if being lectured by a master.

COSMIC

I see.

MARCELLO

Here we are, gentleman.

Marcello turns to Jack and Cosmic.

MARCELLO

Okay, this is going to be a bit
more serious. Let's let the chatter
about fucking and sucking women
stay on the street for now.

COSMIC

Sure.

JACK

Right.

They stop in front of the gate. A sign reading 'Meditation Compound' hangs overhead.

MARCELLO

This is it.

JACK

Meditation?

They turn and walk through a gate into the yard of the meditation compound.

INT. MEDITATION COMPOUND - DAY

A saffron-robed disciple opens the door: Marcello, Jack, and Cosmic enter.

DISCIPLE

Yes?

MARCELLO

We're here for instruction with Dandi Swami.

DISCIPLE

One moment, please.

He walks off.

JACK

Do we have to meditate? I have trouble focusing on...nothingness for extended periods of time.

MARCELLO

It's an essential part of the process, Jack.

COSMIC

Do some pranayama; it'll help you relax.

JACK

Relax? I've already taken two Klonopin.

MARCELLO

You just got out of detox.

JACK

That was for Valium.

Dandi Swami's disciple returns and waves the three inside.

MARCELLO

And Jack, don't make direct eye contact with the Swami - he can see right through you and read your mind.

JACK

He doesn't want to go there.

They walk inside to find Dandi Swami sitting on a cushioned bench against the wall. He is an Indian in his mid-sixties - completely bald and completely naked. Jack and Dandi lock eyes as the three walk over and sit on the floor in front of him. Marcello and Cosmic each bow their heads to the floor.

MARCELLO

This is our friend from America. He's come to meditate with you today.

Dandi Swami gives Jack a subtle scowl and then closes his eyes. Marcello and Cosmic do the same. Hesitant, Jack follows. All sit cross-legged in meditation posture.

Dandi Swami starts his meditation instruction. He speaks in Hindi.

DANDI

(Hindi)

Meditation is the way to end the cause of suffering.

CLOSE UP: MARCELLO, JACK, AND COSMIC

As Dandi speaks, the camera slowly pans across their faces...from Marcello to Jack to Cosmic. They are relaxed with their eyes closed. As the camera moves across the faces of the three men, their interpretation of what Dandi Swami is preaching is revealed through Dandi's voice.

As we pan over Marcello's face, Dandi's voice is normal.

DANDI (O.S.)

Practice being mindful of all that we do...how we torture ourselves ...yes, abandon expectations. Out of Mindfulness, we develop awareness about the way things really are. Life is frustrating and painful. Suffering has a cause. We are all constantly struggling to survive.

The camera pans by Jack. Dandi's voice morphs into the voice of a sexy woman. Jack is smiling.

DANDI

(as Sexy Woman in half-whisper)

Jack...come on, concentrate, you silly boy. Ooo, I just love running my hand across your chest...give the girl a kiss, baby...ha ha ha...let's take these off and see what we find...yeah, that's what I like, ha ha ha....

The camera pans by Cosmic's face, and Dandi's voice changes to that of his mother.

DANDI

(Mother's voice)

I said, pick up your room young man, and I'm not going to tell you again! Do you want me to get your father in here?! He'll take you out to the woodshed, sure as hell!

EXT. MEDITATION COMPOUND, GATE - DAY

The three walk out as the gate closes behind them.

MARCELLO

Wow. It leaves one with a sense of emptiness that is somewhat euphoric. I think that was very beneficial. Didn't you?

COSMIC

I guess.

JACK

Absolutely.

MARCELLO

Now, in addition to meditation, we should each concentrate on another spiritual discipline. I'm going to be taking yoga classes every morning. Jack?

JACK

Yeah, I think I'll stick to meditation - I think I can make it work.

MARCELLO

Great, Jack.

Marcello and Jack look over to Cosmic, who is looking off, trying to avoid the question.

MARCELLO

Cosmic?

COSMIC

Yeah...uh, I'm thinking of taking a course in tantric sex. I heard that it's an excellent way to bring your mind and body together...you know...in the moment.

JACK

Tantric sex?

MARCELLO

That's great, Cosmic.

JACK

Perhaps that's something I should look into -

MARCELLO

I'd stay with the meditation, Jack.

Four giggly Australian girls come bouncing up to Jack.

GIRL #1

Are you Jack Bogart?

JACK
(smiling)
I am.

GIRL #2
My mother has always had an incredible crush on you.

JACK
(slightly disappointed)
Really?

GIRL #2
Oh yeah, for decades. She'd love a photograph...would you mind?

JACK
Of course not.

Girl #2 stands next to Jack as Girl #1 snaps a shot.

GIRL #2
Thank you, Mr. Bogart.

All but Girl #2 huddle around the camera to look at the picture.

Girl #2 stands there, staring at Jack.

Jack reaches out and swings her into his arms. He gives her a long passionate kiss on the lips. As he releases her, she seems faint and stumbles back into her friend's arms.

GIRL #2
Wow.

Girl #2 turns to her friends, and the four walk off.

Jack turns and smiles at Marcello and Cosmic.

JACK
Well, guys. I guess the old boy has a few more years left.

COSMIC
Wow.

EXT. RISHIKESH, PEDESTRIAN STREET - DAY

Marcello, Jack, and Cosmic stroll down the street.

COSMIC

You seem so confident with women, Mr. Bogart.

JACK

Why shouldn't I be?

Jack reaches over and wipes Cosmic's forehead.

JACK

You've got a little sweat going here, pal. Did those chicks make you nervous?

COSMIC

No.

JACK

You sure about that, Cosmic? You seem a bit shaky and -

MARCELLO

I think by tomorrow, you should decide on a suitable spiritual name for yourself.

JACK

What?

MARCELLO

A name; perhaps in the Buddhist or Yogic tradition, that you believe represents your being or spiritual personality.

Jack points at Marcello.

JACK

You prick! I know you. You've already got a name picked out for yourself, don't you?

Jack grabs hold of Cosmic's shirt and pulls him over.

JACK

It's just like him to have already selected the coolest name for himself and then decide we all need names!

COSMIC

I have a name, Mr. Bogart.

JACK

What?

COSMIC

Cosmic.

JACK

Oh, right.

MARCELLO

Cosmic and I had this conversation before you arrived.

Jack releases Cosmic and steps back - looking from one to the other.

JACK

Well, la-di-fucking-da. I suppose you've already picked one out for me, too.

MARCELLO

You can do that yourself.

COSMIC

It's cool.

JACK

Fine. That's why I'm here.

EXT. VED NIKETAN ASHRAM - MORNING

The sun is rising over the Himalayan foothills as the day comes to life. Birds are chirping, and monkeys are playing around the grounds of the ashram.

INTERCUT: MARCELLO AND COSMIC'S ROOMS - MORNING

MARCELLO'S ROOM

A small single room with a smoky haze, as incense and several candles burn in the diffused early morning sunlight. There are Buddhist votive figures on the table and pictures hanging on the walls. Dozens of spiritual books neatly line the shelves. Marcello is meditating, his body is wildly contorted in a yogic posture, his eyes are closed as he breathes slowly and deeply.

COSMIC'S ROOM

Same size as Marcello's, only it is in shambles. There is nothing organized about it. Clothes are strewn about the floor along with trash, and disheveled CDs. Cosmic lies asleep on the small bunk, wearing nothing but a pair of thong underwear - a copy of Hustler magazine lays over his chest with the centerfold opened.

INT. KITCHEN, VED NIKETAN ASHRAM - MORNING

Cooks, Waiters, and Kitchen help hustle around the kitchen. A TEA BOY (18) finishes preparing a pot of filtered coffee on a tray at the counter. He puts some wildflowers in a small glass as decoration, lifts the tray, and leaves.

EXT. VED NIKETAN ASHRAM - MORNING

Carefully carrying a tray, the Tea Boy walks across the courtyard.

INT. JACK'S ROOM, VED NIKETAN ASHRAM - MORNING

Jack, several pillows stacked behind him, lies up in bed reading a script. He's wearing reading glasses and a red satin robe. The walls of his room are covered with colorful Indian print fabrics, and the room is smartly furnished with a small lounge, tea table, and chairs.

Pen in hand, Jack makes notes and turns the pages in frustration.

There is a knock at the door.

JACK

Come in!

The Tea Boy enters Jack's room. He walks into the bedroom and stands there holding the tray. He gives Jack a flirtatious smile.

TEA BOY

I have your coffee, Mr. Bogart.

JACK

I can see that. Just put it over here where I can get to it and go.

Jack tosses a ten Rupee note onto a side table as the Tea Boy walks over to a small table next to Jack's bed and sets the tray down.

TEA BOY

It is told that you are a famous Bollywood actor, Mr. Bogart.

JACK

Bollywood? Do I look Indian to you?

TEA BOY

No, you look -

JACK

Then how can I be a Bollywood actor? I'm from Hollywood...that's Hollywood with an 'H'.

Jack pours himself a coffee and goes back to reading the script. The Tea Boy meanders down to Jack's feet and stares at them.

TEA BOY

May I please give you a massage, Mr. Bogart?

He reaches out and puts his hands on Jack's leg. Startled, Jack sits upright.

JACK

No! I don't want a massage.

The Tea Boy rubs Jack's leg. Jack angrily pulls his leg back. Just then, Marcello and Cosmic enter the room.

MARCELLO

Good morning, Jack. How did you sleep?

JACK

I slept fine.

(gestures to the Tea Boy)

Can you keep these freaks out of my room?

MARCELLO

What can I do? You're the caffeine junky.

The Tea Boy smiles at Marcello and Cosmic and walks out of the room.

JACK

That guy's so sexually tight, the first chick he fucks is going to explode.

MARCELLO

I don't think so.

JACK

Also, this is the worst hotel I've ever stayed in -

COSMIC

It's not a hotel; it's an ashram.

JACK

Look, this place needs to be cleaned, and all I've got to shower with is a God damn bucket and cold water.

MARCELLO

That's what all of us have, Jack.

Jack shakes his head in frustration.

JACK

This enlightenment thing better be worth it because I can see it severely trying our friendship.

MARCELLO

You better get up now; we've got a remarkable acquaintance to make.

EXT. RISHIKESH, DIRT PATH - DAY

Dressed in their white kurtas, Marcello, Jack, and Cosmic walk down the road.

Jack takes out his cell phone and puts it to his ear. He shakes it - then back to his ear.

JACK

But I don't want to destroy my ego. It's one of the few things about me that I really, really like.

MARCELLO

Jack, it's like being controlled by a little devilish puppet master in your head.

JACK

I don't have a problem with that.

Frustrated, Jack taps his phone, trying to get it to work - he can't.

MARCELLO

A great mind once said, that if Buddha or Jesus looked at us now, they'd be shocked because we're all emperors acting like beggars.

COSMIC

When one loses their ego, they find a hyper-reality...it's like an orgasm.

JACK

Orgasm?

Just then, the three stop and watch as another Jesus figure walks by. He has long hair, is bearded and robed, and is trailed by several followers.

Jack looks to Cosmic.

JACK

What would you know about orgasms?

Cosmic looks away. Marcello grabs hold of Jack's arm and whispers in his ear.

MARCELLO

Cosmic's got a little problem with women, Jack.

JACK

I think he's got a problem with more than that.

Jack shakes his phone and listens.

JACK

What's wrong with the service out here?

MARCELLO

Put that away, Jack. Try to find the moment.

JACK

I'd like to find a moment with my fucking phone, is what I'd like to find.

EXT. TEMPLE, MAHARAJA QUARTERS - DAY

Marcello, Jack, and Cosmic walk up to the rear of a temple. There are dozens of the Maharaja's disciples sitting on the ground leaning against the temple wall - many are Western, others Indian. Most are meditating, and a few are reading books or newspapers. All wear colorful loose-fitting new-age-ethnic-chic clothing.

There are two doorways covered with white drapery. Some disciples enter while others exit. One of the Maharaja's Attendants stands by the entry door, controlling who gets inside.

Marcello goes over to a metal trunk, pulls out some pillows, and hands them to Jack and Cosmic.

MARCELLO

Let's have a seat against the wall and meditate while we wait for our turn.

JACK

Wait our turn for what?

COSMIC

We're going to have an audience with the Maharaja.

EXT. TEMPLE, MAHARAJA QUARTERS - DAY

Eyes closed, Marcello, Jack, and Cosmic are sitting on pillows in a meditative posture. They're leaning against a wall in a long line of worshipers working their way toward the door to the Maharaja's quarters.

Jack opens his eyes to find a male dog sitting just a few feet in front of him. Jack watches as the dog starts licking its genitals. Jack elbows the disciple sitting next to him and breaks his trance. Several other meditators look over as Jack gestures for them to slide over to him.

CLOSE UP: JACK AND NINE DISCIPLES

The Disciples lean towards Jack as they huddle up.

JACK

(half-whisper)

These two salesmen were walking across a hotel lobby when they came upon a dog licking itself.

(he nods toward the dog)

One salesman says to the other, 'I wish I could do that', the other salesman retorts, 'Really? I wish I could do it to myself.'

The crowd of disciples breaks out into hysterical laughter, disrupting the concentration of all within earshot. Jack quickly reverts back to his meditation posture as the Maharaja's ATTENDANT rushes out of the door and angrily quiets everyone down. He then signals for Marcello, Jack, and Cosmic to come inside.

The three stand and follow the Attendant.

INT. MAHARAJA QUARTERS - DAY

Marcello leads Jack and Cosmic inside. The Attendant signals for them to step into the foyer and wait. A muffled conversation is heard from inside the Maharaja's quarters.

The door to his quarters is slightly ajar. Jack reaches over and opens it a little further. Marcello frowns at Jack as he mischievously smiles back. The voice of a VALLEY GIRL emanates out of the private chamber. Unable to help themselves, the three lean forward to listen.

VALLEY GIRL

I guess what I'm saying, Raj, is like; this is, like, totally not working. I mean, there are too many girls around here, and I'm a very jealous person.

MAHARAJA

Well, perhaps -

VALLEY GIRL

And how can you, like, totally not love me, too? I mean, I know you're holy and sacred, and enlightened, and everything, but -

MAHARAJA

Reality is a parable of what we perceive as -

VALLEY GIRL

No. Stop. So, anyway, like, I think this is, like, goodbye. The Buddha, like, is so totally out! Bye, little Buddha boy. Bye, fat sumo Buddha.

MAHARAJA

The actual Buddha should only be -

VALLEY GIRL

Like, my Mom was totally right about what she said after my bat mitzvah. Older men are just relics not worth collecting. So this is it, Raj - guess I'll see you in the next life, or the afterlife - well, maybe.

The Valley Girl leaves through the exit of the private chamber.

MAHARAJA

Goodbye, my dear.

Jack and Cosmic look back at Marcello with amazement.

The Attendant steps into the foyer, holding the door open for the three to enter.

As he enters, Marcello turns to Jack and whispers.

MARCELLO

This guy is totally equal to the Buddha.

Dumbfounded, Jack turns and looks back at Cosmic as they follow.

INT. MAHARAJA'S PRIVATE CHAMBER - DAY

Jack sits on the floor as Marcello and Cosmic bend over and prostrate themselves to the living deity. The Maharaja is a frail old man with long white hair and a long white beard. He is lying on a bed and looks very feeble.

He mumbles something to his Attendant. The Attendant turns to the three.

ATTENDANT

Is there anything that you would like to ask his holiness?

MARCELLO

Yes. We are seeking a mindful path to enlightenment. Can you help us to understand life's contradictions that create obstacles to this path?

The Maharaja looks upward for a moment as if gathering strength and knowledge from the heavens. His head slowly tilts back down, and he looks at all three sitting on the floor before him. He speaks in a weak, strained voice.

MAHARAJA

We live in a world of duality. Happiness with sadness, love with hate, selflessness with selfishness. All these attributes are two-sided coins. We all consist of these characteristics, and our struggle to have one side without the other causes us to suffer. Accepting yourself as you are and dropping the desire to change will create transformation. It might seem paradoxical, but it is the only way.

COSMIC

So, acceptance of our imperfections will release the suffering we feel?

MAHARAJA

Kind of like that, yes. Have you been to the great tree?

MARCELLO

Not yet.

MAHARAJA

Go there.

The Attendant signals with a wave of his arm for the three to stand up to depart.

JACK

Wait a minute. Listen, Raj, I've got a meeting with Marty Scorsese when I get back to L.A. It's for a very important part in his new film that would help jump-start my comeback -

Marcello and Cosmic stand up - together with the Attendant, they look down at a pleading Jack.

MARCELLO

Jack, that's not what this is about.

JACK

Give me a minute, guys!
(to Maharaja)
So, what do you say, Raj? Am I going to get the part or what?

The Maharaja stares at Jack for a moment. Raising his hand to his head, he slowly leans forward as if he's about to speak to him when...the Attendant slips a cell phone into the Maharaja's hand, and he starts speaking Hindi into it.

Marcello and Cosmic lean over and pull Jack up to his feet.

JACK

He was going to say something!

COSMIC

He's on the phone, Mr. Bogart.

MARCELLO

Time to go, Jack.

Together with the Attendant, they lead Jack out of the Maharaja's chamber.

EXT. TEMPLE, MAHARAJA QUARTERS - DAY

Marcello and Cosmic help a stunned Jack out the door and back among the disciples in the waiting area. A dazed Jack stares off into space.

MARCELLO

Let's go have a lassi.

EXT. RISHIKESH, GRASS PATCH NEAR BRIDGE - DAY

Marcello and Cosmic are sitting cross-legged while Jack is leaning back on the grass. The three are drinking lassi as they watch the passers-by.

COSMIC

Have you selected a spiritual name yet, Jack?

JACK

Mr. Bogart.

COSMIC

I'm sorry. Have you selected a spiritual name yet, Mr. Bogart?

JACK

You don't understand. Mr. Bogart is my spiritual name.

MARCELLO

Everyone in Los Angeles is so affected. All they do is sit around people watching...passing judgment on everyone that walks by.

JACK

That might be true, but at least it's something we take very seriously.

MARCELLO

Look at that group over there. The El Segundo New Age Club.

COSMIC

And there's a Yogananda wanna-be if I've ever seen one.

JACK

Is he wearing mascara?

COSMIC

Two o'clock - I do yoga as an excuse so I can eat like a fucking pig when I'm alone in my room.

Marcello and Jack give a surprised look over to Cosmic.

COSMIC

What?

Jack looks up to some passers-by.

JACK

These guys remind me of you two.

ANGLE ON:

Two Indian men are walking together, holding hands.

MARCELLO

Here she is, Cosmic.

ANGLE ON:

The three look over to find CHER, a young, pretty, western girl walking by. As it happens, she looks just like the singer Cher did in the 1960s. She glances over and smiles at Cosmic.

JACK

Hey, what's that all about?

COSMIC

Nothing.

MARCELLO

Jack.

JACK

Come on, Cosmic. Make a move on her.

MARCELLO

Leave it alone, Jack.

Jack stands up and signals to the Girl to come over to them. She does so.

JACK

Hello. I'm Jack Bogart, the actor.

CHER

Yes, I recognized you.

JACK

And what would your name be?

CHER

Cher.

JACK

Cher?

CHER

My father was a huge fan of the singer in the eighties and so -

JACK

Yes, I get it. Well, Cher, have you met my friend Cosmic here?

CHER

No, but I noticed that he's always watching me.

JACK

And for an excellent good reason, Cher.

Jack and Cher look over to Cosmic, who is staring off.

JACK

Cosmic, this lovely little thing here, is Cher.

CHER

Hello, Cosmic.

COSMIC

Hello, Cher.

JACK

Cosmic's a graduate student at the uh, Institute of Shadow Reading.

MARCELLO

The Colorado Institute of Integral Studies.

CHER

Oh, I've heard so much about that school. What's it like?

Cosmic looks up to Cher.

COSMIC

It's okay. I'm studying to be a life coach and holistic learning counselor. Jeez, you're pretty. You're even prettier than Cher, Cher.

JACK

Well put, Cosmic. Are you enlightened, Cher?

CHER

No, I'm not.

JACK

Well, Cosmic here is going to become enlightened in a couple of days.

MARCELLO

It might take a little longer than that.

JACK

Okay, then, a week...whatever. You know some people are slower than others.

CHER
That's great, Cosmic. Good luck.

COSMIC
Thanks, Cher. When I'm enlightened, I'll reach nirvana. And if nirvana is anything like being near you, I think it'll be fabulous.

CHER
Thank you, Cosmic. Well, I'm off to my yoga class.

Marcello's eyes perk up.

CHER
It was nice meeting you, Cosmic.

MARCELLO
You're taking yoga?

CHER
Yes, I love it.

JACK
Marcello, down boy. Cher, Cosmic is going to be taking a course in tantric sex. I think you should take it with him.

CHER
Tantric sex? I don't know -

JACK
Oh, come on, it's not real sex. For Cosmic, it'll be just like masturbating; only you'll be there to help.

COSMIC
It's okay, Cher.

JACK
It's my treat. I mean...I'll pay for the course...you know, tantric sex on me.

CHER
Well, I have wanted to try the class.

JACK
Done. Where are you staying, Cher?

CHER
I'm at the Sri Yoga Ashram.

JACK
Great, I'll send you a note as to the schedule.

CHER
Okay. Yeah, great. See you then, Cosmic.

COSMIC
Bye, Cher.

Cher bounces off as Cosmic and Marcello give Jack a questioning stare.

JACK
What?

EXT. VED NIKETAN ASHRAM - DAY

Jack is leaning against a column of the veranda, smoking a cigarette. Together with KARINA (32), a pretty Danish woman, Marcello is doing some stretching exercises.

The three watch as the ashram Desk Clerk and some other workers drag a struggling, tussling YOGI from the building.

YOGI
(Hindi)
Let me go!

They leave him in a heap of dust on the dirt road in front of the ashram.

DESK CLERK
(Hindi)
You'll never work in this town again!

Jack looks over to Marcello.

JACK

Marcello?!

KARINA

The ashram's guru died last night, and now there's a power struggle.

JACK

Great! I arrive, and a day later, our fucking guru dies. I'm out of here.

MARCELLO

He's not our guru.

JACK

No?

MARCELLO

He's the ashram's guru. He's not even on my critical list of local holy men.

JACK

Was he enlightened?

MARCELLO

Perhaps.

KARINA

Tomorrow you can watch his cremation at the river.

MARCELLO/JACK

Cool.

Just then, Cosmic comes bolting out of his room, naked and cringing, with only a towel wrapped around his waist.

COSMIC

Oh, man! I need some toilet paper! Quick!

JACK

What the fuck!?

Cosmic holds out a single sheet of toilet paper to prove his point. Marcello takes it from him and eyes it.

MARCELLO

You don't need more toilet paper, Cosmic...you need to learn origami.

Marcello quickly folds the toilet paper into an elaborate geometric bird that is considerably larger than the single sheet of paper Cosmic had.

Cosmic turns and leaves, holding the origami sculpture as he passes the Tea Boy.

TEA BOY

That is a lovely object. What are you going to do with it, Cosmic, decorate your room?

COSMIC

No. Use it to wipe my ass.

Cosmic rushes off, leaving the Tea Boy stunned.

JACK

This might sound cruel; but I wish Cher were here to see this.

INT. YOGA CENTER - DAY

Marcello is among twenty other people doing yoga. The INSTRUCTOR is an Indian Master and has them all doing very challenging postures. Apart from Marcello, the students are all western women.

Marcello eyes all the beautiful girls in class. In their extreme contortions, the contours of their bodies become exaggerated, and Marcello can't help himself for spying on the women. They are all beauties and eye Marcello flirtatiously as they catch his wandering eyes.

EXT. RISHIKESH, NARROW ALLEYWAY - DAY

Jack is sitting on top of a walled embankment in a cross-legged meditative posture. He is wearing sunglasses, and he is seemingly in deep meditation. Three OLDER INDIAN men walk past and notice him.

OLDER INDIAN #1

(Hindi)

Get a load of this one.

The three laugh and then turn their heads away from Jack. Just as they turn away, Jack's head twists to look at them - they turn back to him just as he jerks his head back to a meditative posture.

OLDER INDIAN #2

He must have started with a huge ego.

The three laugh and again turn their heads away from Jack. Just as before, Jack's head turns, and he looks at them - they quickly turn back to Jack just as he snaps his head back to his meditative posture - again missing eye contact with each other.

Jack turns his head and watches as a small funerary procession marches by. Several men sing and play clumsy make-shift instruments as they carry a body on a hand-made wooden gurney. The three pause as they stare at Jack for a moment, then turn and walk off.

Jack jumps down from the wall and follows.

INT. COMSIC'S ROOM, VED NIKETAN ASHRAM - DAY

With a mixed expression of fascination and horror, Cosmic peruses a diagram of tantric sex postures made up of tiny graphics of men and women.

INT. YOGA CENTER - DAY

Marcello is doing yoga but is heavily involved in multiple flirtations at the same time. Several of the women in the class show interest in him. Marcello smiles at them as they change postures while following the Instructor's commands.

Just as Marcello is exchanging smiles with a gorgeous fellow student, he cuts loose and audible fart. The woman's smile instantly turns into a frown. He panics and looks away from her, only to find that all the women in the class are frowning at him now. What was once a blissful cloud of flirtation has become a storm of disappointment.

EXT. ASHRAM COURTYARD - TWILIGHT

Cosmic and Jack are sitting on the stoop of Marcello's room when Marcello steps out.

MARCELLO

The Tea Boy said he saw you following a funeral procession down to the Ganga.

JACK

Yeah, I marched with the group down to the rocks.

COSMIC

How was the funeral?

JACK

I didn't stay. I figured they're torching our guru tomorrow, so -

COSMIC

He's not our guru.

JACK

Whatever.

Marcello wipes his face with a towel.

COSMIC

How was your yoga class?

MARCELLO

Fine.

JACK

Any cute chicks?

MARCELLO

A few.

JACK

So?

MARCELLO

I don't know; everything was going great until -

COSMIC

Until what?

MARCELLO

Until it just, stopped.

JACK

You blew it, uh?

MARCELLO

Something like that - anyway, I'm calling it a day.

Marcello walks into his room.

EXT. RISHIKESH, VED NIKETAN ASHRAM - MORNING

To the backdrop of a frightening shrill sound - a group of small Indian children is huddled in a corner outside the ashram. Their faces are contorted in horror.

ANGLE ON:

Cosmic, arms shrunken against his body, hands shaped like claws, and mouth gnawing as he shrieks - he's doing his famous 'raptor' imitation and scaring the hell out of the kids.

Jack walks outside to find Cosmic in full raptor glory - the kids screaming.

JACK

Hey!

Shocked, Cosmic and the kids stop and turn to Jack.

JACK

What the fuck are you doing?!

COSMIC

I'm just playing with the kids.

The children take the opportunity to turn and run off. Jack and Cosmic watch them.

JACK

Sure you weren't playing with yourself, Cosmic?

COSMIC

No. I did that earlier.

Jack eyes Cosmic as Marcello walks up.

MARCELLO

Good morning, my fellow spiritualists.

JACK

You seem chirpy this morning.

MARCELLO

I feel chirpy, Jack.

The three walk off.

JACK

Were you with Cosmic earlier?

EXT. RISHIKESH VILLAGE ROAD - MORNING

Marcello, Jack, and Cosmic talk as they walk the road.

MARCELLO

So, in my dream, there was a path - a path on which there was no coming and no going.

COSMIC

Like the eternal home?

MARCELLO

Exactly. A place where nothing ever happens. Nothing changes, nothing is born, nothing dies - the eternal present moment.

JACK

Sounds to me like you're suicidal.

They walk by another man who looks like Jesus Christ. He is sitting on a log with his legs crossed while reading a book entitled "Jesus Lived In India."

Jack stops to ponder the scene. Marcello and Cosmic linger with Jack.

JACK

Jesus lived in India. Did Jesus live in India?

Marcello smiles as the three continue their stroll.

MARCELLO

Many believe that in search of wisdom, Jesus made his way to the Indus region and studied under Hindu and Buddhist masters.

JACK

You'd think he'd just talk to his old man.

Marcello and Cosmic eye Jack.

JACK

You know, God.

COSMIC

It's also believed he went to Ephesus and Persia during the missing eighteen years.

MARCELLO

They say he sailed across the Arabian Sea and back to Palestine.

JACK

Why didn't he just walk?

Marcello and Cosmic eye Jack.

JACK

You know, he could walk on water.

COSMIC

Through references in the Buddhist text, researchers have documented that a remarkable man had passed through Persia, Afghanistan, and Pakistan. All the way to Kashmir.

MARCELLO

He was accompanied by his mother, who died along the way.

JACK

Well, what did he expect? I mean, making her walk through the fucking desert.

Marcello and Cosmic eye Jack as they arrive at a small shop.

JACK

Okay...so Jesus lived in India. Hallelujah. Where are we headed?

COSMIC

To see an astrologist.

Jack freezes at the door, as Marcello and Cosmic step inside

INT. ASTROLOGIST STUDIO - MORNING

Inside a colorful room, surrounded by pictures of great holy men on the walls, Marcello, Cosmic, and Jack sit on a carpeted floor across from an ASTROLOGER.

ASTROLOGER

Death is the beginning, not the end.

COSMIC

Aloneness is our ultimate nature.

ASTROLOGER

Exactly. When death knocks on the door, you will have to leave everything as it was.

COSMIC

One comes empty-handed, and one leaves empty-handed, and still one goes on accumulating.

MARCELLO

Well put, Cosmic.

Jack smiles at Cosmic.

JACK

Yes, very profound, Cosmic.

Jack locks eyes with the Astrologist.

MARCELLO

This is Jack Bogart. Jack, this is Krishna. His family has occupied this shop for eighty-four years.

COSMIC

He's going to give us a cosmic reading of our past and destiny.

ASTROLOGER

My wife is a big fan of yours, Mr. Bogart.

JACK

Thank you, Krishna. I'd be happy to give you an autograph for her if you have a piece of -

ASTROLOGER

That won't be necessary. Shall we continue?

INT. ASTROLOGIST STUDIO - LATER

The three are sitting around the Astrologist as he speaks.

COSMIC

So, there is nothing more you can tell me about my future?

ASTROLOGER

I'm afraid all I keep getting is grave darkness -

COSMIC

Like I have no future?

ASTROLOGER

It's more than that - like you have no - existence. Like you were a mistake.

They all look at Cosmic.

A LITTLE LATER

The Astrologer is giving Marcello a reading.

ASTROLOGER

These coming months will bring you a great awakening - you should continue to follow the path you are on -

COSMIC
How long will he live?

ASTROLOGER
He will live a full life -

COSMIC
When will he die?

ASTROLOGER
He will die on December -

MARCELLO
No, no, no! Shit, don't tell me that!

ASTROLOGER
Sorry.

MARCELLO
Fuck. Now, for the rest of my life, every December is going to be absolute hell.

COSMIC
At least he didn't tell you the date.

ASTROLOGER
The twentieth.

Marcello looks at the Astrologist and shakes his head in disbelief.

JACK
What year was that?

MARCELLO
No!

EXT. RISHIKESH, NARROW ALLEYWAY - DAY

They walk down an alleyway. A line of small horses carrying rocks from up in the hills passes them as they talk.

MARCELLO

What we learned from Krishna will help us to interpret the karmatologist's analysis.

JACK

Karmatologist?

MARCELLO

We're going to have a complete karmic breakdown.

JACK

When?

MARCELLO

Now.

COSMIC

We have to determine any karmacalatical adjustments that we have to make before we can become enlightened.

JACK

Karmacalatical is not even a word.

Marcello and Cosmic stare at Jack.

INT. KARMATOLOGIST STUDIO - DAY

Similar to the Astrologist's studio, but different - the KARMATOLOGIST has a large book opened on his lap as he reviews Jack's karma scale. Marcello and Cosmic watch.

KARMATOLOGIST

Your ledger seems heavily tilted towards the negative. That is why you're so sad.

JACK

Sad? I'm one of the most upbeat people I know.

KARMATOLOGIST

But your wife, she left you in the middle of an important project.

JACK

What are you talking about - that was the happiest day of my life. I had a twenty-two-year-old girlfriend I was banging four times a week.

KARMATOLOGIST

Yes, but your wife got the house in Palm Desert and the Lamborghini.

JACK

Right. Now that was fucked-up.

KARMATOLOGIST

Any intentional action in the present or past life. Mental, verbal, physical - they're all karma.

JACK

How can you expect me to be responsible for a past life?

The Karmatologist scans the ledger and looks up.

KARMATOLOGIST

Your past lives are not so bad.

JACK

Well, that's encouraging.

KARMATOLOGIST

And your children. They all condemn you.

JACK

I uh, don't have any kids.

COSMIC

Do abortions count?

The Karmatologist ponders the question.

JACK

Shit, I hope not.

They all stare at Jack.

MARCELLO

So how does Jack balance his karmatic ledger?

The Karmatologist scans the ledger again.

KARMATOLOGIST

In this life, he doesn't.

INTERCUT: MARCELLO, JACK AND COSMIC - NIGHT

MARCELLO'S ROOM

In the mist of a yellow glow, Marcello finishes lighting the final of many candles - incense is burning - he reaches over to an iPod and puts on some soft Indian music.

COSMIC'S ROOM

Cosmic's eyes focus on a mosquito flying around his room - his hand out, ready to swat it. The mosquito flies around his head, and Cosmic slaps the insect into his face. His hand lowers as the flattened mosquito sticks to his forehead.

JACK'S ROOM

Jack is wearing a red satin robe. A beautiful INDIAN WOMAN follows him to his bed. She helps him off with his robe exposing a pair of red satin pajama bottoms. He lies down on his stomach as she pulls out some oils and starts giving him a massage.

WOMAN

You just relax, Mr. Bogart. This will put you to sleep in no time.

JACK

Sleep? Let's hope not.

EXT. RISHIKESH VILLAGE STREET, RESTAURANT - MORNING

Marcello and Jack are sitting at a table having breakfast. A monkey sits on top of the table.

MARCELLO

Quantum entanglement refers to situations wherein the properties of several discrete objects cannot be described simply by considering them separately, even after taking account of the history of their past interaction. A quantum interaction can affect the entangled quantum entity in a similar manner even though the two are widely separated.

Jack looks over to Cosmic, rolls his eyes, and then looks back to Marcello.

JACK

So, what you're saying is that you can feel this?

Jack reaches out and pokes his cigarette into a cow standing next to the table. The cow groans as Marcello raises his hand.

MARCELLO

No! Jack, that's not cool.

JACK

A better example.

Jack reaches over and grabs hold of the monkey. He stretches out the monkey's right arm, lifts a large meat cleaver from the table, and chops it off at the elbow - the monkey shrieks and runs off, blood splattering everywhere.

Jack gestures towards the monkey, now running off, its horrific shriek fading in the distance.

JACK

Anything Marcello? A little tingle?

Marcello and Cosmic silently look on in shock.

JACK

Okay, one more example.

MARCELLO

Jack. You're absolutely twisted.

JACK
I guess what I'm saying is -
really, what the fuck do we know?

MARCELLO
Understood.

Jack looks at Cosmic.

JACK
Big day today, uh, stud?

COSMIC
Yeah, you know, guys, I'm not feeling too good. I might just skip it.

JACK
No fucking way, Snow White!

MARCELLO
I'm sure it's just a case of nerves.

JACK
You're going to walk into that class, go down on your knees and take all that chick wants to give you.

COSMIC
What?!

MARCELLO
Cosmic, I think what Jack's trying to convey is that as uncomfortable as you feel about it now, you'll feel a sense of accomplishment and unique spiritual insight into an ancient practice by completing the class.

Jack stands from the table.

JACK
Exactly. Now, let's get to it.

EXT. RISHIKESH VILLAGE STREET, DAY - MORNING

The three talk as they stroll the shop-lined pedestrian path through the town.

MARCELLO

So, Cosmic, it's very important that you listen to everything that Mama Love teaches you, but try to simultaneously flat-line all the nervous energy and random thoughts that are sure to be bouncing around in your skull.

JACK

Don't flat-line your cock, though.

MARCELLO

Remember, at its base, this is a meditative, spiritual endeavor. Try to keep all things physical and mental, relaxed…quiet.

JACK

If she starts to give you a low hum followed by short body jerks, you'll know you've found pay dirt.

MARCELLO

Jack, please.

Jack looks over and smiles at Cosmic.

JACK

You look all cleaned up. What did you get, a haircut?

COSMIC

Yeah, a number one.

JACK

What?

COSMIC

A number one. All over.

Jack looks over to Marcello.

JACK
What the fuck is he -

MARCELLO
He's had his entire body shaved using the number one setting on an electric razor.

Jack turns to Cosmic.

JACK
Your entire body?

COSMIC
Head, chin, chest, and balls.

JACK
That's fucking sick, man.

COSMIC
The ladies love it.

JACK
And just how would you know that, you little shit?

MARCELLO
Jack.

JACK
I'm serious, man. Do we have to put up with this punk's -

MARCELLO
Jack, you and Cosmic are brothers. Besides, the tantric sex thing was your idea.

JACK
Yeah. Well, perhaps it'll make a man out of him. Now he's a bloody fairy.

COSMIC
Happy trail.

JACK
What?

COSMIC

I also shaved my happy trail.

Jack gives Marcello an exhausted look.

EXT. TANTRIC STUDIO, DAY - MORNING

The three arrive outside the tantric sex studio. A sign above the curtained door reads, "YOU'RE ABOUT TO MAKE MAMA LOVE." Cher and a couple of other students hurriedly make their way to the door. Cher stops and looks over to Cosmic before she disappears inside. Mama Love, the large, busty, blonde woman introduced earlier, steps outside and looks over to Cosmic.

MAMA LOVE

You comin' honey?

Marcello pats Cosmic on the back as he walks him over to her.

COSMIC

I guess so.

Mama Love looks over to Jack.

MAMA LOVE

What about you, big shot? I'll give you hands-on instruction.

JACK

I appreciate the offer, madame. But I've got my own technique.

MAMA LOVE

I give advanced lessons some evenings.

JACK

As do I.

MAMA LOVE

Okay, then.

Mama Love smiles and disappears behind the curtain.

Marcello turns to Jack.

MARCELLO

How 'bout the best cappuccino you've ever had?

JACK

No shit?

MARCELLO

No shit.

INT. TANTRIC STUDIO, DAY - MORNING

Cosmic and Cher are sitting on the floor atop large padded mats. Along with twelve other couples, they are looking up to Mama Love as she paces the front of the class while delivering her lecture.

MAMA LOVE

Women, if you want to keep your man, you have to be willing to fuck him to God!

She excitedly points upwards.

MAMA LOVE

And, ladies, I don't want to hear how you can't feel it or how he's not doing it right because it's all bull shit! You're going to fake it 'til you make it!

Cher looks over to a nervous Cosmic. He returns her look with an uneasy smile.

EXT. GERMAN BAKERY, DAY - DAY

Marcello and Jack are perched at a shady table at a restaurant overlooking the Ganges River. Shanti, a white-haired, middle-aged woman wearing an off-white dress, sits at their table while speaking to them. She is holding her hands out, demonstrating a massage technique. Marcello is engrossed in what Shanti is saying, while Jack is lackadaisical.

SHANTI

Through your hands, the earth's energy and life force is conducted to the receiver. Those powers transmitted into the body will help induce a meditative state and calm and heal the body.

MARCELLO

And that's called reiki.

SHANTI

Yes. I teach classes four days a week just down that road.

A WAITER arrives and puts a couple of cappuccinos down on the table. Marcello and Jack lift their glasses to each other as a toast and then take a sip.

JACK

So, you're telling me that this massage is done with both parties completely clothed.

SHANTI

Of course.

JACK

Is there such a thing as nude reiki?

MARCELLO

Jack, not all human contact has to have a layer of sexuality imposed on it.

JACK

No, but it makes it much more enjoyable.

SHANTI

More enjoyable?

Jack smiles at Shanti as he reaches over and cups her hand under his.

JACK

Exactly, can you feel it?

BEAT

SHANTI

No.

INT. TANTRIC STUDIO - DAY

All the students in the class are fully clothed and are following Mama Love's instructions.

MAMA LOVE

Men, keep moving around but no hands, all body - a woman needs about forty-five minutes of foreplay before she is ready - where a man needs about five seconds.

CLOSE UP: COSMIC AND CHER

Cosmic is on top of Cher - their faces are only an inch apart as Cosmic's body undulates over Cher's. Cher is smiling, but there is still nervousness on Cosmic's face.

CHER

I think you're the one that needs forty-five minutes.

MAMA LOVE (O.S.)

Okay, close your eyes, everybody - keep moving, but close your eyes. Let your imagination go with it.

Cosmic and Cher each close their eyes as Cosmic continues his handless foreplay.

MAMA LOVE (O.S.)

A woman's G-spot is just under her clitoris. A man, his G-spot is in his anus, and when it gets excited, it gets as hot as a poker.

Cosmic's eyes quickly open as his face turns to terror. Cher opens her eyes, smiles at Cosmic, then reaches up and softly closes his eyes with her fingers.

MAMA LOVE (O.S.)

Keep it up, everyone. The tantric wave of pleasure is always there, and anytime you want, you can jump in and surf it.

A subtle smile creases Cosmic's face as we zoom closer to him - foggy haze envelopes us as we enter Cosmic's imagination.

EXT. WATERFALL, COSMIC'S IMAGINATION, FOGGY-HAZE - DAY

Cosmic and Cher are standing nude in each other's arms as water showers over them. They kiss each other's shoulders, neck, cheeks, and lips. They are blissfully smiling as they lean back - holding hands, they start spinning around.

EXT. GERMAN BAKERY - DAY

Marcello and Jack are sitting alone, halfway through their cappuccinos.

JACK

I bet that little fucker is shaking in a corner somewhere.

MARCELLO

It was a nice gesture on your part, Jack. I'm going to meditate for a few minutes and send Cosmic some positive energy.

Marcello leans back and closes his eyes. Jack gives Marcello a half-hearted smile.

Looking O.S., Jack spots something of interest. He drains his cappuccino, gets up, and walks off.

EXT. ARTISAN'S SHOP - DAY

Standing at the shop are three men dressed in light-colored robes. One is a Jesus wanna-be, and he holds up a small wooden crucifix and eyes it.

JESUS

Has either of you ever seen such a thing?

OTHERS

No. Never.

JESUS

What a peculiar item.

Jack walks up.

JACK

Hello.

JESUS

Good afternoon, brother.

Jack takes the crucifix out of Jesus' hand and places it on the counter with other collectible items.

JACK

So, tell me, are you, Jesus? The messiah?

JESUS

Messiah? True, my name is Jesus, but I'm just a carpenter from Nazareth.

JACK

A carpenter? Listen, I've got a little bungalow in Ojai that needs new kitchen cabinets. Could you give me an estimate?

JESUS

Ojai?

TANTRIC STUDIO - DAY

Cosmic is lying on top of Cher - their faces only inches apart. Cher looks concerned. Cosmic's face is wearing a spacey surreal smile as he speaks in a deep, suave, playboy falsetto.

COSMIC

(playboy)

It's alright, baby. I'm in complete control.

CHER

Cosmic. Are you okay?

COSMIC

(playboy)

I've never been better than I am at this moment, in this place, with this woman.

He slides around Cher's body as his eyes roll back in his head.

CHER

Cosmic. You're starting to make me uncomfortable.

Cosmic moans as he reaches some sort of climax.

EXT. GERMAN BAKERY - DAY

Marcello is sitting lotus style in meditation. As we enter the emptiness of his mental, meditative state, an act of Jack's past is replayed.

FLASHBACK: JACK

INT. CHIC HOLLYWOOD RESTAURANT - OTHER WORLD

Jack is with a beautiful WOMAN walking through a chic Hollywood eatery. There's a fuss about him as photographers follow Jack with cameras flashing. Arm around the woman, he winks at the doorman as they walk out the front door.

EXT. CHIC HOLLYWOOD RESTAURANT - SAME

Jack and the woman step out of the restaurant as a CRAZED WRITER approaches them, confronting Jack.

CRAZED WRITER

Jack Bogart!

Jack hands him his valet ticket.

JACK

It's the silver Carrera.

CRAZED WRITER

I'll call you! I'd love to work with you! That's what you said.

JACK

Have we met?

CRAZED WRITER

Eight months ago at the Sunset Marquis. We had drinks together. I gave you my screenplay, and you promised you'd read it and call me.

JACK

Let me guess. I didn't.

CRAZED WRITER

That's right!

JACK

Pal, if you knew anything about Hollywood, you'd know that nobody reads random screenplays. "I'll call you" is just a line to blow people off.

CRAZED WRITER

What?

The Crazed Writer pulls a revolver out from his jacket and points it at Jack's chest.

JACK

Get the fuck out of my way.

Jack reaches out to brush away the Crazed Writer. As he does, the Crazed Writer fires a shot into Jack's chest.

Jack falls backward into the arms of the Woman and the Doorman as the Crazed Writer runs off.

Jack lies dying in the Woman's arms.

EXT. GERMAN BAKERY - DAY

Marcello, sitting lotus style, suddenly breaks out of his meditative state as if awakening from a bad dream.

EXT. GANGES RIVER - DAY

Cosmic and Cher are in a rowboat at a calm part of the river. Cosmic works the oars as Cher, her face hardened, looks O.S. - Cosmic speaks in his normal voice.

COSMIC

Wow. That was the weirdest sensation I've had since...since I tried to have my nipples pierced.

CHER

Just forget it. Can we get out of this thing? I need some time alone.

COSMIC

But Mama Love said that it would be good for us to spend some quiet time together.

CHER
I don't give a shit what that fat pimp thinks.

COSMIC
I'll get us ashore.

CHER
Did you really have your nipples pierced?

COSMIC
Well...nipple. Singular.

Cher looks down at the water.

ANGLE ON:

A human body floats in the water near the boat. The body rolls over as it drifts. The body is the mirror image of Cosmic, eyes closed, dead.

BACK TO:

Cher looks on in terror as she watches the body float off.

COSMIC
Jeez, what's wrong with you?

CHER
Did you see that?

COSMIC
What?

CHER
A dead...you.

COSMIC
Cher, you're freaking me out.

EXT. RISHIKESH, DIRT PATH - DAY

Marcello and Cosmic are talking as they walk.

MARCELLO

Well, Cosmic, it's true that an essential aspect of tantric sex is to minimize the energy lost during sex - which means you don't -

COSMIC

I couldn't help it!

MARCELLO

It's okay. You just have to keep working it.

Cosmic looks up ahead.

COSMIC

There's Mr. Bogart.

EXT. RISHIKESH, DIRT PATH, LINE OF SADHUS - DAY

Chillum in hand, Jack is standing next to a SADHU MASTER in front of a group of queued-up sadhus.

CLOSE UP: JACK, SADHU MASTER, SADHU FASHION SHOW

The Sadhu Master is dressed in an elaborate polychromatic robe and headdress. He's also tricked out with many strands of beads and bangles on his ankles and wrists. Like he's the host at a beauty contest, the Sadhu Master describes his brethren as they step forward.

Jack takes a massive drag off of a chillum. He coughs, and his head jerks about as he tries to hold the smoke in his lungs.

A sadhu, with his head shaved up to a single lock of hair and wearing an orange costume, steps up and poses.

SADHU MASTER

(Hindi accent)

The Vaishnava ascetic must undergo a shaving and bath ceremony and wear an ochre-colored achla and longoti.

The Sadhu Master points to different articles of clothing on the sadhu's body.

SADHU MASTER

He places twelve sectarian marks on his body and is given a new spiritual name after the ceremony. This sadhu's name is Sampradaya, and he's from Varanasi. His hobbies are begging and smoking ganja.

Sampradaya walks off.

Jack blows out some more smoke.

JACK

Cool. We have spiritual names.

SADHU MASTER

What is your spiritual name, sir?

JACK

Mr...uh....

Jack spots Marcello and Cosmic.

JACK

Hey, Marcello! Guys, come over here.

Another sadhu, dressed in red and holding a long walking stick, steps up.

Marcello and Cosmic walk up to Jack and the Sadhu Master.

SADHU MASTER

This sadhu's name is Mahaprabhu. He's a Namawat sadhu. The Namawat bears two vertical lines of clay on their forehead with a central black spot. They carry a rosary of sacred tulsi wood and roam throughout the entire year. Mahaprabhu is from Pushkar, and his hobbies are begging and smoking ganja.

Jack laughs, then takes another hit from the chillum as Mahaprabhu walks off, and another sadhu, dressed in black and carrying a three-pointed spear, steps up.

SADHU MASTER

This is the Tridandis sadhu.

The Sadhu Master's voice drifts off, as the focus turns to Marcello.

SADHU MASTER (O.S.)
The Tridandis always dress in black, and they carry a trident, or three-pointed staff with them.

MARCELLO
Jack, I thought that we agreed to stay away from mind-altering distractions.

Jack looks over to Marcello and Cosmic.

SADHU MASTER (O.S.)
...and his hobbies are begging and smoking ganja.

JACK
This is nothing, really, just tobacco in a weird stone pipe.

SADHU MASTER
It's yak bone.

JACK
Yak bone?

MARCELLO
And that's not just tobacco.

JACK
(looking to Sadhu Master)
Yes, it is...right?

SADHU MASTER
No. It is a unique mixture of tobacco, cannabis, and hashish.

JACK
Well, anyway, it must be okay because all these guys are enlightened, and they smoke it.

Jack looks to the Sadhu Master.

JACK
We're going to become enlightened.

MARCELLO

None of the sadhus are enlightened, Jack.

JACK

They're not?

Jack looks back to the Sadhu Master - he shakes his head.

SADHU MASTER

None of us are enlightened here, man.

MARCELLO

Let's go. It's getting late, and there's one more person to see before leaving for Kashmir.

JACK

Kashmir?

MARCELLO

His name is Swami Dharmabum, and I think it's vital for you to see him.

JACK

For me to see.

MARCELLO

Us. For us to see...I mean hear.

COSMIC

He's coming here?

JACK

You okay, Marcello?

MARCELLO

Let's go.

EXT. THE BOHEMIAN YOGI JAZZ AND BEAT CLUB, RISHIKESH - NIGHT

Marcello, Jack, and Cosmic arrive at the entrance of the club. The small neon sign flashing overhead seems out of place.

JACK

Yogi, jazz, and beat club. I like it.

MARCELLO

There's an enlightened guru that owns the place.

JACK

Of course, there is.

They watch as a couple of long-haired, goateed, and robed dudes walk in, followed by a couple of cute hippie chicks.

COSMIC

Sweet.

Marcello and Jack turn to give Cosmic a surprised and comical look.

INT. THE BOHEMIAN YOGI JAZZ AND BEAT CLUB - NIGHT

The three enter to find a lively ensemble playing Indian music with a jazz flare. People are dancing, groups of bohemian beat yogi types sit encircled smoking from hookahs. Marcello, Jack, and Cosmic make their way over to a small table and sit, just as the music softens. An MC walks up to a microphone on a small stage among the musicians.

MC

(into microphone)

Buddha buddha dharma.

CROWD

(in unison)

Buddha buddha dharma.

MC

Good afternoon my dharmic brethren. I hope you're all sufficiently purified, indemnified, meditatified, yogified, and buddhafied - because you are about to receive instruction from the holy book of the master entitled 'The Beat of Enlightenment'...here he is all...Swami Dharmabum!

There is general applause as a middle-aged western man, sporting a beard, colorful robe, and a garland in his hair, steps onto the stage.

He stands there in dead silence as he surveys his audience for a moment. Then, suddenly he breaks out - speaking in a lyrical tenor with soft jazzy music accompaniment.

SWAMI DHARMABUM

Everything is ecstasy inside; we just don't know it because of our thinking minds. But our true blissful essence of mind knows that everything is alright forever and forever and forever and forever. Close your eyes...let your hands and nerve ends drop...stop breathing for three seconds. Listen to the silence inside the illusion of the world, and you will remember the lessons you forgot, which were taught in immense milky-ways of innumerable cloudy worlds long ago and not even at all. It is all one vast awakened thing. I call it the 'golden eternity.' It is perfect. We were never really born - we will never really die. It has nothing to do with the imaginary idea of a personal self. Other selves, many selves, many selves everywhere, or one universal self: self is only an idea. A mortal idea. That which passes through everything is one thing...it's a dream that has already ended.

He stops and stands there...again, he is surveying his audience.

Getting the message that their instruction is over, the group shows its approval with a chant.

CROWD

Buddha buddha dharma! Buddha buddha dharma!

The Swami steps off of the stage and walks over to the table of Marcello, Jack, and Cosmic, and sits down.

SWAMI DHARMABUM

Buddha, buddha, dharma.

COSMIC

Buddha, buddha, dharma.

JACK

Would you shut up?

COSMIC

What?

MARCELLO

Take it easy, guys.

SWAMI DHARMABUM

I hear you cats are looking to get lit up.

MARCELLO

Lit up?

SWAMI DHARMABUM

Enlightened, man. Get with it.

JACK

We're looking to get streamlined, if you know what I mean.

SWAMI DHARMABUM

Streamlined, I like that.

MARCELLO

I was told that you -

SWAMI DHARMABUM

I recommend that you cats follow the spiritual path of the rubber soul.

MARCELLO

The rubber soul?

COSMIC

You mean Yogananda? Didn't he meet a guy that could tie himself up in knots?

SWAMI DHARMABUM

Transcendentalize, man. Like sexy Sadie and the magical mystery.

MARCELLO

I'm sorry, but -

SWAMI DHARMABUM

Do like that, who created Western Civilization's single most elegant spiritual opus?

MARCELLO

Ramakrishna?

SWAMI DHARMABUM

No.

COSMIC

Swami Rama?

SWAMI DHARMABUM

No.

MARCELLO

Vivekananda?

SWAMI DHARMABUM

No!

COSMIC

Paramahansa Yogananda?

SWAMI DHARMABUM

No!

MARCELLO

Amma? The hugging saint.

Jack's head jerks toward Marcello.

JACK

Let's do her.

SWAMI DHARMABUM

No! No! No! The White Album, man...the Beatles! The Maharishi Mahesh Yogi's ashram is just up the road from here.

JACK

The Beatles?

MARCELLO
Yes, but it's empty. The Maharishi was banned from the ashram years ago.

SWAMI DHARMABUM
Have faith, brothers. Go. Transcendentalize.

Swami Dharmabum stands.

SWAMI DHARMABUM
Oh, and you'll find them in bungalows six, seven, eight, and nine.

A WAITER walks up with a bill in hand. Swami Dharmabum grabs it.

SWAMI DHARMABUM
This one's on me.

COSMIC
We didn't have anything.

SWAMI DHARMABUM
You had me....gentlemen.

He walks off.

EXT. RISHIKESH, BEACH - DAY

The three are walking along the Ganges shoreline.

MARCELLO
I'm not sure how we're going to get into this place; it's been closed for a couple of decades.

COSMIC
And it's guarded by the Indian Forest Service.

JACK
What do you think he meant..."have faith, transcendentalize?"

MARCELLO

I think he meant for us to just go with it; we'll see when we get there.

The three stop at the point where the beach converges with a jungle cliff. They can't walk any further.

COSMIC

I hear there's a path leading up to a fence we can jump over into the Beatles ashram.

MARCELLO

Let's go.

They start hiking up the jungle cliff.

EXT. JUNGLE CLIFF PATH - LATER

The three struggle up the small jungle trail. Snakes and giant spiders lurk in the bushes and small trees about the path. Suddenly a brown monkey comes bounding down, screeching wildly as he jumps from tree to tree.

JACK

Jesus Christ! Couldn't we just have bribed someone to get into this place?

COSMIC

I think we're almost there, Mr. Bogart.

Jack looks at a snake clinging to a tree limb a few feet away.

JACK

Hey, snake, go eat that spider. They're delicious, ask Cosmic.

EXT. BEATLES ASHRAM - LATER

Marcello climbs through an opening in a broken part of a fence - Jack and Cosmic follow. The three stand for a moment taking in their stunning surroundings.

ANGLE ON:

The neglected, overgrown ashram of the Maharishi Mahesh Yogi. The tendrils of creeping vines seem to be strangling the small crumbling buildings - there are dozens of single-person 'bee-hive' shaped bungalows made of undersized white river rocks mortared together. It all has a lost-world quality.

BACK TO:

The three walk around, exploring the eerie surroundings. They walk over to a group of bee-hive bungalows numbered six, seven, eight, and nine - all in disrepair.

MARCELLO

These are them.

COSMIC

The Beatles' bungalows.

JACK

What now?

MARCELLO

We transcendentalize. Meditate.

EXT. BEATLES ASHRAM - LATER

CLOSE UP:

The faces of Marcello, Jack, and Cosmic. Eyes closed and silent - all in deep meditation.

MAHARISHI MAHESH YOGI (O.S.)

Okay, all, open your eyes and rise.

WIDEOUT:

Marcello, Jack, and Cosmic open their eyes and are surprised to find themselves sitting with company. John Lennon, Paul McCartney, George Harrison, Ringo Starr, Mia Farrow, her sister Prudence and an Old Western Man.

The Maharishi Mahesh Yogi is sitting across and facing them in full glory with his colorful wraps and garlands.

They all stand.

MAHARISHI MAHESH YOGI
Mia, I'd like you, and these other gentlemen, to come with me for more intimate instruction.

Mia walks towards Mahesh as he gestures to Marcello, Jack, and Cosmic to follow.

JOHN
There's something I don't trust about this Maharishi bloke.

Prudence disappears into her bungalow.

PAUL
(singing)
Dear Prudence, won't you come out to play, ah, ayy....

GEORGE
(singing)
Let me see you smi, ah, ah, ile....

JOHN
(singing)
She's like a little chi, ah, ah, ild....

RINGO
(singing)
The sun is up, the sky is blue, it's beautiful, and so are you, dear Prudence -

Paul, George, and John turn and scowl at Ringo.

GEORGE
Has anybody seen my sitar?

George looks at Cosmic.

COSMIC
Uh, no. I haven't seen it.

George walks off.

JACK
What's this Old Man doing here?

JOHN
That's Paul's grandfather.

PAUL
Come on, John. Let's go write some music.

Paul and John walk off, leaving Ringo standing and looking uncomfortable in his own skin.

MARCELLO
Ringo, I wanted you to know that I've always really liked your...nose.

RINGO
Well, thank you very much, mate.

Mahesh, standing at the entry door to the meditation hall, looks back.

MAHESH
This way. Gentlemen.

Marcello, Jack, and Cosmic follow Mahesh and Mia into the hall.

INT. MEDITATION HALL - MOMENTS LATER

Smoke from burning incense floats through the air - colorful fabrics and pillows cover the floor and lean against the walls. There is a low rhythmic chanting audible from somewhere.

MAHESH
You three sit here and work on your meditation while I work on Mia. Remember, silence your minds.

Jack and Cosmic sit down on the floor as Marcello watches Mahesh, arm around Mia, walk off behind some curtains.

Marcello remains standing - Jack and Cosmic follow his eyes to the curtain, still swaying slightly. Suddenly, John Lennon comes charging into the room and abruptly walks behind the curtains.

JOHN (O.S.)
Well, isn't this cute. We're getting out of this place, Mia.

John drags Mia from behind the curtains and heads for the door - Mahesh hurries behind them.

MAHESH
Wait, John. Why are you leaving?

At the door, John turns back to Maharishi Mahesh Yogi.

JOHN
You're the metaphysical one; figure it out.

John and Mia exit the door. Mahesh crumbles to the floor, sobbing.

Marcello, Jack, and Cosmic - their eyes meet.

MARCELLO
We don't belong here.

Jack and Cosmic pop up.

JACK
Let's blow this joint.

MARCELLO
This way.

They turn and make their way to a second door - Marcello opens it, and they hurry out.

EXT. RISHIKESH, PEDESTRIAN STREET - LATER

The three talk as they walk the street.

JACK
Marcello, this journey of yours is starting to make me nervous.

COSMIC
Do you think that they were really the Beatles -

MARCELLO
I don't know.

JACK
I'm getting the hell out of this place.

MARCELLO

Jack, somehow I think that we're on the right track. We head up north tomorrow morning.

JACK

North?

Okay, but this is your last chance to make something happen.

Jack walks off.

INTERCUT: MARCELLO, JACK AND COSMIC - NIGHT

MARCELLO'S ROOM

Marcello sits in cross-legged meditation. He is surrounded by many candles - incense is burning. In the midst of the yellow glow, the head of a traditionally dressed figure of a man, a BODHISATTVA, appears in front of him and speaks in a deep monotone.

BODHISATTVA

The tree.

Marcello's eyes blink open.

BODHISATTVA

The tree.

MARCELLO

The tree? What tree?

BODHISATTVA

North. The great tree is your answer. Go to the tree.

The Bodhisattva fades.

MARCELLO

Where is the tree? Wait!

The Bodhisattva disappears as Marcello takes a deep breath in disbelief.

JACK'S ROOM

Bored, Jack lies on his bed, smoking a cigarette.

His eyes light up. Putting the cigarette out, he pulls out the chillum and ganja mixture he got from the sadhus.

COSMIC'S ROOM

The Tea Boy sits, watches, and listens while Cosmic is changing into his bedclothes.

COSMIC

Yeah, my friend got so much pussy because he did steroids. But in Europe, they dig dudes like I'm built.

TEA BOY

You are beautiful.

COSMIC

I shot my burgers up with steroids, and my shit came out five times its normal size.

TEA BOY

No?!

COSMIC

Really.

TEA BOY

May I give you a massage tonight?

Cosmic stares at him for a moment.

COSMIC

Okay. But not like last time.

The Tea Boy smiles.

EXT. VED NIKETAN ASHRAM, OUTSIDE JACK'S ROOM - MORNING

Marcello and Jack talk while waiting. In the distance, Cosmic walks out of the door to his room. They are all carrying small backpacks.

JACK

I've got a urologist that takes care of that.

MARCELLO

You don't need a urologist for UT. It's about drinking your own urine; how complicated can that be?

JACK

For me, pretty fucking complicated.

MARCELLO

It's the living water within...life's elixir.

JACK

You really have taken this whole thing too far, Marcello.

MARCELLO

There are documented results from using urine therapy to treat intestinal parasites, herpes, sarcoma lesions, colitis...it has anticancer agents like DHEA, retine, antineoplastons, and uric acid.

JACK

So, next time I have to take a leak, will you get on your knees and let me piss in your mouth?

MARCELLO

I only drink my own urine, Jack.

Cosmic walks up.

JACK

Could I piss on your face then?

MARCELLO

No.

COSMIC

You can piss on my face.

JACK

I know.

MARCELLO

Let's go.

EXT. TRAIN STATION, SMALL TOWN, KASHMIR - TWILIGHT

A train eases to a stop. Marcello, Jack, and Cosmic climb off. Dressed in their white kurtas as always, the three stand on the platform observing the place.

JACK

A little further north, uh?

MARCELLO

Relax. We're here.

COSMIC

Who are we going to see?

MARCELLO

Leonard Cohen's guru. He's up in Kashmir.

JACK

The Beatles' guru, Leonard Cohen's guru. I want my own fucking guru.

MARCELLO

I'm working on it, Jack.

JACK

You'd better be.

EXT. SMALL ADOBE HUT, SMALL TOWN, KASHMIR - NIGHT

Marcello, Jack, and Cosmic arrive at the entrance of the hut. There are two INDIAN MEN standing by the door. One of them, MAN #1, is leaning against the wall, eyes closed, hands held up in a meditative stance. The other, MAN #2, is guarding the door.

MARCELLO

Namaste.

JACK

Namaste?

MARCELLO

It means 'the divine in me honors and recognizes the divine in you.'

Jack looks at Man #2.

JACK

Are you divine?

Without expression, Man #2 performs the Indian 'head wiggle.'

JACK

Is that a yes?

MAN #2

May I help you?

MARCELLO

We would like to meet with Ramesh. Sushila, our mutual friend, recommended we come for spiritual guidance.

Jack and Cosmic are looking at Man #1.

COSMIC

Is he meditating?

MAN #2

He's waiting for a divine delivery.

JACK

Namaste.

Man #1 opens his eyes and looks at Jack.

MAN #2

The three of you may enter.

JACK

(to Man #1)

You can go back to sleep.

INT. SMALL ADOBE HUT, SMALL TOWN, KASHMIR - MOMENTS LATER

Ramesh, a small, frail, white-haired man, sits in a chair. He is dressed in a white, lightweight cotton robe.

Marcello, Jack, and Cosmic enter the room and step over to Ramesh. Marcello bows, Cosmic follows Marcello's lead, and they both sit down on the floor. Jack remains standing as he lights a cigarette.

JACK

Are you really Leonard Cohen's guru?

RAMESH

I have the pleasure of dispensing spiritual advice to Mr. Cohen on occasion, yes.

Marcello turns and gives Jack a look of frustration, then smiles.

MARCELLO

Would you like to join us, Mr. Bogart?

Jack flops down on the earthen tile floor. Marcello makes a slight gesture toward Jack's cigarette.

Jack huffs and flicks it out of an open window, and it strikes a MAN (O.S.) standing outside.

MAN #3 (O.S.)

Ouch!

Watching Jack, Ramesh rolls his eyes over to Marcello.

RAMESH

Precisely what is it that I can do for you, gentlemen?

MARCELLO

We -

JACK

We want to become enlightened.

MARCELLO

Jack.

Ramesh looks across the faces of the men. Cosmic gives him an ear-to-ear smile.

RAMESH

Do you want to become enlightened? Why is it that I'm resisting an awkward laugh right now?

MARCELLO

Please, we're here for guidance to help us on our path. Call it a path of inner clarity, spirituality, or, yes, enlightenment.

JACK

What is the meaning of life?

Marcello and Cosmic turn and look at Jack.

RAMESH

There is no meaning in life. There are, however, two distinct facts of life that are meaningful.

BEAT

MARCELLO

We're listening.

RAMESH

Life...or in the case of human beings...the body-mind-organism has total freedom to do whatever it wishes, and nobody has any control over the result of their action.

COSMIC

So, what are the two facts?

RAMESH

The body-mind-organism has total freedom to do whatever it wishes, and nobody has any control over the result of their action.

COSMIC

Oh.

RAMESH

Both are the basis of daily living, while the basis of life is uncertainty. Any reaction is a biological reaction, and the ego reacts to the biological response.

MARCELLO

What if one has renounced their ego and therefore is detached from any result or biological reaction?

JACK

Yeah.

Marcello and Cosmic look back at Jack - he is taking a huge drag from a chillum. Smoke wafts from his mouth as he French inhales it into his nostrils.

RAMESH

The ego is the identified consciousness - you also have an impersonal consciousness. Every human is fundamentally a multidimensional being who wants happiness in this lifetime.

COSMIC

But if one releases their ego and is mindful, present in the moment -

RAMESH

Just being present does not help one to be happy. People consider it a birthright to be happy, but we all have to live within the circumstances in which we are placed. God does not spoon-feed people - happiness is found in one's attitude in life, and attitude towards others. Family, loving your neighbors, and everything that happens is according to cosmic law. We don't even know what our next thought will be, because the individual's ego manifests itself into the greater collective ego. Seven billion egos all following the order of the cosmic law. Subliminal intuition is the inner light - thy will be done equals God's will, and God's will is the collective egos' intercourse with the cosmic law.

JACK

Fuck yeah!

All look back to Jack. He's still holding the chillum and blowing out some smoke.

JACK

Shit, Marcello, where did you come up with this dude?

RAMESH

Is he serious?

MARCELLO

Definitely.

INT. JACK'S ROOM, GUESTHOUSE, KASHMIR - MORNING

CLOSE UP: OF A BARREN PATCH OF PALE-COLORED WALL

Suddenly, as the sun rises over the hilltop ridge, the shadow of a small, metal-grated opening in the exterior wall develops on the pale interior wall. At first, it's fuzzy and undefined, but its shadow takes on a sharp, focused, vivid clarity in a matter of seconds.

CUT TO: JACK BOGART, LATER

Jack is lying on his bed while engrossed in telling a story. TEA BOY #2 sits mesmerized at the foot of the bed... listening while staring at Jack.

JACK

I mean, if God is a woman, that is how she would give a blow job. Make no mistake; it was divine.

TEA BOY #2

Wow. Mr. Bogart, do you make a habit out of seducing women wherever you go?

JACK

I wouldn't call it a habit, more like a hobby.

TEA BOY #2

How do you know when a woman is ready to receive you?

JACK

Receive me? Uh...a man in my position just assumes that all women are always ready to...receive them.

TEA BOY #2

I have never been received by a woman.

JACK

You think you needed to tell me that, pal?

There is a knock on the door.

JACK

Come in!

Marcello, Cosmic, and VAJRA (35), an attractive Indian woman, file inside Jack's room and walk up to his bed. Marcello and Cosmic wear ochre turmeric powder centered on their foreheads.

JACK

Cosmic. You're letting your hair grow.

COSMIC

I don't shave myself every day, Mr. Bogart.

JACK

Aren't you afraid people will confuse you for that guy...what's his name?

COSMIC

Adrian Grenier from 'Entourage'?

JACK

No, G.I. Joe, from Mattel.

MARCELLO

Hasbro.

JACK

Whatever.

Marcello gestures to VAJRA.

MARCELLO

Jack, this is Vajra Bhramavadin. She's enlightened.

JACK

Well, woop-de-fuckin'-do. Are we the only schmucks in this country who aren't enlightened?

VAJRA

What is a schmuck?

MARCELLO

It's a...uh -

COSMIC

Dick.

Everyone looks at Cosmic.

COSMIC

It's Yiddish. It means dick.

VAJRA

What is dick?

Vajra looks down at Jack, who's smiling on his bed.

VAJRA

You used the word for penis and enlightenment in the same sentence - that's blasphemous.

JACK

Blasphemy? Yeah, I've been to that church.

MARCELLO

Jack.

VAJRA

I'm leaving here.

MARCELLO

No, please stay. He didn't mean anything by it.

VAJRA

Then why did he say it?

JACK

Yeah, Marcello. Then why did I say it?

VAJRA

You, sir, are no gentleman.

Jack lights a cigarette.

JACK

I'm from Hollywood, what were you expecting?

JACK

What's with the red marking between the -

MARCELLO

It's a religious symbol. The third eye.

JACK

Is that anything like a third leg?

VAJRA

What does he mean by that?

JACK

Can you give me a massage?

VAJRA

Yes, but I wouldn't.

JACK

Come on, baby. My neck is killing me.

MARCELLO

Jack.

VAJRA

Mr. Bogart, you are a scoundrel.

They all watch as Vajra turns and walks out of the room. Marcello turns and glares at Jack.

JACK

Shall we have lunch?

EXT. LUNCH TABLE, SMALL TOWN, KASHMIR - LATER

The three are sitting at a table on the roof of a restaurant overlooking a lake. Jack and Cosmic each eat a whole fish with the head on, while Marcello eats a vegetarian dish of rice and vegetables.

MARCELLO

Sexual repression is a big problem here - being married and non-sexual is psychologically dangerous.

COSMIC

That's why a tantric lifestyle is so valuable.

ANGLE ON:

Jack is meticulous in the way he manages his fish, and he fillets and de-bones it with the elegance of a Viscount, lunching in the garden of his estate.

JACK

Being non-sexual is just fucking psychotic.

BACK TO:

The three are seated at the table. Frustrated, Cosmic is pawing at his fish with a fork and spoon.

COSMIC

Well, in my tantric sex class, I'd say that I achieved something that no one else at this table could claim.

JACK

And just what would that be, you fucking twerp?

COSMIC

Cher said that I was the first man ever, to give her an orgasm.

MARCELLO

Really?

JACK

Right!?

COSMIC

It's true, multiple orgasms.

Marcello reaches over the table and shakes Cosmic's hand.

JACK

'A' multiple orgasm?

MARCELLO

That's great, Cosmic.

JACK

Save your breath. That's a story you're going to be telling for the rest of your life.

COSMIC

Jealous, Mr. Bogart?

JACK

Son, when you've reached the triple digits, then we'll talk.

MARCELLO

Jack, it's not all about quantity.

JACK

Of course, it is.

Marcello looks over to a couple of FRENCH WOMEN sitting at a table next to them.

MARCELLO

Excuse me. I was wondering if you could give me a general observation.

FRENCH WOMAN #1

(French accent)

Yes.

MARCELLO

Looking at these two plates of fish - if you had to choose one of the men who ate them as a lover, which would you select?

Marcello pulls Jack's and Cosmic's plates out to the center of the table as the two Women lean over to look at them.

ANGLE ON:

Both plates. Jack's is nearly barren; the fish are gone, with only the skeletal remains in a neat, organized arrangement. Cosmic's plate is a horrific explosion of leftover fish flesh, skin, and bones in one scrambled mess.

BACK TO:

The two women are standing over Marcello, Jack, and Cosmic seated at the table. They peer down at the dishes.

French Woman #1 gestures towards Cosmic.

FRENCH WOMAN #1

(French accent)

Well, this boy is not a considerate lover. I am confident that he does not know how to seduce a woman...I am speaking of the French tradition of seduction obviously -

FRENCH WOMAN #2

Perhaps that is so, but he does not lack passion - many women would forgo subtle foreplay for a heated, primal, ravishing lover - it depends on the circumstance, of course.

FRENCH WOMAN #1

Well, perhaps, if you don't mind being physically injured - I'm also certain that it would not only be messy, but it would be over quite quickly. While Mr. Bogart here - I'm sorry, but it's pretty obvious who you are -

JACK

(in French)

Please call me Jack, Mademoiselle.

FRENCH WOMAN #1

Merci. Jack is a slow, methodical lover that would ease a woman's sexual tension as well as develop her interest so that by the time of penetration, she is more than ready...shall I say eager, for the insertion of his -

MARCELLO

Thank you very much, ladies. I think we understand what you're saying.

Jack smiles at Cosmic.

JACK

I think it's evident that they both believe that in terms of human lovemaking, I'd be the preferred choice-

COSMIC

That's not what they said.

JACK

Perhaps not in so many words, but -

MARCELLO

I think that I'd call it a draw.

JACK

What!

MARCELLO

A draw - giving Jack the art of seduction while Cosmic scores points for passion.

JACK

Bullshit!

COSMIC

I agree.

BEAT

JACK

With what?

EXT. DUSTY ROAD, SMALL TOWN, KASHMIR - LATER

Marcello, flanked by Jack and Cosmic, walk uphill, flanked by small single-story buildings on each side of a rocky pathway. Tired, they labor as they walk.

JACK

Shit, Marcello. Do you have any idea where we are?

MARCELLO

North. Way north.

COSMIC

Like Pakistan north.

MARCELLO

Not that far.

JACK

Well, I’m ready to give up on this shit.

Marcello looks up and stops. Jack and Cosmic follow suit.

POV MARCELLO:

The rooftops of the buildings have half a dozen men. All are dressed in Kashmiri para-military uniforms and hold rifles aimed at Marcello, Jack, and Cosmic. The three stand looking up at the men.

INTERCUT BETWEEN: ROOFTOP GROUP AND THE DHARMA KINGS

A COMMANDER and his SECOND are crouched down behind the armed men. They look down at Marcello, Jack, and Cosmic. The Commander and Second look at each other and then back to the three Americans.

Marcello, Jack, and Cosmic stare up at the armed rooftop men.

COSMIC

Is this Pakistan?

The Commander shakes his head.

JACK
Are you Indian?

The Commander shakes his head.

MARCELLO
Are you Muslim rebels who want Kashmir as your homeland?

The Commander nods his head.

MARCELLO
We don't want any trouble. We're just travelers in search of enlightenment.

Time freezes for a beat.

BEAT

The Commander turns to his Second.

COMMANDER
(Pakistani/Urdu language)
Let them -

SECOND
Fire!

The rifles of the dozen militants fire.

BLAM BLAM BLAM BLAM BLAM BLAM BLAM BLAM BLAM BLAM BLAM

SLOW MOTION as bullets tear through Jack and Cosmic - deep red blood sprays from their white kurtas as they float to the ground...dead.

Marcello stands in shock - he looks down at his dead comrades.

The Commander gives his second a look of surprise.

COMMANDER
(Pakistani/Urdu language)
I was going to say let them pass.

He looks back to Marcello standing - Jack and Cosmic lying on the ground.

SECOND

Oh...sorry, I just assumed that we'd -

COMMANDER

It's fantastic; not one bullet struck the one in the center.

SECOND

That's easy enough to handle -

COMMANDER

No! It must be written.
(louder)
Let him pass.

SECOND
(English)
Where are you going?

Marcello points to the large bodhi tree in the square just up the road.

MARCELLO

To the great tree.

SECOND

You may pass without threat to your life.

MARCELLO

Thank you...I think.

Marcello again looks down at Jack and Cosmic. They lie bullet-ridden in blood-soaked white kurtas.

In complete shock, Marcello hesitantly walks on.

All atop the roofs watch in silence as he passes.

ZOOM OUT:

Marcello continues the walk towards the great bodhi tree visible ahead.

THE END

MUSIC/FINAL CREDITS ROLL:

EXT. THE GREAT BODHI TREE SQUARE, KASHMIR - LATER

Marcello sits under the tree, legs crossed in meditative silence as animals hesitantly approach him - deer, monkeys, goats, an eagle lands next to him.

FADE TO BLACK

About the Author

Paul Charles Bailly has written over twenty-five screenplays as he's traveled the world. He's lived and written in West Hollywood, Chiang Mai, Rishikesh, Buenos Aires, Logroño, Vina Del Mar, Tucson, Naples, Girona, Quinta da Marinha…wherever.

Published December 2023

www.ingramcontent.com/pod-product-compliance
Lightning Source LLC
Chambersburg PA
CBHW081133300726
48982CB00005B/958

* 9 7 9 8 9 8 8 8 8 9 9 1 5 *